"Wendy M. Wright writes like no one else in the field of spirituality today. Travel with her on this fascinating Marian pilgrimage, and you will discover worlds that extend far beyond Mary and Los Angeles—and ultimately, you will be brought home to yourself."

—Fr. Edward L. Beck
CBS News Faith and Religion Contributor and
author of God Underneath: Spiritual Memoirs
of a Catholic Priest

"Here is a pearl of contemplative wisdom formed from layers of insight, discernment, friendship, expansive maternal sensibility, and the author's own 'soul moments.' It is a treasure of art, local history, and multicultural experience, perceptive theology, and awareness of how images of Mary could reinforce both women's oppression and freedom."

—Joann Wolski Conn
Neumann University (Professor Emerita)
Past President, Society for the Study
of Christian Spirituality

"These pages take us into the very heart of Mary and the marvelous City of Angels. This book is a treasure for pilgrims or anyone who wants to become one."

—Jeanne Hunt
Author of Celebrating Saints and Seasons

"This book is a major contribution to the place of Mary in contemporary Catholic spirituality. Accompanying the author and her photographer as they criss-cross the busy freeways of this bafflingly diverse megalopolis, the reader is led through the web of Marian devotions and the history of the many communities who make up today's Los Angeles, and brought to see how figure of Mary combines faith with culture. Readers who love Mary, those who are fascinated by southern California, or those who seek to understand why the figure of the Virgin continues to compel will all find in this poignant and elegantly written text things to inform and delight."

—Rev. Dorian Llywelyn, SJ
Loyola Marymount University, Los Angeles

"Nobody brings together popular piety and serious theological reflection better than Wendy Wright. The heart and the intellect can go together. This book is proof!"

—Fr. Ronald Rohlheiser
Oblate School of Theology (San Antonio, TX)
Author of Our One Great Act of Fidelity

The Lady of the Angels and Her City

A Marian Pilgrimage

Wendy M. Wright

Foreword by
His Emminence Cardinal Roger Mahony
Archbishop Emeritus of Los Angeles

LITURGICAL PRESS
Collegeville, Minnesota

www.litpress.org

Scripture texts, prefaces, introductions, footnotes and cross references used in this work are taken from the New American Bible, revised edition © 2010, 1991, 1986, 1970 Confraternity of Christian Doctrine, Inc., Washington, DC All Rights Reserved. No part of this work may be reproduced or transmitted in any form or by any means, electronic or mechanical, including photocopying, recording, or by any information storage and retrieval system, without permission in writing from the copyright owner.

Scripture texts in this work are taken from the New American Bible with Revised New Testament and Revised Psalms © 1991, 1986, 1970 Confraternity of Christian Doctrine, Washington, DC, and are used by permission of the copyright owner. All Rights Reserved. No part of the New American Bible may be reproduced in any form without permission in writing from the copyright owner.

Scripture texts in this work are taken from the New Revised Standard Version Bible © 1989, Division of Christian Education of the National Council of the Churches of Christ in the United States of America. Used by permission. All rights reserved.

© 2013 by Order of Saint Benedict, Collegeville, Minnesota. All rights reserved. No part of this book may be reproduced in any form, by print, microfilm, microfiche, mechanical recording, photocopying, translation, or by any other means, known or yet unknown, for any purpose except brief quotations in reviews, without the previous written permission of Liturgical Press, Saint John's Abbey, PO Box 7500, Collegeville, Minnesota 56321-7500. Printed in the United States of America.

1	2	3	4	5	6	7	8

Library of Congress Cataloging-in-Publication Data

Wright, Wendy M.
    The Lady of the Angels and her city : a Marian pilgrimage / Wendy M. Wright.
        p.   cm.
    ISBN 978-0-8146-3470-7 — ISBN 978-0-8146-3495-0 (e-book)
    1. Wright, Wendy M.   2. Christian pilgrims and pilgrimages—
California—Los Angeles.   3. Mary, Blessed Virgin, Saint—Devotion to—
California—Los Angeles.   4. Los Angeles (Calif.)—Church history.   I. Title.

BX4705.W773A3   2013
263'.04279494—dc23   2012039195

Contents

Foreword

Mary's was a pondering heart. In quiet and in stillness, she was alert to the signs of God's coming in her midst, attentive to the very life of God within her.

Wendy Wright, native of Los Angeles and Professor of Theology at Creighton University in Omaha, returned to her home place numerous times over the course of several years in search of the woman for whom our city is named; Our Lady whose presence was no small part of Wendy Wright's decision to become a Roman Catholic in young adulthood.

Professor Wright was in our midst in much the same way as Mary: tranquil, observant, unobtrusive, and vigilant. She searched for the presence of Mary in her various manifestations in architecture, art, sculpture, tapestry, and stained-glass window. She is Our Lady of Refuge, Guadalupe, Immaculate Heart, Our Lady of La Vang, Our Lady of the Angels, and so much more. And still more. She is consolation, protection, first of the disciples, mother of the church, wounded heart. Her presence penetrates this city named for her, and Wendy Wright found her in streets, fiestas, parades, Sunday Masses, and popular devotions. She finds the woman wrapped in silence in her own pondering heart as she beholds the Madonna of Korea, the Mother of Good Counsel, the Protector of the Child and the world's children of every race, land, and language. She is here in her city, assuring her children that God is with them in their joys and their hopes, in their suffering and their anxiety. And Wendy Wright discovered her here. Again.

More than a historical account with an alluring array of photos, *The Lady of the Angels and Her City* charts the spiritual movements of an author who is woman, wife, mother, and theologian. Aware of contemporary scholarly perspectives on Mary of Nazareth, Wright places herself in the midst of the mothers of the despised, the sisters who serve the wounded and the weak under the protection of Notre Dame, the women young and old who struggle to keep faith and manage to do so in no small measure due to the woman whose words are echoed in choirs, pews, prayer books and on the lips of countless millions across the miles and throughout the years: "God has cast the mighty from their thrones and has lifted up the lowly."

Lift this volume into hands poised for prayer. Let the eyes of your heart gaze on the one who is the Lady of the Angels even as she whispers to those who may seem farthest from heaven.

His Eminence
Cardinal Roger Mahony
Archbishop Emeritus of Los Angeles

Acknowledgments

A host of gracious individuals have made this book possible. In particular Fr. Michael Engh, SJ, and Dr. Michael Downey offered invaluable help in both the research phase and the writing phase of this book. Their intimate knowledge and love of Los Angeles and its Catholic Church gave me access to people and places I could never have found on my own and enriched my sense of the living community in the archdiocese. I am likewise utterly indebted to photographer Dorothy Tuma who traveled with me in the later phases of research and whose contemplative eye is evident in most of the photos reproduced here.

In California innumerable people were generous with their time and expertise, including Msgr. Francis Weber and Kevin Feeney from the Los Angeles archdiocesan archives; Pat Livingston and Lynn Bremer of the Santa Barbara Mission archives; Br. Timothy Arthur, OFM, of the Franciscan archives at the Old Mission Santa Barbara; Hermine Lees and Mike Nelson from the staff of *The Tidings*; Tod Tamberg from media relations at the L.A. archdiocese; Anna Maria Prieto of the IHM archives, Immaculate Heart High School; Dr. John Ford, Sr. Leanne Hubbard, SND, and Mrs. Rita Faulders, all connected to Saint John's Seminary in Camarillo; Carol Carrig, IHM, and Anita Daniel, IHM; Fr. Dorian Llywelyn, SJ; Dr. Douglas E. Christie; Fr. Daniel Peterson, SJ, at the California Province Jesuit archives; Dr. Richard Hecht; Frs. Michel Hoang and Alex Kim of the diocese of Orange; and Fr. Aldon Sison and all the other wonderful pastors, pastoral associates, sacristans, and parishioners of the L.A. archdiocese who are mentioned in the text.

Conversations with others outside California also enriched my thinking. Thus thanks are due to Dr. Damian Zynda; Paul Burson; Tim Swisher; Nancy Wynn, director of the Clare Gallery in Hartford, Connecticut; Louise Bernikow; Dr. Aurelie Hagstrom; the staff of the Marian Library at the University of Dayton, especially Clare Jones, Fr. Thomas A. Thompson, SM, Cecilia Muchenheim, Fr. Johann Roten, SM, and Fr. Francois Rossier, SM; Mary Ann Zimmer, ND; Fr. Edward Beck, CP; Fr. Ted Bohr, SJ; Fr. Joseph Chorpenning, OSFS.

Thanks are due as well to the following for various monetary grants and academic leave time that made research possible: the Kripke Center for the Study of Religion and Society at Creighton University, Dr. Ronald Simkins, director; funds from the John C. Kenefick Chair in the Humanities at Creighton; Dr. Timothy Austin and Dr. Robert Lueger, Deans of Creighton's College of Arts and Science.

Finally, I am immensely grateful to Hans Christoffersen and the staff of Liturgical Press for their willingness to take on the publication of *The Lady of the Angels and Her City.*

By Thomas Merton, from THE COLLECTED POEMS OF THOMAS MERTON, copyright © 1977 by Trustees of the Merton Legacy Trust. Reprinted by permission of New Directions Publishing Corp.

Excerpts from *Prayers for New Millennium* (Liguori, MO: Liguori Publications, 1998) and *Mary the Peacemaker: A Novena* (Erie, PA: Benetvision, 2002) by Mary Lou Kownacki, OSB, director of Benetvision, www.joanchittister.org. Used by permission of Mary Lou Kownacki.

Permissions for use of photographs have been granted by the following:

Dorothy Tuma Photography

Santa Barbara Mission Archives (p. 12)

Franciscan Sources Room, Old Mission Santa Barbara (p. 10)

Directors of the Archives of the Immaculate Heart Community (pp. 44, 49)

Los Angeles Archdiocesan Archives (pp. 51, 136, 137, 139)

Tod Tamberg, Media Relations, Archdiocese of Los Angeles

Janet Weber, Immaculate Heart High School (p. 49)

Marian Year Procession, Old Mission Santa Barbara, 1954.

Chapter 1

The Pilgrimage Road

I have joked with my friends that I am making up for missing it twice. My first lapse occurred in 1954, the year I turned seven. This year was designated by Pope Pius XII as a "Marian Year." His encyclical *Fulgens Corona* announced a worldwide observance intended to celebrate the centenary of the dogmatic proclamation of the Virgin's immaculate conception in the womb of her mother, Anne. The celebration also acknowledged the recent 1950 proclamation of a second Marian dogma, the assumption of the Virgin, the teaching that the mother of Jesus at the end of her life had been taken up, body and soul, into heaven.

The 1954 Marian Year was to be celebrated in each local church and on the diocesan level by festivals, conferences, and devotional events. Universally, pilgrimages to Mary's shrines were organized. I have seen photos of that year from the Franciscan archives at Mission Santa Barbara of elaborate processions of Southern California area priests and nuns in full religious regalia following a white marble statuette of a demure Madonna held aloft by vested choir boys, as well as photos of uniform-clad Los Angeles parochial school children piously saying their rosaries. I know as well that if a devout Catholic, wishing to gain the plenary indulgences merited by a Marian Year pilgrimage to Rome or to the Guadalupe shrine outside Mexico City, was unable to do so, he or she could gain the same grace by making a pilgrimage to designated Marian shrines in the local area. The parishioners of San Fernando Valley, just west of Los Angeles, for example, organized a pilgrimage to the Mary shrine in Burbank built by the nineteenth-century peregrinating Italian foundress of the Missionary Sisters of the Sacred Heart, Frances Cabrini, who trekked over the American frontier ministering to her fellow immigrant nationals and left Marian devotional sites in her wake.

I faltered once more in 1987 when Pope John Paul II did it again, issuing *Redemptoris Mater* to proclaim another Marian Year—this time as one of several designated years leading up to the millennium. The then-archbishop of Los Angeles, Roger Mahony, responded at the time by commissioning a mural in Watts and creating several Marian sanctuaries for that special year: in Santa Maria, Santa Barbara, Oxnard, and Camarillo. He also presided over a procession and Mass at St. Vibiana Cathedral at the close of the year.

I missed both Marian Years, not only in my native Los Angeles, but in consciousness. The first occurred long before I, an L.A. grade-school student from an unchurched family, had joined the Catholic Church. The second occurred after I had converted. But while it was on the periphery of religious awareness, that Marian Year did not make much of an impact, my attention being fully directed at that point toward three children, aged nine, four, and two, and a family move from the East Coast to the Midwest with all the attendant upheavals which that move entailed. And, frankly, in the post–Vatican II ecclesial world in which I circulated in the late eighties, Marian fervor was distinctly muted. So, I have jokingly told inquiring colleagues that this work I have been doing, this shuttling back and forth between my present home and university career in Nebraska and my native West Coast to sleuth about in dim sanctuaries and hunt up people to converse with about the Virgin Mary in, of all places, Los Angeles, a city famed in the 2009 *Guinness Book of World Records* for the most internationally watched TV program, *Baywatch*, with its scantily clad performers, is my way of making up for those missed Marian Years. I may have kidded about the plenary indulgences I have earned in the process, but as I have lived into what began as no more than an insistent urging, the true nature of what I had been doing has become clear. This is in fact a pilgrimage story.

It certainly did not start that way. It began as a longing to circle back to my home-place: the city of Los Angeles. It was as though at this specific point in my life as a late-middle-aged, empty-nested, Midwestern college professor I had little choice but to home westward, lured once again by the salty sting of ocean air and the olive, grey-green, and burnt-umber palette of the sloping California coastal range. Home: landscapes, natural and constructed, that long ago shaped my emerging consciousness. To explain myself to myself I found myself conjuring up the 1986 classic Horton Foote film *The Trip to Bountiful* in which the aging Geraldine Page slips away from the urban apartment where she lives with her son and boards a bus that will take her back to Bountiful, the rural home-place whose scent and texture has invaded her waking dreams. But while Page's character was drawn by a country idyll, my "Bountiful" is the sprawling, car-clogged, cacophonous urban environment of Los Angeles—bounded, of course, for miles around by stately palms, pristine beaches, and those sloping olive hills and seasoned by that salt-sharp ocean air.

When did the search expand beyond my private homecoming? I am not clear about the process, but at least a year into my frequent forays to the West Coast, I found myself seated across the desk from Jesuit Michael Engh, an administrator at Loyola Marymount University and specialist in the religious history of Los Angeles. One qualifies for sabbatical leave from one's university by proposing a project that will lead to publication. Because I had already published and not perished in the tenure process, I felt that I could afford to be a bit "wooly" about what it was I intended to accomplish. My sabbatical proposal did, however, state that I would be consulting with scholars such as the historian now seated before me. As our conversation meandered, I allowed myself to express the tentativeness I felt about what it was that I was actually doing (or not doing) on this initial sabbatical trip. Then I heard myself ask, "What's been written about Mary in Los Angeles?"

Although the question surprised me, once it was uttered I knew it was the right one; it was my question. My conversation partner seemed as struck by the thought as I was, and, after rummaging around in his memory, he unearthed a couple of articles written mid-twentieth century. Of course, he advised, various aspects of Marian devotion have been the subject of scholarly investigations. But most of these studies would take me well beyond the confines of Southern California and that home-place that continued to tug at me so insistently.

One might ask, why Mary in Los Angeles? The answer, at once personal and historical, is that I became a Catholic because of Mary. The unfolding process that this conversion entailed took place in the very landscape that I call home. So the memories that this trip to my own Bountiful evoke are also those of that slow turning. But L.A. is not only my city; it is hers. The sprawling, humming, magnificent, and tawdry urban environment that is my hometown is not, strictly speaking, the City of the Angels. For decades historians have waffled back and forth among several possible original names: the City of Our Lady of the Angels, the City of Our Lady of the Angels of the River Porciuncula, the City of Our Lady of the Angels of the Porciuncula, or the City of the Queen of the Angels. Whatever the historical accuracy of the matter, it is indisputably true that the city is Mary's. The angels may have come to stand in for her in common discourse, mine included, but this does not negate the fact that the city is hers. Nor does the name alone identify it as such. Here in the city she is powerfully and palpably present. She has been from the very beginning.

Once initially articulated, the academic Mary in L.A. project gained its own momentum. I shifted the personal itinerary to the background. At first, I wondered, how would I go about capturing the Virgin in her city? Monographs, scholarly histories, newspaper articles, mission archives were the obvious starting points. Yet my surest sense was that I needed to touch, feel, and see for myself. I wanted to participate in the devotional practices associated with the Virgin. I needed to be present in the actual spaces themselves—both temporal and geographical—that were placed under her protection, the sites where her presence is palpable. I longed to visit her through the people who love her, through the gestures and material objects with which those same people encounter her. If I might identify this approach and give it a scholarly name, I would describe it as the study of "lived religion," not an appellation unique to me but one that fits, as it takes into account the interconnections between faith expressions, social structures, cultural horizons, bodily existence, everyday lives, and the local circumstances of practitioners. At the root of the search, however, was the insistent pull of Mary herself and the sense that somehow, at this late midlife moment, she and I were intimately intertwined.

Thus began my solitary, intermittent peregrination around the greater archdiocese of Los Angeles, a vast 8,762-square-mile landscape stretching well beyond the city proper. The ecclesial region extends east to the San Bernardino County line several driving hours inland, south to the busy commercial port of Long Beach, north past Malibu Beach nested in the Santa Monica mountains, along the coastline, over the Gaviota Pass, inland to where the Sierra Madre mountain range slopes off to form the Caliente range, and beyond to its northeastern-most boundary in the desolate rangeland beyond New Cuyama. So richly diverse is the archdiocesan population that cultural geographers have described the metropolitan region contained therein as a "minority majority" city. The archdiocese reflects this reality; its directory refers to "ethnic services" offered to seventy-two different groups in this culturally mixed environment. The 2012 Catholic directory estimates that nearly 4.5 million Catholics reside in the ecclesial jurisdiction which in turn is divided into five pastoral regions. These Catholics live among a total population of nearly twelve million located in 120 cities where

287 parishes, seven missions and chapels, nine Eastern Rite Catholic Churches, and nearly 225 Catholic elementary and fifty Catholic high schools provide ministerial services.

As time progressed, I came with a professional photographer, Dorothy Tuma, to capture some of the images that continued to haunt me. I spoke with pastors, sacristans, pastoral associates, missionaries, priests-in-training, seminary professors, abbots, women religious, parishioners, laity—young and old—and along every part of the fiercely contested political, cultural, and theological ideological spectrums. In so doing, my pilgrimage became one of global Catholic experience. This archdiocese, whose heart is the city named for her—the city of Our Lady of the Angels—is a microcosm of the universal Catholic Church.

My work has always been interdisciplinary, and this project was as well. At times I felt like a journalist; at other times, an ethnographer; certainly my theological and historical training was always in mind. When I interviewed pastors or religious educators, I heard beneath their words the echoes of ministerial training, church politics, and academic theological arguments. When I visited shrines, I felt compelled to research the colonial origins of many of the devotions practiced there. In the process, the surprising adventures of the religious orders and the heroic yet flawed individuals who carried devotions across the oceans came startlingly alive, as did the tales of miraculous events, apparitions, and otherworldly encounters in the "new" world. The work of art historians, sociologists, and social psychologists shed light on what I saw and heard. Entire peoples, raw and bleeding yet resilient, presented themselves through their Marian patronesses: Armenia's Queen of Martyrs, Mexico's Guadalupe, Poland's Czestochowa, and Vietnam's Our Lady of La Vang. Mary in Los Angeles was a sacred window into multiple worlds, ancient and modern, that were simultaneously present. Being a scholar of Christian spirituality identifies me as an academic who admits the self-implicating nature of my studies. Thus, although my work is not "apologetic" in the formal sense, I write as someone who shares this wide, broad Catholic world with those whom I have interviewed. More than that, I share this city. If Mary and her devotees have a history in this complex urban environment, so do I. Eventually it became clear to me that the personal intertwining of stories was an essential piece of the project.

This was the landscape that surrounded me from 1947 to 1984, and my story, as well as Mary's, is inscribed here in Los Angeles. Moreover, a pilgrimage is always more than a geographical journey, just as an academic project in the field of spirituality is more than simply the collection and interpretation of data. The action of returning to homeplace brought me to memories buried in the landscape itself, parts of my story that perhaps had not been integrated with my present self-identity as mother, professor in a Catholic department of theology, and spiritual guide. I needed to own the young woman who thought she would grow up to have a theater music career and who flailed around, moved from school to school, relationship to relationship, in search of something she only vaguely could name. I needed to own as well the ecumenical and interfaith sensibilities that still animate my faith. Yet I wanted at the same time to own the profoundly Catholic sensibilities that drew me to and still hold me firmly, if not always easily, in that faith tradition. I needed to make a pilgrimage to my Los Angeles.

If you were to ask, "Where in L.A. do you come from?" I will volley back, "L.A." There really is a Los Angeles. The metropolitan area is a mosaic of towns but the city proper has its own integrity. Both the city itself and the wider metropolitan basin are made up of discrete, classic neighborhoods. My natal neighborhoods are Silver Lake, Echo Park, Griffith Park, and Los Feliz. These neighborhoods extend backward to the early civic years long before the suburban sprawl and the paths that automobiles laid down became the dense web of freeways that today ensnares the entire Southern California basin. Silver Lake is now a trendy, bohemian enclave; Echo Park was once the center of the early film industry and later home to such notable Angelinos as children's book illustrator Leo Politi and Aimee Semple McPherson, the flamboyant Foursquare Gospel foundress of the Angelus Temple; Griffith Park is famous for its landmark hilltop observatory and picturesque outdoor Greek theater; Los Feliz was part of one of the first Spanish land grants in California as well as the place where, at a later time, Mickey Mouse was "born" in the garage of Walt Disney's uncle's house; homes designed by architects Frank Lloyd Wright and Richard Neutra still stand in yet another of these contiguous neighborhoods.

I grew up with these colorful stories. As heir to them, I was expected to be creative and do notable things. After all, my parents identified themselves as belonging to the "upper middle-class bohemian" segment of the population: my father was a contemporary jewelry designer, and my mother was a writer in early radio and film. Although my parents were not formally affiliated with a particular church, in elementary school I was enrolled in the choir programs at Hollywood First Presbyterian because choral training was considered essential for an aspiring singer. After graduating from John Marshall High School, I rotated in and out of a variety of institutions of higher learning interspersed with professional work interludes as a singer-actress. When I finally burned out of the L.A theatrical scene, I became a religious studies graduate student at the University of California at Santa Barbara. And there I stayed for a full decade.

This is where, with the guidance of several inspiring mentors, the foundations for the next thirty years of my life were laid: a doctorate, marriage and family, and formal entry into the Catholic faith. When, in 1984, degree in hand and two children in tow, we moved to Boston, I left the Los Angeles area behind. Certainly, I had returned to Southern California over the intervening years before this recent pilgrimage. Yet never until these last six years had I returned as a pilgrim, heart-honed and oriented by an inner compass wavering in a direction I could not envision. What has emerged in the pages that follow is not personal memoir but a spiritual peregrination taken in concert with others. Here, my own story is intertwined intermittently with the stories of thousands of other Catholics refracted through the seemingly infinite expressions of Mary's presence in this vast metropolitan basin. What draws these many layers of discourse together are the "spaces"—material, rhetorical, performative—that relate to Mary in her many guises. From Our Lady of the Rosary of Talpa in the barrio of east L.A. to Mary Star of the Sea whose majestic golden image is a beacon for seafarers above the harbor of San Pedro, from affluent suburban parishes to poor churches gated against graffiti and vandalism, I visited her under her innumerable titles. And in dozens of languages I listened to stories, noted the gestures, opened my heart, and was taught by those whom I met.

These spaces and my exploration of them are, in my estimation, at once profoundly catholic and essentially Catholic. They are catholic in the sense of being universal. They represent a wide spectrum of global religiosity. They suggest the many ways that human beings live deeply into the depths of joy, grief, fear, exaltation, hope, and freedom of which the human heart is capable. They open up into the realm of religious symbol and archetype. In addition, they are, of course, Catholic in that the Virgin Mary has long been one of the most identifiable figures defining Catholicism. The spaces I have entered through visits, conversations, historical research, and personal memory take me into a conceptual cosmos that undergirds the Catholic faith: a world of intertwined presences that transcend linear time and bounded space, a cosmos shot through with intimations of the divine. This incarnational religiosity issues an invitation to a serious engagement with flesh, with matter, with the entire material world and its environments, whether natural or humanly constructed.

The narrative of this book is particular: it is about a very personal story set in a particular place. But, I believe, that particularity opens out into a larger reality. It affords glimpses into the history of Los Angeles Catholicism. It peeks into the founding of the faith in the frontier region (*conquistadors*, *padres*, the vast Spanish land grants, the romance of the *ranchos*, the sad despoiling of Mexican Catholics by the Anglo-American takeover); it touches on the heroic labors of the religious orders that went on mission there and their sometimes dramatic destinies; and it intersects with the colorful personalities (Edward Doheny of Teapot Dome scandal fame, Fr. Patrick Peyton of the Hollywood Family Theater of the Air) that shaped the church in the 1950s and 1960s. Powerful leaders such as Bishop Thaddeus Amat and Archbishop John Caldwell appear in these pages, stamping the West Coast diocese with their own theological and ecclesial visions.

The narrative also gives access to the history of the Catholic Church in the United States as experienced on the West Coast as waves of immigrants arrived on American shores. Italian and Portuguese fishermen settled in San Pedro harbor in the nineteenth century; Vietnamese refugees flooded into the region mid-twentieth century. They brought their traditions and practices with them. The forcible internment of many Californians of Japanese descent during the Second World War is glimpsed, as are the disparate stories of the many Eastern Rite Catholic communities that established themselves in the region: Coptic, Ukrainian, Armenian, Lebanese, Russian, and Greek, each with its own style of worship and vivid relationship to the figure of Mary. Here, there is evidence of centuries of ever-changing demographics.

In addition, the living history of particular communities as inscribed on the layered physical space (architecture, statuary, renovations, *ad hoc* spatial revisions) is described: a parish may bear an Irish saint's name or the name of a Roman martyr favored by an ultramontanist bishop, have windows representing a time when Polish parishioners dominated, and now have elaborate devotional displays featuring El Salvador's and Honduras's beloved virgins. The book's narrative is particular to L.A. but mirrors the experience of many contemporary U.S. dioceses.

My lens widens as, with the insights of scholars of varied disciplinary expertise, the subtexts of the encounters I have are illuminated. With my academic colleagues and with my many Los Angeles conversation partners, I explore the vast global, cultural, linguistic, and ideological sweep of the Catholic Church. Most touchingly, I am gifted with the personal stories of men and women of faith. These stories entrusted to me with moving vulnerability, while different in almost every specific, mirror my own. These Marian spaces are inhabited by fellow pilgrims who also follow Mary's star toward the urgent longings of their hearts.

Finally, I find in these spaces the ecclesial *point vierge*, Catholicism's still center. The immense diversity of this global tradition comes together in this one figure, Mary. Her meaning and identity is certainly contested, parsed out in thousands of ways by devotees of seemingly endless ideological and cultural orientations, all the while being shored up through theological distinction and pastoral oversight. Yet she is generous and welcoming enough to hold them all together under her sheltering cloak. She is a splendid example of the centrality of paradox that lies at heart of Catholic faith. I make no attempt here to collapse all of her singular identities into one generic one, yet at the same time I hold her in my heart as the unifying "point" where the tensions hold, the conflicts find common ground, and Catholic diversity dances its miraculous and—when all is said and done—celebratory common dance.

Blessing before Our Lady of Refuge, Marian Year, Old Mission Santa Barbara, 1954.

Chapter 2

Our Lady of Refuge
Refugio

If through the centuries this most worthy mother of Our Lord has shown all goodness and compassion to all peoples and nations; if she has ever shown favor even to the most ungrateful and forgotten sinners, what will she not do for those people who bind themselves to her, who have recourse to her love, who invoke her, who call her their own, their solace, their recourse, their refuge, and special patroness?

—Francisco García Diego y Moreno, first bishop of California

The quiet of a grey-green winter morning. Through wisps of fog, glimpses of the offshore islands are visible. From my vantage point at the tip of the weathered wooden pier, I am cradled between the watery expanse of the Santa Barbara channel and the low crests of the Santa Ynez Mountains. What is it about returning to a place saturated in memories? To stand at the edge of this pier facing the olive-hued hills is to call up a decade of graduate studies at the university campus whose much-expanded outline is just visible on the distant promontory to my left. It is to summon the voice and gestures of a long-gone beloved graduate school mentor. It is to recall a wedding, two births, the slow inexorable turning of soul that when complete is, quite surprisingly, a conversion. It is to lapse into a reverie that cannot quite capture a distant decade's transformations or the blessings and the bruises that brought them about.

This morning the Pacific's expanse is not my surest compass; instead, the mountains' sheltering reach guides me, that and the city of Santa Barbara named for the saint once known as patroness of sailors

Our Lady of Refuge, Archives, Old Mission Santa Barbara. Used by permission.

and the saint to whom they appealed when high seas threatened shipwreck. Although the city nestled in the shadow of the Santa Ynez reach and the mission founded by the Spanish Franciscans still retain her name, St. Barbara has long since been dismissed from the official role of canonized saints. Her legend, in the light of historical-critical analysis, has been deemed just that, a legend. It is not, however, Barbara who is the object of my contemplation this early fog-strewn morning. I turn instead to the queen of saints, the Virgin Mary in her guise as *Nuestra Señora Refugio de los Pecadores*, Our Lady Refuge of Sinners.

To the north of the pier on which I stand is Refugio State Beach, a family friendly haunt dotted with picnic tables and swing sets. Long ago this place was entrusted to Our Lady of Refuge and baptized with her name, although the reference has long since disappeared from public memory. The vast Spanish land grant stretching from Gaviota Pass to Goleta, of which this strip of sand formed the southwestern perimeter, was deeded to the Ortega family at the end of the eighteenth century and put under the protection of *Nuestra Señora Refugio de los Pecadores*. It was fitting that *Refugio* should spread her mantle over the region. She came to this area by way of northern Mexico where during the colonial era she was one of the most popular of devotional images. (Art historians estimate that a full 25 percent of the ubiquitous painted wooden retablos in viceregal Mexico were of *Refugio*).

Her first arrival in the New World can be credited to the Jesuits, Italian Juan José Guica in particular, who in 1729 was missioned by his order to the new colonies in Mexico. Back home, Guica had been deeply moved by the theatrical preaching of Anthony Baldinucci, his Jesuit confrere who attracted overflow crowds on his tours of the Italian peninsula. At the front of the penitential processions he staged, Baldinucci carried a painting of Our Lady Refuge of Sinners and urged his rapt listeners to repentance. The priest assured them that if they entrusted themselves to her she would plead on their behalf to her son, the Redeemer. So popular did the Italian image become that Pope Clement XI had it crowned—an official ritual gesture reserved for the most venerated and reputedly powerful religious images—and enthroned in the chapel of the Jesuit church of the Gesù in Frascati outside of Rome.

Fr. Guica had been present for the coronation ceremony in Rome, and when he was sent overseas he carried with him a copy of the painting of the compassionate lady. Guica began his work in Mexico where he met a group of Franciscans from the Apostolic College at Zacatecas that included Friar José Guadalupe Alcibía. The Jesuit's heartfelt love for this particular Marian image and the stories of its power to draw devotees communicated itself to Alcibía. Guica offered the painting to Alcibía for use in the Franciscan Indian missions. *Refugio*, he felt, seemed to want to accompany the friars northward and bless their work. Soon the patronage of the Indian mission was officially transferred with Rome's approval from Guadalupe, patroness of the Zacatecan seminary, to Our Lady of Refuge.

When in 1840 a new diocese to the north was established, Francisco García Diego y Moreno from the Franciscan community at Zacatecas became its first bishop. García Diego brought with him a tender devotion to Our Lady of Refuge and proceeded to name her the new diocese's patroness. In a pastoral address to his flock in January 1843, the bishop's enthusiasm is clear:

> We make known to you that we well *had* to name, as we *do* name as principal patroness of our diocese, the great Mother of God under her precious title, *Del Refugio*. . . . Yes, beloved sons you are now under the patronage and special protection of the most beautiful queen, Mary most Holy, Refuge of Sinners. What felicity is yours. What ineffable happiness. With so great a patroness and protectress, what can you not promise yourselves? What can be wanting to you? Whom need you fear?

Throughout the new diocese images of *Nuestra Señora del Refugio* or *Refugium Peccatorum* (her Latin title) appeared. In each of the chain of Franciscan missions that snake up the Pacific coastline, her image can still be found. For a time in the mid-nineteenth century, a seminary operated by the Franciscans and bearing her name operated at Mission Santa Inés. Likewise in the historical archives of Southern California, one can often find references to the devotion she inspired. The name of Refugio State Beach is such a remnant in cartographic form.

The many mission images, while they reproduce the recognizable *Refugio* iconography, each have a distinctive charm of their own. Two especially, discovered in Santa Barbara at the Queen of the Missions during my pilgrimage, have become my favorites. I was no stranger to the parish of St. Barbara: it had been the site of hundreds of conversations with my first spiritual mentor, the remarkable Franciscan, Virgil Cordano, as well as my first parish after I was welcomed into the Catholic Church. Despite my long familiarity, I did not know of the *Refugio* images until my Marian peregrination began.

The first image I discovered unexpectedly in the anteroom of the mission archives propped against the wall where it sat fresh from storage. The sweetness and delicacy of the image struck me, although it clearly was a "folk" rendering. Mary and child are at the center, she visible from the just below the waist up, he standing on her knee swathed in a gauzy gown through which his chubby torso is visible. Both figures are elegantly crowned, heads slightly inclined toward each other. She looks out of the frame directly at the viewer while he gazes at his mother. Radiating halos tipped by small stars frame their two faces. The Virgin, draped in an embroidered cloak with a double strand of pearls at her neck, holds him up as if to present him.

The archivist Lynn Bremer identified the image as Our Lady of Refuge. There was, I learned, another more formal *Refugio* crafted in the European style upstairs in the Friars' Chapel. Brother Timothy Arthur, the Franciscan in charge of the community archives, was gracious enough to guide me through the cloister garden to the alcove just outside the friars' private chapel where an elegant Italianate version of *Refugio* hangs. García Diego y Moreno, the first bishop, planned to establish his episcopal seat in Santa Barbara and to have it bear Our Lady of Refuge's name. The cathedral, however, was not destined for that location or for *Refugio*'s patronage. After the California territory was ceded to the ever-expanding United States, the third bishop, Thaddeus Amat, a member of the Congregation of the Mission (the Vincentians) and a man fueled by a desire to have his far-flung diocese orient not south but eastward to Rome, oversaw the construction of his cathedral further south, in the city of Los Angeles. He replaced *Refugio*'s patronage with that of St. Vibiana, a Roman martyr whose freshly discovered remains were attracting attention in the Eternal City. It is thought that the *Refugio* image now hanging in the Friars' Chapel was commissioned for the Santa Barbara cathedral that was never built.

I learn more about this image as I read about artistic renewal in the era of the Catholic Reformation, to which this image owes its genesis.

To emphasize a personal and mystical approach to religion, close contact between the faithful and the divine was encouraged in artistic design. This I see in the Virgin's eyes that gaze out at the viewer. She has stood the test of time and even today *Refugio* compels. The sweetness of the image is not saccharine, its delicacy not cloying. When I am in her presence, I enter into an imagined world of infinite compassion, innocence, and tender mercy, a world in which I can find refuge.

In 2006, July 5, Our Lady of Refuge's feast day (made an obligatory diocesan celebration by California's bishops in 1981), fell during one of my visits. Intent on finding out the extent to which she is still consciously memorialized in the diocese, I made inquiries. To my dismay, I discovered that no official celebrations were planned. Even the one parish in the archdiocese that bears her name, Our Lady of Refuge in Long Beach, with its

Our Lady of Refuge, Our Lady of Refuge Church, Long Beach. Artist: J. Pikner, 1960s.

contemporary bronze statue by artist José Pirkner of a standing Mary hovering high above the busy intersection of Los Coyotes, Stearns, and Clark Streets, had not planned an observance for that day. Conversations with Dr. Joan Bravo de Murillo, the energetic young principal of the parish parochial school, indicate that the parishioners of Our Lady of Refuge are mainly Anglo or affluent, assimilated Hispanics for whom Marian devotion is not a focal point of faith; the only formal reference to *Refugio* in the school curriculum is confined to a formulaic "Our Lady of Refuge, pray for us" included in daily prayer. It is clear that this particular devotion, once lively in the region, no longer captures the imagination of present-day Catholics here.

Still, she lingers—not only as an artifact enshrined in mission archives, but as a palpable presence—in this land and its people entrusted to her tender mercies by Bishop Francisco García Diego y Moreno and the members of the Ortega family. I too have known this place as refuge, even before I knew her name. This south-facing triangle of earth cupped in the sheltering arms of the Santa Ynez range was the home-place of my slow turning, a reorientation of self. When I arrived here in 1974, I was fleeing the shards of a failed marriage and a theatrical career. In 1984, during the final week of my residence in St. Barbara's city, in a momentary break from the vagaries of packing the detritus of a decade's graduate studies, I drove to the top of Mission Ridge, high above the cityscape of Santa Barbara, got out of my car, and sat at the edge of a sun-drenched precipice. Below me stretched the familiar sites. That day the fog had cleared enough to afford a crystalline view of the Pacific and the far islands. Memories came flooding back, too many to parse them all out, so I simply sat, holding the years in some inarticulate way in my heart. Then, quite distinctly, I felt as though I had been kissed. Yes, kissed: by the Universe, by God, by the land itself. I did not know it then but I had taken refuge in Our Lady of Refuge's home-place and had received her blessing.

ECCE
ANCILLA
DOMINI
FIAT MIHI
SECUNDUM
VERBUM
TUUM

AVE MARIA GRATIA
PLENA DOMINUS TECUM
BENEDICTA TU IN MULIERIBUS
ET BENEDICTUS FRUCTUS
VENTRIS TUI JESUS

SPIRITUS
SANCTUS
IN TE
DESCENDET
MARIA
ET VIRTUS
ALTISSIMI
OBUMBRA-
BIT TIBI

WILLIAM EARLEY
CHURCH ART STUDIOS
DUBLIN CAMBERWELL

Annunciation Window, St. John's Seminary, Camarillo.

Chapter 3

Lady of the Angels
Nuestra Señora de los Angeles

As Mary listened to the voice of an angel,
may you be open to God's voice
and respond to God's will
each day of your life. Amen

—From the *Solemn Blessing*, *Cycle B*: August 2, 2007, Feast of Our
Lady of the Angels at the Los Angeles Cathedral of Our Lady of
the Angels

It means "little portion" and it reflects the Franciscan spirit from which it was born: *portiuncula* (Latin) or *porziuncola* (Italian) or *porciúncula* (Spanish) as in *Rio Porciúncula*. This was the name the Spanish explorers in Captain Gaspar de Portola's 1769 expedition to Alta California gave to the thin ribbon of water that threaded through the coastal villages of the native Gabrielino tribes. Among those explorers was Franciscan diarist Juan Crespi, who made note of the expedition's arrival on August 3, the day following the feast of Our Lady of the Angels of the Porciúncula. Littleness, minority, the least, the poor, poverty (material and spiritual)—these were the themes dear to Francis, the medieval saint of Assisi who modeled his life on Jesus the Christ who entered the world as a naked, vulnerable infant and left it naked and abandoned on a cross.

Aptly, the site on the Italian peninsula where many of the pivotal events in Francis's life took place was given the name the *Porciúncula*, the Little Portion. A small Romanesque church was the site of Francis's discernment to follow the naked, cross-hung Christ, the site of the

19

founding of his order, the Friars Minor, of the consecration of Chiara Offreduccio (Clare of Assisi) to an enclosed variant of the mendicant life he followed, and the site where he welcomed Sister Death. The Little Portion is nestled in an Umbrian region known as the Valley of the Angels, perhaps because angelic voices are reputed to be audible there. Over the valley hovers the protective presence of Our Lady of the Angels.

Historians still quarrel about the name given to the California town that was founded in 1781 along Rio Porciúncula by settlers from Sinaloa and Sonora. Perhaps the most trustworthy possibility is *El Pueblo de Nuestra Senora de los Angeles del Rio Porciúncula* (the town of Our Lady of the Angels on the Porciuncula River). The hamlet, initially comprised of a mere forty-four persons of mixed Spanish, Native, and African ancestry, was served by the Franciscan friars who ten years before had established nearby San Gabriel Mission. As the tiny community grew,

Annunciation Mosaic, "*La Placita*," Piczek Studios Mosaic.

the pueblo received its own church. It was dedicated to the Lady of the Angels and became known as *Iglesia de Nuestra Señora Reina de los Angeles* or, in more familiar parlance, *La Placita*, the little plaza.

On a typical Sunday the courtyard alongside *La Placita* is humming. Worshipers at one of the twelve weekend Masses, eleven of which are conducted in Spanish, file in and out of the tiny ornate mission-style church. In the courtyard they fill bottles with holy water available from a spigot, purchase tamales or candies from vendors, or pause to admire the holy cards and devotional trinkets at the gift shop run by the Claretian Fathers who now staff the parish. This church, the plaza across the road, and colorful Olvera Street with its historic adobes and rows of *puestos* offer tourists and Angelinos alike a sense of the Mexican city's life as it was first experienced over two hundred years ago.

Long before I became a Catholic and could share in the liturgies at *La Placita*, I knew Olvera Street and the Spanish and Mexican heritage

"*La Placita*," Los Angeles's Original Church.

that is so central to L.A.'s identity. In my mother's telling, the California past was first and foremost the romantic rancho period when elegant Mexican families presided over vast tracts of cattle land and held festive dances at which closely guarded *señoritas* peered out from behind their fans at handsome potential suitors. Before the Franklin Elementary public school curriculum introduced me to pilgrims and Mount Vernon, these California stories were mine. Thus my sense of American history could be summarized by the novel *Ramona*, a widely read 1884 potboiler by Helen Hunt Jackson that spun out the melodramatic tale of an orphan raised by wealthy rancheros of Southern California in the era when the Americans had begun their dismantling of Mexican culture in the lands they had recently acquired as war booty.

The romance of these imagined early days were reinforced for me by the colorful images of the city captured by L.A. illustrator Leo Politi. Politi's world, like Ramona's, was profoundly Catholic in some way I, during these unchurched years, could not have articulated. My first Politi book, one he signed for me in 1953 with his signature colored pens creating swirling loops and flowers upon the inside page, was *Pedro, the Angel of Olvera Street*. In those pages I dreamed with the little boy who lived on the narrow founding street adjacent to *La Placita* with the red-tiled pavement and the little *puestos* where *piñatas* and *piruli* were sold. The warmth of Politi's world drew me in. It was a world where angels and saints intermingled with mothers' kisses and tamales, and prayers were offered up under a shining star. Leo Politi honored the little things: children, small animals, ordinary gestures of kindness, people of no import in the great dealings of nations yet crucial for the nurture of the world.

It is a little person, an unimportant girl from a backwater village in the Middle East, that the Christian tradition places at the center of its sacred story. Within the womb of this girl, a mortal human being, tradition locates the incarnate Godhead. It is within her fragile flesh that the unfathomable mystery of life, death, and the cosmos is revealed. The tile mosaic that since 1981 has graced the front portico of *La Placita* is a replica of a fourteenth-century image by Prete Ilario da Viterbo at the *Porziúncola* in Assisi. The tile version in L.A. is the creation of Isabel Piczek of the fabled Piczek sisters whose art is everywhere evident in the archdiocese. This multicolored mosaic of Italian Renaissance style shows Mary at the moment of the annunciation, the moment reported in the Gospel of Luke when this unassuming young Palestinian girl said yes to an angel's confounding invitation to become the Mother of God.

It is about this obscure girl-child that Franciscan Fr. Richard Juzix speaks to me on the foliage-shaded patio behind the rectory at St. Francis of Assisi Church in L.A.'s Silver Lake district during a morning conversation. Being here in this neighborhood brings memories flooding back, for it was in St. Francis's sunlit sanctuary, thirty-five years ago, that one of the pivotal moments of my early soul-turning took place. I had recently abandoned my theater career and enrolled in a history course at the state university just off the San Bernardino Freeway. St. Francis Church was on my homeward route and I, the non-Catholic, had taken to stopping by in the late afternoons, drawn by the stillness and the rainbow of colors filtering through the vertical stained-glass windows—their light flooding across the pews. Generally

Annunciation,
St. Vincent's Church, L.A.

alone, I wandered about gazing at the windows of the unknown holy men and women through whose images the light flowed. Above the central altar the Umbrian saint, Francis himself, hung as an oversized wooden bas-relief.

One day, it is difficult to describe, in that warm womb of a space, half-dreaming, I clearly yet terrifyingly saw myself for the first time and understood with precision that God was the one absolutely essential fact of my life. Simultaneously, I saw exactly how far I was from actualizing that truth. All the energies of my personhood, which rightly belonged at the still center, were flung wide with the inexorable power of centrifugal force and were scattered in a thousand directions. At that moment I grasped how impossible it would be for me to draw them back. I flung a desperate, instinctual prayer out into the universe, but half knew that only a miracle could effect any change; and, as I exited the church, the inner sight faded and fear that I would lose the precious knowledge took its place. Yet I know now, in retrospect, that the years that followed were in fact an answer to that inarticulate prayer.

Fr. Richard has no notion of my history nor am I here today to reminisce. Rather I have come to speak to him of Marian devotion. He and his Franciscan confreres, says my host, harkening back to the medieval theologian Duns Scotus, have long emphasized the centrality of the Virgin Mary both in their theology and their spirituality. She is the instrument of the incarnation, and it is her openness to the divine invitation that is the key to the Gospel. It is because of her openness that she became fruitful and gave life to the world. That is the way she is best understood, Fr. Richard affirms. He calls her the model of the church and the model for each member who, like her, is called to be open to the Gospel and to bear its fruits in the world. Recalling one of the salutations from Assisi's prayerful litany

Annunciation Window, St. Francis of Assisi Church, L.A.

of Our Lady—"Hail Virgin, made Church"—my conversation partner continues to stress that Mary for Francis himself was a model of the church. Franciscans, he informs me, vow to live the Gospel life. They do not merely vow poverty, that would be too narrow, but vow to do what Mary did, become fruitful and sing of glorifying the Lord, and of the lowly raised up and the rich sent away empty. It is this Mary, the little one, who turns an attentive ear to an angel's invitation, who is at the center of the Marian mystery of the city that bears her name.

In this same listening posture, Mary is found in numerous stained-glass versions all over the region, wherever the biblical scene or the mysteries of the rosary are illustrated. Most notably, in terms of local history, she is remembered this way at Mission San Gabriel Arcángel, the "mother church" of the archdiocese and the "godmother of the pueblo of Los Angeles." The parish, founded in 1771, honors the archangel Gabriel who greeted Mary; and the nearby Chapel of the Annunciation, built in 1956 to accommodate the growing congregation, features the scene of their encounter above the main entryway.

This angelic encounter is the focus of a liturgy I attend at St. Andrew's Abbey in Valyermo in the high desert at the far edge of the archdiocese. It is December 8, the feast of the Immaculate Conception, and a passing winter storm has dusted the San Gabriel Mountains with a thin patina of snow, making my two-hour drive northeast from downtown a glittering, gleaming one. This is my first visit to the Benedictine abbey famed for its charming ceramic representations of angels and saints. Today the air temperature hovers just above freezing, and the local worshipers gathered for the feast day keep their fleece jackets hugged around them in the pine and brick-floored chapel that once served as a horse stable. For this solemn observance, the sung Mass parts, in Latin and set to the traditional pattern of Gregorian chant, are led by one of the youthful, robed monks who directs the assembly from a spot next to an expansive floral arrangement of red roses and white lilies set out for the feast. The assigned Gospel reading for this liturgical observance, which turns our attention to the singular grace that Mary received at the moment of her conception in her mother's womb, is the familiar one of the annunciation from the first chapter of Luke. The angel approaches, Mary hesitates and then assents.

This feast, our monastic presider suggests, applies to all of us. Although it features the Virgin as unique—in that to prepare her for the coming of her son she was dispensed from the effects of original sin—we too as human beings, like Mary, must be prepared. The Advent refrain "Prepare ye the way of the Lord!" is meant for each of us. The emphasis of the priest's homily is not surprising. Benedictine spirituality is profoundly scriptural and liturgical. For centuries monastics have looked to the Virgin Mary as the model for their life, indeed as model for the ideal human life: a life of increasing openness to the Word of God, a life of gradual and insistent being unmade and made over again into the divine image in which humans were created. For each of us is called to receive and gestate and bring into the world the Word. Each of us is called to be a mother of God.

Following the Eucharist, I seek out my host who with his fluffy salt-and-pepper beard looks the very picture of a seasoned Benedictine. Fr. Philip has graciously agreed to chat with me about Mary and the monks, and we take a seat in the lounge of the retreat house after I have been plied with characteristic Benedictine lunchtime hospitality. My host is a bit nostalgic, for it was on the eve of this feast day many years before that he entered this monastery, and he had also awakened on that first morning to the wonder of a snow-shrouded desert landscape. Fr. Philip, I learn, came to Catholicism and his monastic vocation from an evangelical Presbyterian background so elements of the faith were foreign, especially the idea of Mary and the communion of saints. He tells me that he gradually came to see that when you are with Jesus you are with Mary, for at every significant point in the sacred narrative about Jesus she is there. And, my host contends, the Virgin is a very apt model for a Benedictine because she is steady, present to her son at the beginning, middle, and end, always reflecting, always quietly but earnestly pondering the meaning of what takes place. The monk's words suggest the vow of stability and dedication to seek God in contemplative silence that he and his confreres have taken, the vow to show up day after day, to continue searching, to live into the questions, to ponder them in the heart.

St. Andrew's is a missionary branch of the Benedictine family birthed out of the German monastic revivals of the nineteenth century and affiliated with a cluster of Benedictine communities known as the Congregation of the Annunciation. In fact, this house was founded by a mission from China. The primary mission work in which they engage now is their mail-order ceramic business and running the retreat house. After Fr. Philip apologetically interrupts our conversation to attend to the inquiry of one of the gift-shop employees, he returns, having remembered an important Benedictine contribution to the Marian tradition: Our Lady of the Sabbath, a favored observance from the Cluniac Benedictines of the tenth century, an observance which one of the present monks here is eager to revive. As I tour the property after our time together, I am struck with the wilderness quality to the landscape recessed far back into the arid hills studded with Joshua trees: a sabbath place where reflection and perspective can be cultivated, where time is experienced not as slipping away but as opening out into infinity. This is a place where angels might easily appear, and one who listens and ponders might find a home.

The high desert is not the only place where I discover traces of a Mary who consorts with angels. Under the title of Our Lady of the Angels she manifests herself in visual form in various places in the Los Angeles archdiocese. On a prominent corner of busy Wilshire Boulevard, along the edge of the parking area belonging to the austere modernity of St. Basil's Church, she flings her dark bronze arms up and reaches toward the sky with a contemporary abandon unthinkable to a long-ago religious sensibility. She appears more conventionally in polychrome plaster-of-paris guise surrounded by clouds of *puti* at Our Lady of the Angels parish on the outskirts of Santa Maria in the northeastern sector of the archdiocese.

And, of course, I find her downtown at the magnificent new Cathedral of Our Lady of the Angels. She is there in two distinctive incarnations, the older one, a gorgeous life-sized Majolica statue, transferred from the former Cathedral of St. Vibiana before its closing. Her more recent incarnation, cantilevered above the great bronze entrance doors of the newly consecrated cathedral, is as a girl of unidentifiable biracial identity who might be any girl in this modern metropolis. The late Mexican-born L.A. artist Robert Graham has presented her unforgettably here in bronze as the woman of the Book of Revelation, clothed with the sun, the moon beneath her feet, with the halo shaft surmounting her gathered hair which allows the California sunlight to move imperceptibly across her features as the day unfolds. Barefoot and bare armed, she is wrapped in a simple smock, her palms turn up in a gesture of welcome to the diverse throngs of faithful and tourists who enter beneath her gaze. Our Lady of the Angels's gesture recalls as well that similarly expansive "yes" breathed back two millennia ago to the messenger to whom an unassuming girl hesitantly, then boldly, learned to listen.

He was a little man, physically at least, as well as in terms of material wealth. During his 2008 funeral Mass, the superior of his Franciscan community spoke of how he had lived and died in the spirit of their founder—chaste and poor—and of the few personal possessions he had left behind: a modest number of books, a small suitcase of clothes. He was buried in a small pine box in his plain brown habit belted with its white cord knotted three times expressing his three lifelong vows of poverty, chastity, and obedience. But for the funeral Mass held on the red-tiled steps and the lawn fronting the Old Mission Santa Barbara where he had lived for most of his eighty plus years, two thousand folding chairs had been set up to accommodate those attending because Fr. Virgil Cordano, this unassuming padre, had so profoundly touched each of their lives.

He certainly touched mine. During a 1975 private retreat at the Immaculate Heart Spiritual Center in Montecito, I was lent a tape recording of one of Fr. Virgil's homilies on the biblical book of James. Seated on the slim single bed in my retreat room, one window flung open to welcome the scent of the sage-covered hills, everything changed. One phrase spoken in Virgil's unprepossessing voice lodged itself in my consciousness and never left. "God is greater than your own condemning heart." With those eight slight words, a man and his Gospel-inspired spiritual vision entered my listening ear and moved to my heart. What followed was a year and a half of Saturday morning forays to the mission's adobe-walled anterooms where Virgil and I sat on adjoining brown Naugahyde sofas, and his listening gradually drew me into a new, deeper life in the Catholic faith. Over the years our friendship grew.

Our final 2008 visit took place at Santa Barbara's Cottage Hospital. When I arrived at the hospital room, a solicitous nurse withdrew and left us alone, a gesture I guessed was one she had repeated dozens of times since his latest admission. I perched on his bedside, we exchanged words of gratitude, and Virgil uttered the refrain that I took to represent the divestment taking place in this great spirit, now stripped of

Our Lady of the Angles, Cathedral of Our Lady of the Angels. Artist: Robert Graham.

physical strength and all the honed capacities of a lifetime. "I guess I am my own sort of Catholic." For him it had become so utterly simple. All of the complexities of theological argument, rubrics, and ideology: all dissolved in the imperative to love.

Among the two thousand mourners shading their eyes from the bright south coast sun that May morning of Fr. Virgil's funeral were rabbis, Buddhists, Unitarians, the unchurched, as well as Catholics and every variety of Christian, all gathered because this man had personally touched them in some inexpressible way. My own kind of Catholic, he had said, speaking rhetorically to the architects of rubrical guidelines and splitters of theological hairs. We clasped hands and wept, a sign of the remembered hours we had shared in the anterooms of the Old Mission, me hesitantly, then boldly, probing the hidden recesses of my spiritual longing. He listening, attuned, attentive, willing to hear beneath my words, bend to the spirit, and form in me a listening heart.

Our Lady of the Angels, St. Basil's Parish, L.A. Artist: Ernest Shelton, 1975.

Chapter 4

Our Mother
Nuestra Madre

Mother of dark soil,
morning star
and vast ocean–
Mother who births plants,
winged creatures,
fish of the sea
and four-footed beasts–
Mother who nurses the stars,
the planets,
the black universe–
Mother who suckles the children of the earth–
Mother who holds creation in strong arms,
rocking it through the ages,
with the lullaby of life–
Show us your face, O Divine Mother,
Show us your face.

—Mary Lou Kownacki, OSB, *Prayers for a New Millennium*

Alert as always to the devotional energy that pulses unceasingly like a heartbeat beneath the frenetic surface of the city, my Jesuit mentor Fr. Engh informs me of the fervent Armenian devotion to St. Rita of Cascia, known as the Saint of the Impossible, that occurs the first Thursday of

Korean Madonna, St. Gregory Nazianzen Church, L.A.

each month at Our Mother of Good Counsel parish in the Los Feliz district. On the Thursday I visit, the church is abuzz with milling devotees: votive candles and sandwiches are for sale in the side vestibules and petitioners deposit offerings of various kinds. While I didn't realize it during my first childhood visit to this parish four decades previous, it was the Augustinian order that brought to the archdiocese not only devotion to St. Rita but to Our Mother of Good Counsel as well. These men, members of the order inspired by the great North African theologian, traveled in 1922 from Philadelphia at the invitation of Bishop John Cantwell in order to staff schools and parishes. The graceful carved wood image at the parish on Vermont Avenue of Our Mother of Good Counsel, her gaze cast affectionately toward her toddler son who in turn wraps his small arms around her neck, is placed to the right of the altar and set against a tasteful white marble background. The image, I learn, is a copy of the original at the Augustinian shrine at Genezzano near Rome that has attracted veneration since the late fifteenth century.

My Thursday visit occasions a flood of memories as well as interest in the present-day parish, and I seek out a conversation partner at the rectory behind the church. There Fr. Walter Vogel, an older, welcoming gentleman, presents himself and, leaving whatever he was busy with, is gracious enough to sit with me awhile beneath the Marian image and comment on life at Our Mother of Good Counsel. Unlike most L.A. parishes, the Augustinian tells me, Good Counsel is mostly Anglo, although increasing numbers of Filipinos and Hispanics frequent the liturgies. Devotion to Mary is thus not as lively here as in many more diverse congregations. However it still thrives among members of his own Augustinian community and its secular order. Fr. Walter lowers his head slightly and leans toward me and speaks tenderly of the onset of each day when he and his confreres begin with prayer to the Mother of Good Counsel. Directing my attention to the statue beneath which we sit, he gestures fondly upward: "See, the hands of the Christ Child: they hold on to her for security. In this way too we Augustinians lean upon our good mother."

I cannot claim that from my own first immersions in Roman Catholic waters I emerged with a sense of a compassionate maternal presence such as Fr. Vogel described. My maiden voyage inside a pre–Vatican II Catholic church was during elementary school and took place in this very sanctuary. I was visiting with Chris, a sixth-grade friend whose

Augustinian Our Mother of Good Counsel, Our Mother of Good Counsel Church, L.A.

family belonged to the parish. Chris let me follow the incomprehensible Latin service in her fist-sized missal but, child of only marginally churched parents, I possessed no frame of reference with which to orient to the ritualized actions. My time at Mass was spent anxiously trying to determine on which knee worshipers were supposed to genuflect, an action which appeared to be rigidly codified and observed by all others present.

Nor were things much better at Christ the King parish for my next Catholic foray in my early twenties when I attended the Pre-Cana sessions obligatory for those planning a wedding. My husband-to-be, a nonpracticing Catholic, did not attend, being occupied with theater rehearsals. My memory of those dreary sessions is partial, but I do recall the green paperback cover of the pre–Vatican II pamphlet that contained our assigned readings and that I tearfully shook at my fiancé when he cruised by to pick me up. The (now effectively defunct) teaching on limbo that consigned unbaptized infants to a Dantesque nomadic

oblivion between heaven and earth horrified me. Despite this, what convinced me to sign the agreement that I would raise any children of this union as Catholics was the utterly compelling thought that such children might travel anywhere in the world and, on entering a Catholic church, find themselves at home. In retrospect, it is this intuition that undergirds my Marian peregrinations undertaken decades later. Mary's maternal presence gradually made itself known to me. But it was only after the slow dissolution of that early childless marriage along with the move from the world of show business to graduate study of religion in Santa Barbara that this happened.

In fact, I became a Catholic because of Mary. The university class that occasioned my encounter was entitled "From Augustine to Luther." The professor, Walter Holden Capps, was destined to become my dear friend and dissertation director, but all I knew at the time, as I haunted the eight-storied UCSB library building in search of a research topic, was that what entranced me about the course were the oblique references to the medieval cult of the Virgin Mary. I began to chart her various titles and appellations, organizing them in graph form on generous sheets of poster paper: Second Eve, Queen of Saints, God-Bearer, Throne of Wisdom, Enclosed Garden, Bride, Mystical Rose, Fountain of Joy, Woman Clothed with the Sun. The graphs were complex and recorded the classic literary, theological, and pictorial evidence of Mary's identities as I came across them. More than any other source, however, I was drawn by Henry Adams's classic *Mont-Saint-Michel and Chartres* with its captivating tales of medieval popular devotion to the Virgin that conveyed a compelling sense of her as tender and forgiving yet pragmatic. It was Mary to whom the lost, strayed, fallible, and oh-so-very-human turned. I was not naïve about the literary and historical nature of this encounter, but gradually her world opened to me experientially. A ground of infinite compassion began to reveal itself. It had a maternal, feminine face and her name was Mary.

Professor Capps favored immersion pedagogy, field trips with a purpose, which placed his students in real-life contexts that complemented the theoretical reading we did in class. Several key moments of the slow conversion taking place in me occurred "in the field": on the red-tiled steps of the Old Mission Santa Barbara where I stood with Capps and realized for the first time that I belonged there; in the chapel of the Poor Clares monastery on Los Olivos Street—that fragrant space of parlor grill, hushed corridors, habited sisters, gold chalices, and white lace altar cloths—and registered as accurate the words the mother superior gave to a fellow student's question about how they could possibly know what was happening in the world without a TV: "Ah, but everything important eventually comes to the center." Suffice it to say that these and a thousand other incremental soul movements culminated in a private ceremony of confirmation in the elegant library of the Immaculate Heart Center for Spiritual Renewal in Montecito with Fr. Virgil presiding. As a reading for the ritual moment, I chose a text from a letter written to Christians in Ephesus by the second-century bishop Ignatius of Antioch, the final phrase of which resonates with me still.

> And the virginity of Mary, and her giving birth,
> were hidden from the prince of this world,
> as was the death of the Lord:
> Three mysteries of a cry which were wrought in the stillness of God.

The metropolitan sprawl of Los Angeles is immense, necessitating my spending substantial blocks of time in my rental car trying to locate my Marian spaces. Much of the time I have been ably directed by one or the other of my essential go-to people, Fr. Engh or the Cardinal-Archbishop's theologian, Dr. Michael Downey. The latter has helped me contact Fr. Alex Kim for answers to my questions about Koreans and Marian devotion. I reach Fr. Alex by phone at St. Thomas in Anaheim where he resides just south of the archdiocese, and he confirms my previous research about his community: Marian devotion is very important in Korean Catholicism. Perhaps, Fr. Alex speculates, this is because of the Confucian respect for family, elders, and progenitors that permeates the culture. Or perhaps she is instinctively welcomed in a world visually familiar with Kuan Yin or Gwan-Um, the Goddess of Compassion. Be this as it may, Mary as the Immaculate Conception is patroness of Korea. Yet, unlike other Asian communities, in Korea there have been no Marian apparitions nor are there separate titles for her of which Fr. Alex is aware. She is depicted primarily as a mother with her child, a representation appropriate to a culture in which the family is held in high esteem.

Late one afternoon, after a day driving when my carbon footprint has become embarrassingly heavy, I stop off at St. Gregory Nazianzen Church on Bronson Avenue near Ninth in L.A. I have had it in mind to track down a parish with a sizable Korean population to see if there is iconographical evidence to photograph. The present high-ceilinged

Italo-Gothic sanctuary of St. Gregory, erected in 1938, yields little, but as I wander outside I see two Korean women in religious habits closing up a gift gallery in a storeroom at the side of the church. They honor my request to peek inside, and there I discover a twelve-inch-high statuette of Mary in rose-colored Korean dress, her child held lovingly in the crook of her arm. The elder of the two nuns presses the image on me: Do buy her and have her blessed by the priest. You must put it in your home. You have children? (I do). She will watch over them.

I purchase the graceful statue and have it blessed by my Jesuit confrere (he is sensitive enough to my project to be unfazed by the request). It eventually comes to rest on my bedroom dresser in Omaha, a maternal figure charged with the long-distance care of my own now-scattered brood. Yet as lovely as she is and as genuine the sentiment that bonds the Korean sisters and myself, this particular Mary is not an unambivalent image. She is the radiant mother, without a doubt. But her hair, while tied back in keeping with the style of her national costume, is light brown, not the dark hue of living Korean women, and her sculpted face clearly mimics an Anglo standard of beauty. My Asian theological colleagues would rightly see in this image a dark reflection of the subjugation and exploitation that Asian women have endured for centuries, women who stagger under the multiple oppressions of the historic inferior status of Asian women, colonially imported Western canons of beauty, the brutal reality of the sex trade buttressed by stereotypes of Asian women as compliant partners of male exploitation, and the subordination of women's voices within the church. Despite her sweet smile, my rose-hued statuette might, if she were afforded a voice, have a brutal tale to tell. I allow her to preside on my dresser with her complex message, perhaps because I feel so deeply the solidarity with other women that motherhood affords: a vocation lived out in varied ways in often heartrending and impossibly difficult circumstances, but a vocation that binds us together nonetheless. I allow my Korean Madonna to be a conscience-pricking reminder that my visceral link with women all over the globe must also issue in advocacy.

In L.A.'s historic Chinatown I have less trouble finding a maternal version of Mary that reflects its appropriate cultural origins. Situated not far from the civic center, Chinatown exists in my childhood memories as the idyllic home of Moy Moy and Mr. Fong, the little girl of the dragon dance and the toymaker fashioning shadow puppets for the Moon Festival, who are featured in L.A. artist Leo Politi's books. Today the district is still the densely populated, commercially lively neighborhood that Politi captured, if not exactly his imagined world of childhood innocence. St. Bridget's parish, hidden at the edge of the maze of small winding streets that snake through this historic district, is bustling on my first Sunday visit. The church vestibule is crowded with folding chairs set up for the overflow congregation, and I wedge myself between an elderly matron and a family with three squirming children, grateful that the universal pattern of the Eucharistic service makes it possible for me to follow the Cantonese responses. Touring the church following the liturgy, I find several examples of what I am looking for. At the entrance door is a small stack of prayer cards depicting Our Lady of China, a reproduction of an image originally painted by John Lu Hung-nien, a mosaic version of which hangs in the National Shrine in Washington, DC. This elegant Chinese Madonna in the flowing robes of a noblewoman stands at the center of the composition upon a curling white cumulus cloud. She gazes shyly down at her son while he peeks coyly out at the observer, his tiny hand emerging from his red coat to clutch the fluttering edge of his mother's veil. The duo are framed by two white birds who circle with flower offerings in their beaks. On the left wall of the sanctuary, a boldly colored stained-glass depiction of a contemporary Chinese Mary presents herself. Hands pressed in prayer, she is flanked by a deer, water lilies, marsh reeds, and a soaring bird. Then there are the arresting Stations of the Cross that circle the interior. In one of them the slim, lightly clad

Chinese Madonna Window, St. Bridget's Chinese Catholic Community, Chinatown, L.A.

Our Lady Help of Christians, St. Bridget's Chinese Catholic Community, Chinatown, L.A.

Asian Christ stands before a shogun-like Pilate; in another, he inclines toward his silk-robed mother, the two of them framed by a mountain in the flattened perspective of Chinese landscape painting.

Fr. Lam, a priest of the Salesians of Don Bosco in residence at St. Bridget, supplies substance to my initial observations on a return visit. One of several Chinese communities in the archdiocese, St. Bridget's is the only independent Chinese congregation. Fr. Lam, stressing what I know to be a foundational value in traditional Chinese culture, informs me that Catholics here are *educated* in Marian devotion. Hence devotion is very strong. First Saturdays are carefully observed, the parish plans to participate in a Cantonese rosary at the upcoming Rosary Bowl to be held in the Rose Bowl stadium, and all the L.A. Chinese parishes participate in honoring Our Lady of China the second week in May. Additionally, here at St. Bridget's on the twenty-fourth of each month, Fr. Lam informs, a novena is offered to Mary Help of Christians.

Indeed, the European Mary Help of Christians in regal stance, scepter in hand, crown upon her head, her kingly child held aloft, is also visually present at St. Bridget. She is cast in white plaster in the fenced-in yard where the remains of a recent parish festival are evident, and she appears in polychrome splendor inside the church. This image was St. Don Bosco's favorite. That nineteenth-century Piedmontese founder of the Salesian family of priests, religious, and lay cooperators was quite literally a dreamer of dreams. Among the more vivid nighttime communications that he felt were divinely prompted was an 1862 dream of a large ship commanded by the pope surrounded by fleets of smaller seagoing crafts all feverishly bent on destroying the larger vessel. Two columns appeared in the dream through which the pope steered in these dangerous waters: upon one Mary as the immaculate conception was posed, an inscription identified her as *Auxilium Christianorum* (Help of Christians). The dream catalyzed Don Bosco into a lifetime of ministry to impoverished and marginalized youth

Mary Help of Christians has presided over the global Salesian family since that time, although, Fr. Lam explains, because of government policies, the religious order's work on the Chinese mainland is restricted and they must proceed there prudently under the auspices of a secular organization. Bosco's approach to the destitute children he served was one of gentle persuasion rather than punishment or severity, an approach sometimes referred to as "preventive pedagogy." In keeping with this spirit, the St. Bridget's anniversary brochure Fr. Lam offers me illustrates the prodigious efforts in this Salesian-staffed center to provide holistic nurture to the community's young people. The figure of Mary Help of Christians, through the Salesian family, continues today to preside over their charges with her compassionate and infinitely inventive maternal care.

I know from experience that, although the archetype of motherhood is ever with us, actual motherhood is different in varied cultural settings as well as for different individual women. Yet motherhood is also a great bond that connects women across time and space. Certainly Mother Mary is a complex figure. She is also one that speaks an essential truth. As I gaze at the imagery scattered about the sanctuary at St. Bridget's, I see in the faces of the Chinese Madonna a reflection of other Asian figures like Kuan Yin, in whom motherhood equates with compassion. The sorrowful Chinese mother who kneels ever so discreetly at the foot of the cross on which her only son hangs speaks of still another painful dimension of motherhood as she bears the unspeakable sorrows of her child. Turning to the back of the church, I find in the figure of the Salesian Mary the instructive mother who, while gentle, is fierce in her untiring efforts to rescue and support her forgotten children. My thoughts turn to my earlier visits and the sweet visage of Our Mother of Good Counsel who offers her Augustinian sons and daughters a warm and protective embrace and to my statuette of the Korean mother and child who speak to me of the fierce maternal challenge of carrying hope and love into a world marred by structural sin and human culpability. My mind strays even further to memories of a Mary as the white-veiled icon of the "Mothers of the Plaza" who, during Argentina's dirty war of the late 1970s and 80s, stood against a ruthless military regime on behalf of their disappeared family members. Or of the reports of mothers from indigenous tribes recorded about the same time during Guatemala's brutal civil war, women who leaned on Mary as their *"companera"* because she was a poor woman and knew, as did they, the horror of having sons arrested, tortured, and killed.

Although I first fell in love with Mary as mother through the mediation of medieval Christianity where she is the archetypal maternal presence par excellence, it was my own lived experience of bearing and raising three children that matured and solidified that love. She was the one to whom I instinctively turned, the one in whom my heart found itself at home. This home was not mine by family inheritance but by attunement to her as mother, and as the embodiment of fierce yet gentle and always inventive maternal care. Thousands of remembered moments flood back from my years of child bearing and rearing: pregnant for the first time I kneel before the side altar of Our Lady of the Mountains in Estes Park, Colorado, afraid that the miracle of pregnancy cannot be true; during a tumultuous adolescent period, I bury a small photo of a teenaged daughter at the base of an outdoor statue of Our Lady at a costal retreat center; as serious illness threatens another daughter's health, I weep and plead in concert with the Sorrowing Mother; votive offerings and flickering candles on behalf of our children are placed at innumerable shrines and grottos at far-flung locations across the country and globe.

My own mother was certainly a playful and engaged grandparent who cared as much about the minutia of each offspring's little accomplishments as did I. But it was to Mother Mary that I turned when my own mothering heart could not hold the fulsome joy or the deep anxiety that seems to simply come with the capacity to care about another creature more than you care for yourself. I felt her as always available, ever ready to hear my most trivial complaint and to respond to my most exhausted prayer. She was the one who could be companion to me in all the small joys and tender moments as well as in the frustrations and searing pain of the long, never static years of mothering, years that do not end, only change, even as children grow and mature.

It was Mary, in fact, who, quite unbidden, appeared at one of those perplexing times of parent-child transition that always seemed to catch me unaware. In the fall of 1996, my husband and I sent our eldest daughter to college. She chose Loyola Marymount University in Los Angeles,

Visitation Window, Our Lady of Refuge Church, L.A.

halfway across the nation from our Nebraska home. The upheavals of shepherding this first child out of the nest were major. I went with her for freshmen orientation. It was a good weekend, but one in which I found myself struggling with the welter of paradoxical emotions that threaten to swamp anyone at a time of such transition. Late in the afternoon of the weekend's close, I took a solitary walk out to the campus edge. LMU is situated on a wide bluff that overlooks the central city in one direction and the ocean in the other. Dusk was gathering, and I found myself full-throated with an explosive mixture of pride, sorrow, joy, grief, anxiety, and relief. I watched for a long time as the sun grew crimson over the sea, then started back to the central campus.

As I rounded a tree on a grassy knoll near the campus church, I noted a statue I had neglected previously. At first glance, it seemed to be a statue of the Virgin Mary, which in fact it was, but the Virgin as I had never seen her before. Standing, with her body thrust slightly forward and arms lifted high, she offered an infant child up to the expansive sky. The gesture was charged with the protective love of motherhood that must relinquish to an unknown future those who are more precious to her than life itself. The statue was dedicated "To the Mothers of the University's Students."

Mary's Day Immaculate Heart High School, 1951.

Chapter 5

Immaculate Heart
Inmaculado Corazón de Maria

But Mary treasured all these words
and pondered them in her heart.

—Luke 2:19

"Now, that's my kind of Mary!" she calls out to us over her shoulder as, with her vigorous stride, she mounts the steps that lead up to the campus chapel. We are swept along in her wake by her energetic monologue. My photographer Dorothy Tuma barely has time to pause and focus at each image into whose presence we are briskly ushered before we are hurried along to the next Marian incarnation. "Yes, the Mary of Elizabeth Johnson's *Truly Our Sister*, that's *my* kind of Mary." Our tour of the campus of L.A.'s Immaculate Heart High School is being conducted by Ruth Ann Murray, a retired school president and member of the ecumenical Immaculate Heart Community under whose auspices the school operates. Ruth is anything but the stereotype of a retiree. She seems not to have slowed down a bit, either intellectually or physically. We can hardly keep up with her. Her energetic enthusiasm for the most contemporary theological scholarship—Johnson's is an example—is obvious.

The author of the book to which Ruth refers is a Roman Catholic theologian whose depiction of the Virgin Mary refrains from treating her symbolically as she has so often been—as the feminine face of God, the eternal feminine, the idealized church, the queen of heaven, the co-redemptrix—and treats her primarily as an historical woman, a disciple and companion for those who journey on the road of faith. Johnson's narrative brings critical feminist theory to bear on the figure of Mary, the biblical woman who, she asserts, has been too often used to validate the patriarchal idea that the difference between the sexes assigns women and men to predetermined characteristics and social roles. Johnson's egalitarian theological anthropology envisions not a gender dualism but a redeemed humanity with relationships between men and women marked by mutual partnership.

Ruth is all for this Mary. Everything about her and about the community to which she belongs would confirm an appreciation for an updated image of the Virgin Mary reflecting sound biblical scholarship and contemporary social concerns. In fact, a cursory knowledge of the recent history of this Los Angeles branch of the Immaculate Hearts suggests why this might be so. Ruth's predecessors, the California Sisters of the Immaculate Heart of Mary, were founded by Canon Joachim Masmitjá de Puig in the Catalonian region of Spain in 1848 as the Daughters of the Most Holy and Immaculate Heart of Mary. In the late nineteenth century they came to Southern California at the behest of Bishop Thaddeus Amat, himself from the region of Catalonia. Amat had need of a congregation of women to staff new educational and charitable institutions in the frontier diocese on the western edge of what had been Mexican, and was soon to be American, territory. The historic leadership of the Immaculate Heart congregation included many capable and energetic women charged with doing the yeoman's work of a fledgling Catholic outpost. The community became independent of the Spanish mother community in 1924, exchanged the name of Daughters for Sisters and went about their groundbreaking ministries.

In the wake of Vatican II this talented group of women began a process of discernment. Many of the community felt inspired by the directives of the council as well as by the currents of scriptural renewal sweeping through the church to pursue higher education and expand the boundaries of traditionally practiced religious life. The story is a complex one, the specific arc of whose narrative without the benefit of long hindsight is still a matter of contention. Suffice it to say that what was at that time the unthinkable happened: in the year 1970 the reigning Los Angeles ecclesiastic, Cardinal James Francis McIntyre, presided over the formal dispensation of the vows of 350 of the approximately 400 Immaculate Heart sisters. The traditional Catholic press of the time excoriated the dispensed sisters. From this group a core decided to reorganize as a volunteer lay community in order to continue their ministries, including the all-girls' high school whose grounds we so briskly visit under the tutelage of Ruth. Over the years that community has continued its progressive development: now not only Catholic laywomen but married couples and families from varying Christian denominations form an ecumenical association dedicated to spiritual nurture and the promotion of justice and the common good.

Prior to my tour with Ruth, I had been on the campus of Immaculate Heart High School for the annual spring celebration of Mary's Day. That visit to the garden-laced urban campus had brought back poignant memories of my unchurched parents' rejection of the school as an appropriate choice for my potential high school career because of its religious affiliation. Yet, despite their precautions, I was here. In preparation for the visit I had poured over IHM school archival photos of Marian celebrations in the decades before the new community was formed. In early photos veiled sisters in long sepia-toned habits were visible shepherding their neatly attired Catholic girls' school charges through traditional May processions: white-gloved young women wearing wreathes of flowers in their hair solemnly enact the May crowning of the Virgin Mary. Late 1960s snapshots of the May festivities capture the seismic changes of that turbulent decade: colorfully dressed students and fully habited sisters, all wearing fanciful floral head gear, blow up balloons. A "dragon" parade consisting of serpentine lines of girls crouching under upturned Pop Art–decorated cardboard boxes celebrates John XXIII's justice-focused encyclical Peace on Earth. More habited nuns, one waving a placard of a Hawaiian pineapple advertisement appears amidst a sea of costumed students whose signs protest the commoditization of food–Food Is Holy! Give them something to Eat, said Jesus!

Down the hall from the archives where these photos are stored is the office where the artwork of the late Sr. Corita, known after the events of 1970 as Corita Kent, is marketed. Corita, like most of her sisters in the IHM (although not her blood sister who remained with the contingent whose vows were not dispensed) threw open their windows and embraced the modern world. Corita's art grew with her adventurous spirit. I peruse the plastic display folders that list the prints she created. Her Marian depictions evolve from typical—fiat, Magnificat, heart—to whimsical. My favorite: "the juiciest tomato."

Mary's Day 2005 continues the tradition of IHM transformation. In the fifth year of the new millennium, the now vibrantly multiethnic student body gathers for the opening Eucharistic celebration in the school gymnasium which has been festooned for the occasion with filmy leaf-covered fabric banners and paper vines curling up the walls. A vegetative fabric *"baldaquino"* is looped over an altar set in the middle of the space as visual accompaniment to the theme of this year's Mary's Day,

"Plant the Good Seed." Mass opens with two circles of young women carrying glittery egg-shaped "seeds" and undulating to the subtle beat of Native American drums. As the celebration unfolds, antiphons and texts weave together to amplify the chosen themes: earth, womb, creativity. These young women of Immaculate Heart are to dedicate themselves to mothering the earth and to planting and nurturing the seed of faith within them that will sustain the world. With God all things are seen to be possible, and Mary is named as the role model of creative strength, courage, and faith.

Greg Boyle, a southern California Jesuit known for his ministry to gang members in the troubled barrios of east L.A., presides at the Eucharist. His homily emerges from the reading of the day, the *Magnificat*, that liberating Gospel canticle sung by the Virgin Mary in the second chapter of Luke. The Virgin, our presider affirms, did not merely proclaim the message of the *Magnificat*, Mary became the message. He amplifies his point with a contemporary story about Soledad, the mother of four sons caught up in the L.A. gang wars, two of whom had been murdered. One grim night, as she held vigil in the hospital emergency room for her dying son, Soledad became aware that a sixteen-year-old member of a rival gang had been brought in and placed in a neighboring bed. She overheard as the doctors labored to save his life: "I'm afraid we're losing him," they murmured. Despite the fact of her own pain, this grieving mother found herself praying for the boy and his family. He survived. When the grieving Soledad reached out to the enemy, Fr. Boyle insists, she was like Mary of the *Magnificat*; she not only proclaimed it but was the message. And we, the ardent Jesuit addresses the gathered student body, must be the message as well. It will change the world.

At the conclusion of the liturgy, the girls, free of their customary school uniforms and glorying in their spring attire (the fashion du jour being a hip-hugging, mid-thigh-length flounced skirt), clamor out of the auditorium to a large grassy quadrangle in whose center a maypole has been erected. They assemble facing a foliage-covered hill at the pinnacle of which an antique statue of Mary has been set up. Then a May crowning procession and a musical interlude, which would not have been a surprise to the long-ago student body, takes place. The traditional strains of the Marian hymn "Immaculate Mary," sung a capella by a musically gifted senior, waft in the air, and Mary receives her flowered crown at the hands of a specially honored young woman. But just as the sweet soprano dies away, the vibrant rhythms of African tribal music burst out from the loudspeakers situated at both ends of the lawn. The girls break into the steps of an indigenous dance practiced for the occasion,

Mary's Day Immaculate Heart High School, 1964.

Mary's Day Immaculate Heart High School, 2007.

then swirl spontaneously into a long conga line and shimmy their way over to the refreshment area, laughing and whooping out end-of-the-school-year cries of delight.

On our present visit Ruth has whisked us by Marian statues from an earlier day, especially images of Mary of the Immaculate Heart, her white stone hand pointing to the exposed heart on her breast. That flower-ringed and sword-pierced heart has been from its Spanish be-ginnings the symbol that expressed the vision of the Sisters of the Im-maculate Heart. But what Ruth, the Jesuit preacher, and the undulating young women see symbolized in that heart is not exactly what the first Spanish sisters who journeyed to the new world saw.

My archival outings enrich my understanding not only of the sym-bol of the Immaculate Heart among the IHM community but also of the way in which Mary herself is reconceptualized over time in response to changing social, political, and theological agendas. The roots of this ongoing reflection on the heart—the interiority of Mary—are biblical. Twice she is described in the Gospel of Luke—at the angel's procla-mations of her pregnancy and when, as a child, Jesus was found in the temple teaching the elders—as "treasuring" or "pondering" these mysteries in her heart. (Luke 2:19, 51). That same gospel contains the prophecy of Simeon (Luke 2:35) that foretells a "piercing" of her soul, understood by later commentators to refer to her heart.

But it was in seventeenth-century France that reflection on the qual-ity of Mary's heart came to the fore. Before this, in the late medieval period, Mary was chiefly honored because of her motherhood: for the fact that she bore the Christ into the world. That is not to say that she did not have immense status. She had long been acknowledged as *Theotokos* or God-Bearer, as the Second Eve (paired with Jesus, the Second Adam), had been identified as Mother of the Church, and was regally honored as Queen of heaven and Queen of saints. But as a human individual whose interiority was significant, that recognition had to wait until the early modern period and a shift in the spiritual currents of a newly emerging reformed Catholicism. It was at that point that Mary's heart, as symbol of the nature and quality of her personhood, came to the fore.

Early modern exegetes explored the Lucan passages in new ways in response to changing times. During the European Reformations (both

Protestant and Catholic), faith had come to be understood in a newly interior, spiritualized fashion. Stress was put on inward prayer and moral convictions more than on the external means of communicating with God. The quality of a person's heart now mattered. Virtues, the practiced habits of heart, were to be cultivated. Alongside the traditional theological and cardinal virtues of faith, hope, love, prudence, fortitude (courage), justice, and temperance (restraint), other virtues like purity, humility, faithfulness, devotion, obedience, poverty, patience, mercy, and sorrow became defining Christian virtues.

Alongside this, a fresh image of the Virgin Mary emerged. The Virgin Mary of the period was extolled as an exemplar of the new interiorized piety; self-controlled, virtuous, especially humble and obedient, she was the mirror of what the model disciple should be. This modern Mary of the virtuous, introspective heart was highlighted in the spirituality of the popular writer Francis de Sales (d. 1622) and described in the liturgical writings of John Eudes (d. 1680). While much might be said about the inculcation of these sorts of virtues to create willing subjects of emerging modern nation states, centralized ecclesial polities, and patriarchal family structures, suffice it to say that, on the positive side, these virtues also reflect the increasing literacy, spiritual self-reflection,

Immaculate Heart postulants, 1947.

and moral conviction that characterized the Catholic Church of the early modern era.

Two centuries later the rigorously moralistic and ascetic climate of Catholic Spain in which Canon Masmitjá, the priest-founder of the Sisters of the Immaculate Heart, was raised gave rise to a different vision of Mary. In the wake of the French Revolution and subsequent European political upheavals, antimonarchical and anticlerical revolutionary sentiment swept through Europe. In much of Spain, as in France, religious orders were suppressed, seminaries closed, and the ministries that religious communities sponsored abandoned. Churches were vacant, and young people, flocking to the cities in response to the economic pressures of the industrial revolution, were uneducated, uncatechized, and vulnerable.

In the Parisian capital, the enterprising pastor of Our Lady of Victory Church, Fr. Charles Dufriche-Desgenettes, concerned about his empty pews and the state of souls, in 1838 launched an archconfraternity to pray for conversions. There, under the title of the Immaculate Heart, Mary was invoked to intercede on behalf of sinners. Mary's pivotal role in the continuing redemption of humankind was conceived in the theology of that day as flowing from the intimate connection she shared with her son, the union of her heart with his in charity. The success of the archconfraternity was stunning: dramatic conversions and a resurgence of piety took place.

Other churchmen throughout Europe paid attention. In his own pastoral region of Catalonia, Canon Masmitjá founded a chapter of the archconfraternity of the Immaculate Heart. Then he began to dream of a community of religiously minded women who would have to profess "simple" not "solemn" vows since formally constituted religious orders were forbidden by the government and who would respond to the

Immaculate Heart Rose Window, La Casa de Maria Retreat Center, Montecito.

pressing spiritual and educational needs of young girls who crowded into the cities. These women were to be Daughters of the Immaculate Heart. As the community's aims were evangelical and apostolic—they began with catechesis and soon received permission to teach secular subjects—so was their prayer apostolic. In their earliest rules and customs, Fr. Masmitjá insisted that his charges have a strong devotion to the Immaculate Heart of Mary as a powerful intercessor and dedicate themselves to praying through her for sinners. The evangelizing intent on the part of these Catholics confronted with what they saw as an impious and apostate world is evident.

When Bishop Amat of California requested a women's community from his fellow Catalonian, the community brought with them this devotion to Mary's heart as one that could effect great things on behalf of the faith. Thus their early custom books prescribed, along with widely practiced Marian-focused devotions such as the recitation of the Little Office of Our Lady or the Litany of Our Lady, prayers and practices that relate specifically to them as Daughters of the Immaculate Heart. Each sister wore a Seven Dolors rosary and weekly said the chaplet of the Seven Dolors (Seven Sorrows of Mary), consecrated herself to the Immaculate Heart, made reparation to that heart for the sins heaped upon it by a godless world, and daily after dinner recited the following prayer:

> Immaculate Heart of Mary, pray for us.
> August Queen of Heaven, Sovereign Mistress of Angels,
> You, who from the beginning, have received from God the power and the mission to crush the head of Satan,
> we humbly ask you to send your holy legions,
> that under your orders and through your power,
> they may pursue the demons, combat them everywhere, repress their audacity, and drive them back to the abyss.
> Holy Angels and Arch-Angels, defend and guard us.
> O good and tender Mother, you shall always be the object of our love and our hope. Amen.

While Mary's Immaculate Heart may still be invoked in the twenty-first century, her inner life, at least among progressive women like the IHMs, is conceptualized very differently than it was even a century ago. In 1998 Dr. Alexis Navarro, a member of the contemporary reimagined Immaculate Heart Community, spoke about the history and present charism of the IHMs at a gathering at Mount St. Mary's College. Apropos of the Heart of Mary, Navarro waxed eloquent about the updated devotion that the late twentieth-century ecumenical community now promotes. The new ecumenical foundation, she stated, "saw itself as carrying forward the Deuteronomic command: Love the Lord your God with your whole heart, with your whole soul and with your whole mind and love your neighbor as yourself. It is understood that it is in the heart where freedom dwells; it is in the heart where the spirit is heard." Navarro's view exemplifies what the new leadership of the reconstituted community now understands to be the deepest meaning of having a heart like the Virgin: "A heart prepared for ministry, for generosity, for outgoing joy, for lightness and humor, for compassion and sorrow, for a spirit of courage, daring, and challenge that Mary experienced in giving flesh to Jesus."

The habits of Mary's heart also surface in 2007 at the Immaculate Heart Center for Spiritual Renewal in Montecito as the topic of a conversation I hold with Carol Carrig and Anita Daniels, two members of the ecumenical community who were formed as young religious in the IHM community in the years before the 1970s split. When they entered as novices, Carol and Anita were given manuals of prayer that contained the traditional devotional practices and encouraged to imitate the virtues of Mary. However, they had not entered because of Marian devotion but were drawn to the teaching work of the Immaculate Heart sisters and the joyful spirit they found there.

As they matured, Carol and Anita did in fact begin consciously to model themselves on Mary. Not the Mary who was as a pious girl obedient to conventional expectations or one who summoned angelic help in the fight against evil. Rather they admired her as a woman who listened deeply and trusted enough to be obedient to the voice of God. She was model for those who pondered things in their hearts. In other words, they saw Mary engaging in a thoughtful, often risky, spiritual process of discernment, trying to uncover the often surprising promptings of the Spirit of God amid the conflicting cultural, psychological, and spiritual promptings that assail us all. It was fidelity to the process of spiritual discernment, the two women affirm, that led to the innovations in the Immaculate Heart Community in the 1960s and 70s and it

Traditional Immaculate Heart Statue, Immaculate Heart Spiritual Renewal
Center, Montecito.

is that same fidelity to discernment that they understand themselves to be engaged in today.

The insights offered by Carol and Anita, Ruth's offhand comment, "Now that's *my* kind of Mary," and Alexis Navarro's encomium about the heart of an IHM represent an explicit setting aside of other images of Mary, perhaps the Mary in whose shadow these women had grown up, certainly the Mary under whose aegis the early Immaculate Heart sisters were formed, as well as the submissive, docile Mary of the early modern Catholic Reformation.

I resonate with the task these women have set themselves: the risky launch into the unknown that openness to the Spirit often prompts. And I recognize myself, at least to a degree, in them. For it was here, on this oak-sheltered and orchard-checkered property in December of 1974, with the blessing of the IHMs and the ecclesial fiat of Fr. Virgil,

Fatima Garden, La Casa de Maria Retreat Center, Montecito.

that I took my own risky leap and was confirmed in the Catholic faith. From the beveled glass doors of the elegantly appointed building in which Carol, Anita, and I converse, I can see a traditional white plaster statue of Mary of the Immaculate Heart situated on a stone pedestal at the crest of a rock-strewn path. Whether she is, as she seems in this version, the virtuous exemplar of obedience and submission, or the one who fiercely summons angelic legions, or the mother who forgives her son's murderer, or the woman who defies authority, or simply the person who waits in silence for the stirring of life, I marvel at the mystery of a heart that is responsive to the breath of Spirit the midst of the world's swift turning. And I concur that it—this life of faith—does have to do with heart. Opened, willing, pondering, longing, questioning, audacious, seeking, broken, pierced, sorrowing, courageous, hope-filled, and ultimately joyous. This Spirit-led life is a matter of the heart.

Our Lady of Hollywood (*N.S. de Covadanga*), Immaculate Heart High School, L.A.

Chapter 6

Our Lady of Hollywood
Nuestra Señora de Covadonga

Faint angel whispers in the breeze
in roses,
in pumpkin bread,
chocolates.
The best kept secret in Hollywood
tucked in folded hands,
behind eyelids,
and closed corridors.

—Excerpt from "Monastery of the Angels,"
   Armando P. Ibanez, OP

"And here," Ruth, our speedy guide through the Immaculate Heart campus informs us, halting abruptly at an ochre, navy, and beige Mexican tile image half-hidden beneath low evergreen branches, "is Our Lady of Hollywood." The somewhat worn image looks old and ethnic. And it is. Framed by bright blue-tiled squares of abstract floral design, this Lady is flat and frontal. Her sweeping triangular vestment fans out above a thick crescent moon and protrudes from her neck-less head above which balloons a gold-crowned nimbus. The image came here, we learn, as a refugee to the IHMs in 1982 after a devastating fire that gutted the historic Hollywood branch of the public library where she had been embedded in the entrance wall. Dating most probably from the early 1800s, the Madonna of Hollywood has been identified as the creation of Dominican friars trained in Talavera, Mexico. Most likely she is a version of Our Lady of Covadonga, an ancient image venerated in the mountainous regions of Asturia (now Spain) since at least the seventh century and associated with Christian victories over the Moors on the Iberian peninsula.

Hollywood: epicenter—symbolically if not literally—of the film industry's tawdry glamour. Hollywood: place, like so much of L.A., where just below the shabby surface is a rich lode of spiritual treasure. Hollywood: where episodes from my own youthful story played themselves out. Two churches from my pre-Catholic life loom large as I map out my itinerary one fine fall weekday: Mount Hollywood Congregational on Prospect Avenue midway between the Golden State and Hollywood freeways northwest of Silver Lake and south of Griffith Park, and Hollywood First Presbyterian Church located in the heart of tourists' Hollywood on the corner of Gower just off the 101.

It was at Mount Hollywood Congregational that as an infant I was christened in the arms of my WWII conscientious-objector father by the Rev. Alan Hunter, an ardent pacifist and pastor of this peace-oriented congregation. It was my theatrically inclined mother who, having discovered in grade school that I could sing, led me to Hollywood First Presbyterian where the professional-level choir program might help me develop the musical skills she deemed necessary for one so gifted. Indeed, in retrospect I would have to agree that this was a seminal step in my own development, if not quite as my mother imagined. There is nothing like hymn singing: the great theological truths are married to rhythm and melody and impart a wisdom that is imprinted as muscle memory on the vocal box, on the breath, and in the heart.

During the same years that I was trekking up the blocks from the bus stop at Hollywood Boulevard to First Presbyterian for choir practice, Fr. Patrick Peyton, an Irish Holy Cross priest, was busy nearby marshalling the energies of Hollywood's celebrities for his Rosary Crusade. Peyton's broadcasting evangelism was legendary. With the initial help of Colonel Tom Lewis, the head of the Armed Forces Radio and husband of actress Loretta Young, the Family Theater of the Air was launched. Produced at Jerry Fairbanks Studio on Sunset Boulevard, the radio broadcasts ran from 1948 to 1970. Although the programming was nonsectarian to appeal to a mass listening audience, in fact the radio show was an offshoot of Peyton's Rosary Crusade that had as its motto "The Family that Prays Together Stays Together." The Family Theater had as its raison d'être the strengthening of familial ties as a means of counteracting secularism and communism. The list of performers who appeared on Family Theater or on specially televised programs at Thanksgiving, Easter, Christmas, and Mother's Day reads like a Who's

Who of theatrical royalty of the era: Ethel Barrymore, Cesar Romero, Irene Dunn, Loretta Young, Bing Crosby, Gregory Peck, Don Ameche, Shirley Temple, Maureen O'Hara, Jane Wyatt, Ronald Reagan, Ozzie and Harriet Nelson, Van Heflin, William Holden, Barbara Stanwyck, Jack Benny, Jerry Lewis, Marian Davis, Louella Parsons, Bob Hope, and Gary Cooper at one point or another contributed their talents to Fr. Peyton's crusade. This was the parallel Catholic world that existed just a few blocks away from my own Hollywood.

But the boulevard on which today one can match footprints with celebrities' shoe imprints on the star-studded sidewalk outside Grauman's Chinese Theater is not for me all memories of celestial choirs and progressive Christian witness. It has a darker side as well. And this is, strangely, what draws me now to the Dominican Monastery of the Angels just a few blocks north of the red towers of First Presbyterian. Hollywood Boulevard is riotous with color, sounds, and sights: gigantic neon billboards advertising the latest TV show premier, gaudy store fronts, exotic lingerie purveyors, cheap wares, and endless lanes of cars. The city of the silver screen can be a questionable place. For several years in my twenties I pursued the illusive dream common to thousands of aspiring performing artists in L.A. Although I had some success, earning union cards from the American Guild of Variety Artists and Actors Equity, the truth of the ugly, bottom-line business of it all dispirited me. Having trained in French opera repertoire in the Hollywood Hills studio of Madame Ruth Chamlee of the Metropolitan Opera and having aspired to the necessary elocution to master Shakespearian dialogue, it was, to say the least, depressing to find myself jumping out of tires to advertise Pure Oil products, and being asked to hike up my skirts to show my knees and thighs as a prerequisite for a TV ad audition. There is nothing like seeing Hollywood up close to propel a person into an academic career studying religion!

So it is the reputation of that less-than-savory Hollywood that takes me to the Monastery of the Angels where twenty-some traditionally habited, fully enclosed Dominican nuns who dwell in the cloistered convent at Carmen Avenue are reputed to be concerned for that same sad side of the city. Established in the archdiocese in 1924 at the invitation of Archbishop John Cantwell, the community can today be discovered at the eastern edge of the heart of old Hollywood, a mere mile west

of Immaculate Heart High and two-tenths of a mile from the imposing Scientology Celebrity Center compound. The monastery's beige
bell tower with its simple cross is visible at the end of a short lane as I
turn right off busy Franklin Avenue onto the narrow residential street.
Birdsong issues from the trees behind the cloister walls and floats above
the continuous low hum of nearby traffic. I cannot say I knew anything
of this place until reading of it in a 2006 *New York Times* article which
described the cloistered nuns as "battling the evils of Hollywood with
prayer" and quoted one of the elderly sisters, described as "pale and
innocent as an uncooked loaf" as identifying the neighborhood with
its dopers, runaways, pimps, and surgically augmented inhabitants as
"the Babylon of the U.S.A." I knew I had to visit.

Despite its seamy side, which I have myself experienced, and which
was so colorfully augmented by the rhetoric of the *Times* journalist,
Hollywood is not an impoverished area, not the territory of gangs or
historic racial violence. The winding lanes of the Hollywood Hills hide
elegant tile-roofed Spanish estates and handsome Art Deco dwellings.
Nevertheless, the seedy Hollywood is real: thus the area's residents are
as varied as its Janus-faced character. It is a First Saturday of the month
when I make my visit to the Dominican monastery and, this being a day
special to the Virgin as Saturdays are always dedicated to the Virgin,
I settle in for the scheduled Mass and Consecration to the Immaculate
Heart of Mary sponsored by the "Heart of Mary Ministries."

First, however, I stop in the spacious, well-appointed monastery gift
shop where homemade pumpkin bread, elegant gold rosaries, and baby
caps are offered alongside books such as the *Catechism of the Catholic
Church*. While I browse, an elegant, well-heeled, high-heeled matron
and her distinguished-looking husband drop by for some convent-made
breads and, clearly being familiars, ask to be remembered to a certain
sister. The primary work of these Dominicans is not active ministry, nor
baking and crocheting, but contemplative prayer. Yet they also provide
a space, an oasis really, in the neighborhood for those who seek the
presence of God. Their chapel of Perpetual Adoration is open daily during daylight hours for any seeker. Devotional groups like the Heart of
Mary Ministries use the space for their monthly holy-hour gatherings
on a regular basis.

I am not the first to arrive in the simple chapel before the appointed
worship time: an elderly woman wearing a lace mantilla, muttering over
her prayer book, and a slender black man wearing rimless glasses, jeans,
and sneakers are absorbed in the quiet. As I enter I am struck by the
sight of the floor-to-ceiling metal grating that separates the cloistered

section of the chapel from the area accessible to visitors. Beyond the grating and upon a slatted wooden partition behind which invisible nuns pray is a giant brass monstrance flanked by metal wheat sheaves and topped by a crown that holds the Blessed Sacrament up for adoration. After confessions are heard and Mass is offered, adoration of the sacrament is presided over by the group's elderly Jesuit chaplain. Then the assembled participants continue with a consecration to the Immaculate Heart that could have been heard in the archdiocese in the 1950s and has something of the apocalyptic tone of the prayers that the IHM novices in Montecito would have prayed half a century ago. Mary here is invoked as compassionate mother, but the fallen world's impurity is stressed as is the need to make reparation for the sins of errant humankind.

A glance around the pews reveals my fellow devotees who fit no known stereotypes of a praying community. There are Asian women with tight jeans and Gucci handbags, a young woman who straps athletic kneepads to her legs before making her way up the chapel aisle on her knees, an older African American woman dressed to the nines in a cacophony of bright color, and a thin thirty-something Caucasian fellow with curls circling his entire head who fingers a plastic rosary. Silent middle-aged men line the back pews, Italian grandmother types scurry about setting up flowers and devotional statuary. There are people on crutches, three buff young men who look like they work out daily, and an elderly woman in a shabby sweater and frayed trousers. Across the wooden partition that separates us from the enclosure, the sisters in floor-length habits, some whose native tongue is English and others for whom English is not a first language, kneel silently in their prayer stalls. I think of the phrase credited to James Joyce: Here comes everybody.

The contrast that the nuns and devotees at the Monastery of the Angels experience as a collision between the Catholic sacred and the Hollywood secular worlds is not a new apprehension. Nor is that apprehension confined to Hollywood proper: Catholic values have often been painted in high relief against the backdrop of the secular city. An article dated March 5, 1954, that I discover in the archives of *The Tidings*, the L.A. archdiocesan paper, announced "despite sin, smog and secularism, the east side [a predominantly Latino area] is Mary's land." The piece went on with bruised purple prose to claim that "the siren call of secularism and the treacherous winds of modernism that sweep swank stuccos in Beverly Hills blow just as strong against the frail frames of Belvedere but the flames of love for Our Lady survive on the east side."

It is true that too often Hollywood is a harsh and bitter place driven by false illusions and given to crass exploitation. I can attest to that fact.

It is likewise true that the "east side" of L.A. between Union Station and Coyote Pass, being for the most part immigrant and Spanish speaking, is still, over fifty years later, "Mary's land." As I peregrinate over this familiar terrain with its personal memories of social witness, joyous hymnody, and tawdry glitz and glamour, and as I pray with devotees of Our Lady, I find that it is also true that love has no one address and grace no preferred neighborhood. Hollywood, as part of Our Lady's city, and well beyond the stillness of the Dominican cloister, still feels the sweet presence of the Holy Spirit, a presence Mary herself knew so well.

ROSA MYSTICA

Chapter 7

Mystical Rose
La Rosa Mystica

There is no rose of such virtue
As is the rose that bear Jesu: Alleluia!
For in that rose containèd was
Heav'n and Earth in little space:
Res Miranda (O Thing of Wonder).

—Fifteenth-century carol

"Where do you find these people?" She looks up and hands me the butt end of a celery stalk to toss in the garbage. "I always think of Los Angeles as such a secular city." My young adult daughter in her postage stamp of a kitchen is mincing vegetables. Famished, I reach over and claim one of the unminced jicama pieces. "It's a city with a lot of layers" is all I can think to say in response. It is true. There are a lot of layers to Our Lady's city.

Our eldest has lived here in this slightly worn but stylish Art Deco building a few blocks off Wilshire Boulevard about a year, plying her trade as a graphic designer for a small garment manufacturer. Because I have just begun my L.A. Marian auto odyssey, I would have to agree that, on the surface, L.A. is a very secular city: part trendy boutiques, pricey little cafés and oxygen bars, part pure crass, like the glitzy ostentation of the Flynt Enterprises Building—offices of Larry Flynt, founder

"Rosa Mystica," Litany of Loreto Windows, St. Ambrose Church, West Hollywood.

of *Hustler Magazine* and self-described "smut-peddler"—which I passed on my way toward Wilshire.

As we toss the veggies, I proceed to regale my daughter with a story about "one of those people" she cannot imagine inhabiting this city where liposuction and breast augmentation have replaced apple pie as identifying American icons. His name is Chuck, I inform her, and he is a sort of volunteer sacristan at St. Ambrose's in West Hollywood. That afternoon I had sought out the small parish (founded in 1922) as the result of a chance meeting in Santa Barbara with one of the members of the ecumenical Immaculate Heart Community who volunteered that St. Ambrose's had a unique set of stained-glass rosary windows decorated with symbols from the Litany of Loreto. As this was one of my early trips, when I was simply canvassing the territory, I had arrived at the corner of Fountain and Fairfax unannounced. I know enough to be strategic in my timing. Sunday mornings, of course, and just before and after scheduled liturgies one can gain entry to most L.A. churches and, with the rare exception, during weekday school hours one can generally find a back door through which to slip into a sanctuary and pray. But St. Ambrose no longer has a parochial school, and I found myself on the busy street without access to the gated church. A number of cell phone calls finally yielded an older gentleman with a pronounced Brooklyn accent clad in a flowered Hawaiian shirt who identified himself as Chuck.

Inside the dim interior of the smallish church, Chuck and I craned our necks upward trying to identify the iconography inscribed on the stained glass. Yes, there were her Loreto titles in shimmering blues, back lit by the fading sun of an L.A. afternoon—Gate of Heaven, Sorrowful Mother, Queen of Confessors, Queen of Martyrs, Queen of Prophets, Mystical Rose, House of Gold, Spiritual Vessel, Tower of David, Help of Christians, Vessel of Honor, Seat of Wisdom, Ark of the Covenant, Mother Most Pure—each situated under a scene from one of the mysteries of the rosary. We chat about how he loves the feel of Fairfax—it reminds him of New York—and about the Marian imagery he has never really noticed before. As we do so, his story unfolds. For the past fifteen years Chuck has been helping out at St. Ambrose's parish community, years that were an answer to a desperate prayer. It seems that as a young actor he was often out of work and, in his search for recognition, eventually drifted into the fast lane of the Hollywood lifestyle and a cocaine

Rosa Mística Window, *Nuestra Señora de Guadalupe* Church, El Monte.
Icon and Rosary, Our Lady Queen of Martyrs Armenian Catholic Church, L.A.

addiction. A near-death emergency room experience terrorized him. Drawing upon dim memories of his childhood faith, Chuck prayed in the direction of a heaven he was not sure was even there for one last chance. His current life of service at St. Ambrose was proof, he nodded knowingly, that his prayer was heard.

The 1950s vintage windows from Ireland that loom over Chuck's revitalized life of volunteer ministry are indeed lovely and the specificity of the parish identity fascinating. On a return visit I am welcomed by Alvin Hopkins, the parish business manager, who informs me about the changing demographics of the area over the years. It seems that an early Irish Catholic population gave way to an influx of Russian Jews, then the neighborhood became a haven for gay and lesbian singles.

Many single-family homes were replaced by high-rise apartments. Today the area is multicultural and diverse. There are some younger families, many of whom have inherited pricey neighborhood homes from parents. As its location might suggest, St. Ambrose's has over the years had artists—musical, visual, theater, and film—as parishioners. When I check the website several years after this visit, I learn that the parish also has a Legion of Mary group which sponsors visits to prisons, convalescent hospitals, juvenile detention facilities, and special-needs homes. I am reminded that the Legion, founded in 1921 by Irish layman Frank Duff, was a staple of lay Catholic apostolic energy before the Second Vatican Council. Designed to foster personal holiness through union with Mary in the evangelization of society through participation in practical actions sponsored by the group, the Legion remains—as at St. Ambrose's—a presence in some pockets of the L.A. archdiocese.

While the Litany of Loreto is still the only Marian Litany officially sanctioned by the Roman Church, since Vatican II and the muting of individual devotional practice, the symbolic titles evident on the lower windows at St. Ambrose have become unfamiliar to most parishioners. I know of the titles of Loreto mainly through my academic studies of the early modern era when the House of Loreto, fabled to have been the original dwelling place of the Holy Family and later miraculously transported to the shores of Italy, was a much-visited pilgrimage site. That era, when the Catholic Church was engaged in the process of confessional identity formation over against the emerging Protestant churches, made much of Mary. While theologians worked to correct what were seen as idolatrous medieval tendencies to make more of Mary than her son, nevertheless her importance in the plan of salvation and the honor due her was vigorously promoted. As for the litany's life in L.A., there is evidence that Padre Junipero Serra, considered the founder of the necklace of Franciscan missions spread up the California coast, dedicated Lower California to Our Lady of Loreto and chanted the litany at the blessing of ships sent northward to establish the faith.

The origin of the Loreto prayer is believed to be a medieval rhymed litany influenced by the long-standing devotion to the Virgin that flourished in the Eastern Christian world. In the ancient *Hymnos Akathistos* one encounters a series of Old Testament images which were traditionally read to apply to the Virgin. Here they are in West Hollywood, inscribed in block letters surrounded by the shimmering blue light of stained glass. The annunciation window, depicting the young Mary receiving the angelic messenger, identifies her as *Foederis Arca*, or Ark of the Covenant, because she, like David in the Old Testament, is entrusted with carrying the Divine Word. Beneath the scene of Mary and Joseph presenting their firstborn infant son as a thank-offering to the temple priest is a golden tabernacle. *Domus Aurea*, it reads, House of Gold. *Sedes Sapientia* or Seat of Wisdom is imaged as a throne upon which sits an open book from whose pages a serpent emerges. This figure, which identifies Mary as the throne upon which the infant Christ the King is seated, underscores a larger representation of the Virgin's coronation.

There is a haunting antiquity to these phrases that arrests me. The lower panels of the Ambrose windows speak of a Mary of cosmic proportions. She is not only the mother of the human Jesus but also the chosen woman whose immaculate conception and assumption mark her as the fully realized human person. She is honored in Loreto's litany as much more. She fulfills age-old prophecies. She is the necessary earthen vessel in which divinity is carried to the waiting world. She thus reigns over prophets, confessors, and martyrs, indeed, over the very cosmos itself.

In the St. Ambrose windows, I find my favorite Loreto appellation: *Rosa Mystica*, Mystical Rose, illustrated as a bush with three red-budded branches. Mary's association with the rose is long standing even if its origins are obscure. From antiquity the rose was associated with mystery. For early Christians it was a symbol of both martyrdom and paradise. By the medieval period the identification of the Virgin Mary with the rose was complete. She was the bud that opened to receive the divine sun, the flower at the center of the enclosed virgin garden, the archetype of the mystical union of human and divine, the admired lady whose chivalric courtier adored her from afar, the beloved of the divine lover, the rose of Sharon of which the Song of Songs sings. Mary was "God's rose garden" in Latin hymnody, and Dante in his *Paradiso* lauded her as the rose in which the word of God became flesh. The scented beauty of the rose still clings to the Virgin today.

St. Ambrose's is not, of course, the sole place in the archdiocese where the intimate connection between Mary and the rose is celebrated. The rosary, that most familiar of Marian prayers prayed throughout the L.A. basin, carries the scent of the fragrant flower. The exact manner in which the rose and the beaded cord with its cycle of recited or meditated prayers were associated is somewhat obscure. Suffice it to say that there were a number of elements in the gradually accepted association:

the tradition of offering a series of prayers to the Virgin; the use of the term *rosarium* to refer to a "bouquet" of anecdotes, texts, or prayers; the development of a psalter for laity which contained 150 psalms, in some versions of which Ave Rosa appeared as a repeated salutation; the association of the five-line *Ave Maria* prayer with the five petals of the rose; and a medieval legend. This legend told of a lay brother, in the habit of making a rose crown for the Virgin, who at his superior's instructions began praying *Ave Maria*'s in place of fashioning the floral crown. As he was thus praying in the forest one day, robbers neared but they were stopped from harming him by a vision of Mary plucking from his mouth one rose for each Ave he uttered. The result of this gradual process was that by the fifteenth century the term "rosary," and the prayer beads, and the Virgin, and her flower were linked in Catholic thought.

Here in Southern California she appears under her title as Our Lady of the Rosary, among other places, in the city of Paramount. It is a weekday when I am able to make the trip southeast of downtown through long car-clogged miles of suburban and industrial landscape to Our

Our Lady of the Rosary Window, Our Lady of the Rosary Church, Paramount.

Lady of the Rosary parish located across from the sprawling campus of Paramount High School and next to an outdoor flea market. True to form, from the elementary school yard I find an open backdoor to the church sanctuary. Above the altar area is a light-filled circular window depicting a regal Mary seated upon a throne with her kingly infant, a large brown link of beads cascading down her lap. In the dimly lit church I become aware of the presence of a young mother kneeling with her rosary in one hand and her toddler in another. Another figure, a man, whom I presume is the sacristan as he is rearranging the presider's chair and passing out bulletins, busies himself about the space. Eventually, he asks me if he can direct me somewhere. When I inform him of my Marian project, he opens up about his own devotion to the Virgin.

His name is Mel and, being self-employed and in charge of his own work hours, he has been able for forty years to serve as the volunteer sacristan at Holy Rosary. I learn that for thirty of those years he was a friend of the former pastor and, as his tale unfolds, I am struck with Mel's contemporary theological awareness. The Lord, he tells me, inspired him to help the church in the way he does now. If your faith is mature, he comments, you will always grow in a desire to serve. Mel prays the rosary daily, and knows Mary to be both the Mother of God and his own and our mother. Without her, I am told, the faith makes no sense for she is the one who takes us to her son and helps us to comprehend our struggles. Even if someone is biblically illiterate, Mel assures me, by praying the rosary he or she can get an overview of God's plan. We are here, he continues, to be loyal to the church that Jesus established and by being close to Mary, we stay loyal. He smiles when he speaks of Mary and adds: she makes life beautiful.

The unique set of stained-glass windows that rise above us as Mel and I chat illustrate the fifteen decades of the rosary he loves. He points them out carefully, one by one. First the Joyful Mysteries: the annunciation; the visitation; the nativity of Jesus; the presentation in the Temple; and Mary and Joseph's finding of their lost son in the Jerusalem Temple. Then the Sorrowful Mysteries: Jesus's agony in the garden of Gethsemane; Jesus is scourged after his arrest; he is crowned with thorns; he carries his cross toward the place of execution; and, finally, his crucifixion and death. Last, the Glorious Mysteries: the resurrection; Jesus's ascension into heaven; the descent of the Holy Spirit at the feast of Pentecost; the assumption of Mary into heaven as the first fruit of her son's redemption; and the coronation of the Virgin by her risen son. The windows shimmer in the midday light. Soon Mel needs to be on with his work so he leaves me with a catechetical admonition: We should continue to be informed and grow in our faith. When we learn about Mary, all the rest makes sense.

The classic rosary meditation counted out on fingered prayer beads, along with the omnipresent Novena to Our Lady of Perpetual Help, are the most frequently sponsored devotions here in the archdiocese of Los Angeles. On my visits to churches I often find small groups engaged in murmured multilingual incantations of the rosary prayer. Catholics across the age, gender, theological, and vocational spectrums are forthcoming about the rosary as a cherished Catholic practice. The rosary is, of course, as Franciscan Fr. Richard at St. Francis of Assisi previously pointed out to me, the most universal form of prayer that does not need a priest. Thus it belongs to the laity in a special way. The friar also reminded me that the prayer developed out of the monastic Liturgy of the Hours as a way for laypeople to experience a sort of summary of the Psalter. The prayer does not, of course, merely involve rote recitation but also reflective meditation on the Joyful, Sorrowful, and Glorious Mysteries. Thus the rosary is not only a mirror of the pattern of the psalms but a narrative summary of the Catholic faith.

In its most familiar form, the rosary harkens back to early eighteenth-century France and Louis Marie Grignon de Montfort but the devotion in germ is much older: legend associates St. Dominic in the thirteenth century with its origin and during the Catholic Reformation rosary confraternities proliferated. But it was de Montfort, champion of the spiritual way of going to Jesus through Mary, with whom it is most associated. Most recently, Pope John Paul II added another set of mysteries to be recited between the Joyful and Sorrowful, which he titled "Luminous Mysteries" and which focus on the events of Jesus's life and ministry as outlined in the Gospels. Although he is appreciative of the addition of these latter Luminous Mysteries as they are more inclusive of Gospel material, the Franciscan with whom I speak at St. Francis of Assisi is saddened by the fact that the connection with the Psalter in the pattern of 150 psalms has, by this inclusion, been obscured.

As one might expect, the archetypal practice of fingering prayer beads transcends eras and cultures, and the Catholic variant of this universal kinesthetic prayer—the rosary—has come to the Los Angeles archdiocese not only west from Europe but east from Asia and from south of the U.S. border. Talpa is a small village of about fifteen hundred families in the state of Jalisco, Mexico. Legends from the eighteenth century tell of a miraculous restoration of a petite venerated *virgencita* statue—crowned, aqua-gowned, with infant, rosary and scepter—and a miracle of candles that continued to burn before her unspent. Maria

Our Lady of the Rosary of Talpa,
Our Lady of the Rosary Church
of Talpa Church, East L.A.

de Talpa, the titular patroness of the basilica in Jalisco, made her way north to Southern California, and today her image is found at Our Lady of the Rosary of Talpa in east L.A. Fr. Silviano Calderon authorizes the parish secretary to provide me and my photographer with an informational brochure and access to the church. The interior is dark but fragrant with lush displays of flowers. And, as our eyes adjust, we become aware of several versions of Maria de Talpa. A monumental painting contributed by parishioners in 1944 dominates one side of the church. In it, the miraculous image is borne aloft by a cascade of angelic violinists while members of a Mexican donor family kneel on either side of the canvas. Across the sanctuary seated upon its own pedestal is a porcelain version of Talpa, her tall cerulean crown cantilevered upon her sovereign head, the triangular expanse of her embroidered blue gown, the pearled rosaries that she and her child carry, and a moon—a sliver beneath her feet—are set off by the freshly cut blooms set before her.

The global reach of the rosary is further evident in the L.A. archdiocese at Our Lady of Loreto on Union Street near downtown. Scattered about the church are images of the Cuban *Nuestra Señora de la Caridad* with its recognizable small boat containing sailors and slaves over which the Virgin hovers, as well as Perpetual Help, Fatima, Vietnam's La Vang, and the classic European Our Lady of Loreto. It appears that Marian devotion is alive and well here with rosary recitation before Mass, a Blue Army chapter, the Legion of Mary, and a Guadalupe committee. Our Lady of Loreto parish is staffed by the Divine Word Missionaries but Vincentian Fr. Minh Pham serves as its Vietnamese chaplain. It is he who introduces me to Thomas Khoan Khac Tran, leader of the parish Confraternity of the Rosary. Thomas and I meet after Eucharist in the school yard behind the church where a thermos of fruit punch and paper cups have been set out on school-lunch benches. Since his English is minimal and my Vietnamese nonexistent, our communication is halting, but I do learn that the four hundred–member rosary group, which he founded four years previously, thrives. To belong, Thomas insists, is very easy: one makes an application, agrees to carry a rosary always, and to recite five decades daily. The group also sponsors a weekly Saturday block rosary, a group devotional practice common before the Second Vatican Council, which moves from house to house.

The language barrier is not a problem during one of my most intimate rosary encounters that occurs at the Assumption of the Blessed Virgin Mary Church in Pasadena, a town engraved in my own family memory as the site of my mother and father's meeting on a blind date to the Pasadena Playhouse in the 1930s. Morning Mass is followed by the recitation of a rosary, a parish tradition inaugurated on the feast of the Assumption thirty-seven years before. The parishioners who tend to gather here do so with intent. The Irish pastor, Fr. O'Brien, introduces me after the rosary ends, and the group shares their deeply felt sense of the meaning of the devotional ritual they have just enacted.

Those gathered are a mixed group, and while I hesitate to identify participants as being from a particular ethnic or cultural identity, many do claim one of the many heritages common to this "minority majority" city. Sometimes these family backgrounds as well as length of residency and age help explain a person's view of the devotional practice. Here is Bill, a midlife Anglo who speaks with, to my ear, a nonaccented English about the new birth promised in the Gospels and feels that just as one must have both a mother and a father to be born physically, without both one cannot be born into heaven spiritually. Nor without Mary the mother, Bill asserts, could there be Jesus, the son and hence Christ and the church. Tim, another Anglo male, inherited the rosary as a family devotion. When his mother was ill and dying, she gave her life over to Mary and when she found herself cured, she was moved to spread her devotion. Thus Tim comes to this church in honor of his mother and the Virgin whose compassionate healing he has witnessed.

Among the women present this morning, Dora speaks forcefully in her Spanish-inflected tongue about Mary as promoter of the Catholic faith. The Mother of Heaven, in her view, does not like abortion. Dora excitedly describes an occurrence at a nearby abortion clinic when a pro-life friend surrounded the clinic with Marian medals. Dora is convinced that it was because of this and the intercession of the Virgin that the clinic was eventually removed. Dora also tells of a Pentecostal preacher who studied in order to learn which of the Christian churches was the true church of Jesus. His study led to his conversion to Catholicism. Dora conveys her felt sense of Mary's accessibility: one can easily talk to God's mother.

In fact, Dora has visited the Virgin as she has recently been appearing in the Mojave desert. I learn of this reputed phenomenon as I peruse an *L.A. Times* article that reports that since 1989 on the thirteenth of each month Mary is reported to appear to a middle-aged woman, Maria Paula Acuna. Directed to the visions by a critically ill child, Acuna reports seeing a woman in white who identifies herself as Lady of the Rock, Queen of Peace of Southern California. Although archdiocesan officials have gently tried to dissuade people from doing so, each month large crowds gather to photograph what they believe to be the Virgin in the desert sky. Dora is among them.

Two women who might be African-American or perhaps of Caribbean origin, one wearing a fabulous cowboy hat about which I offer my admiration, report that they belong to the Legion of Mary and recommend that I visit the Passionist Mater Dolorosa Retreat Center garden in Sierra Madre. Another woman, Luisa, who identifies herself as being of Filipino heritage, reports that she has been devoted to the rosary since childhood, as were her parents. Luisa, like Dora, is eager to claim the miracles she believes Mary has performed. Fifteen years before, a jealous colleague of her husband's sent death threats. When Luisa's husband got a gun to defend himself, Luisa was frightened and decided to do a Novena to Our Lady of Bon Secours (patroness of New Orleans). On the third day of her novena, her husband's colleague asked for forgiveness, and the two were reconciled. A grateful Luisa continues to pray the rosary every day.

Macrine, a woman who could be of Asian descent, speaks up. "Oh," I exclaim, recognizing the origins of her name, "for Macrina, sister of Sts. Gregory and Basil!" "You know!" she responds. Macrine radiates a gracious calm, and her soft voice carries gentle authority. Mary, she tells those of us assembled, answers desperate cases. She answers like a mother, beyond expression: it is striking how perfect her answers are. Macrine goes on to describe an intractable problem she encountered with her sister. Her face is luminous as she does so. Desperate, and despite the fact that she does not like the idea of praying on her knees, she did, to the point of getting blisters. Mary was the one to whom she turned. Macrine smiles at me beatifically: the hoped for healing of the ruptured relationship occurred.

I find myself touched by the sincerity of the rosary group, if not quite as prone as some of them to draw the direct connection between the Virgin and the answers to the petitions directed toward her. The stories I hear often end the way Luisa's and Macrine's did, with results that to the teller seem self-explanatory. Unspoken are the sentiments: Mary does intercede for us; Mary is the one who caused this to happen; she can be trusted to take care of us. But the unvoiced implication is clear to those who tell and hear the stories.

"These people," of whom my daughter spoke so wonderingly as we peeled our vegetables in her trendy studio off Wilshire Boulevard, are all over the archdiocese. They gather daily, weekly, monthly, yearly, each bearing her or his own version of the poignant burden of human life. Mary, the biblical woman on whose life they meditate, and the Mystical Rose of ancient invocation, opens for them like a fresh bud and offers the perfume of her presence, consolation, and hope.

Mystical Rose Window, Our Mother of Good Counsel Church, L.A.

Star of Sea: Mary Star of the Sea Statuette, Mary Star of the Sea Church, Oxnard.

Chapter 8

Star

Estrella

Life is like a voyage on the sea of history, often dark and stormy, a journey in which we watch for the stars to show the route. The true stars of our life are the people who have lived good lives. They are lights of hope. Jesus Christ is the true light, the sun that has risen above all the shadows of history. But to reach him we also need lights close by—people who shine with his light and so guide us along our way. Who more than Mary could be a star of hope for us? With her "yes" she opened the door of our world to God himself. . . .

Holy Mary, Mother of God, our Mother, teach us to believe, to hope, to love with you. Show us the way to his Kingdom! Star of the Sea, shine upon us and guide us on our way!

—Benedict XVI, *Spe Salvi*, 49–50

Among the most haunting of Marian appellations, and one rooted deep in the tradition, is "star." She is Morning Star, Day Star, and Star of the Sea. She is often encircled in stars, which symbolize her virtues and recall the twelve stars worn by the sun-clothed woman of the Apocalypse. Mary and the stars, like the rose and Mary, go together. The appellation, like that of Mystical Rose, is included in the Loreto Litany that heralds Mary as Morning Star, the sign of the coming day, and the promise of the light of Christ. The even more ancient Byzantine Akathist litany-like hymn beloved in the Eastern Orthodox Churches similarly invokes her with star imagery: Hail, O Star who manifests the Sun! Hail, O Mother of the Star without Setting! Hail, O Radiance of the Mystical Day! Hail, O Star who manifests the Sun!

As Morning Star, Mary is captured visually throughout the archdiocese, mainly in stained-glass windows such as the angular six-pointed starburst that casts its rays over sky-blue striations at Our Mother of Good Counsel, or in the equally modern five-pointed star radiating upon a field of irregular teal panes at *Nuestra Señora de Guadalupe* in El Monte captioned in Spanish as *Estrella Matutina*. Stars and roses merge visually in the windows of one of my favorite Marian parishes, Our Lady of Guadalupe in Santa Paula. This community composed mainly of farm workers remodeled its charming southwestern-style church in the Santa Clara valley in 1995 with motifs taken entirely from the imagery of *La Virgen Morena* who showed herself to peasant Juan Diego at the Hill of Tepeyac outside Mexico City in 1531. Assistant administrator

Gary Lopez proudly shows visitors the beveled glass doors etched with designs from Guadalupe's mantle and the squared windows whose centers are open-bloomed rose shapes superimposed on bright yellow stars.

Mary the Morning Star has another related title, Star of the Sea. In this guise she is

Estrella Matutina Window, *Nuestra Señora de Guadalupe* Church, El Monte.

Crowned M Window, Our Lady of Guadalupe Parish, Santa Paula.

likened to the lifesaving North Star that oriented long-ago seafarers as they navigated treacherous ocean waters. Like the star that could be counted on to save them from losing their way, Mary was the bright light toward whom one could always turn when buffeted on the seas of life. When Spanish padre Junipero Serra sailed up the California coast in the mid-eighteenth century and established the chain of Franciscan missions in the newly claimed Alta California province, he did so under the protection of Mary Star of the Sea. And it is fitting that with this appellation Mary is still invoked in oceanside towns where fishing, canning, long-shoring, and seagoing commerce have long dominated the local economy.

The coastal city of San Pedro is all about the sea. Explored early by the Spanish who claimed it as part of colonial New Spain, the area that falls now within the city limits was a sizable segment of one of the earliest land grants in Alta California, deeded to Juan Jose Dominguez, a member of the eighteenth-century Portola expedition. In 1906, the city of Los Angeles, then part of the United States, annexed the region. The port of San Pedro was from the beginning its defining feature, being home to important fishing and canning industries and connecting the city with commercial activity from across the globe. The seaside city early attracted European immigration, and today remains the center of the Italian American and Croatian American communities of Southern California. Portuguese, Mexican, Greek, and Japanese presence is also evident. Sailors and fishermen: these people, many of whom are Catholic, are at the heart of San Pedro. It is no surprise then that towering over the city from atop the hill overlooking the port is a ten-foot gleaming gilded statue of Mary Star of the Sea mounted on top of the bell tower of the church of that name, her arms outstretched toward the port. Visible from the water far below, she is the beacon that welcomes sailors and fisherman to safe shore.

I am awed as I circumambulate the ample interior of Mary Star of the Sea, one of the earliest Catholic communities in Southern California. Nick, the full-time sacristan, fills me in on the early history of the fifty-six hundred family parish that supports an academically notable K-through-12 parochial school. We wander down the side aisles appreciating the vivid colors of the low rectangular windows depicting symbols of the Virgin, and Nick tells me the delightful story of the Waterford stained glass being shipped from Ireland in protective crates of molasses. All about us are reminders of the founding eastern European immigrant communities whose progeny are still well represented here. To the right of the altar is a hanging satin banner stitched by the

Croatian Altar Society with the words *Velike Gospe* (Holy Mary). A side niche houses a reproduction of Michelangelo's Pieta. Outside sits an enormous white marble statue of Our Lady of the Rosary of Pompeii, an image from a nineteenth-century shrine near the ancient Roman city, the handiwork of a devoted Italian lawyer who had been converted to the Catholic faith through devotion to the rosary. These varied images are dwarfed by the one that dominates the interior space: a nearly life-sized gleaming white marble Virgin who cradles a fishing boat beneath an oversized gold and striated marble *baldaquino* that rises majestically above the central altar.

She is a fitting counterpart to the bronze Star of the Sea who rises on the parish bell tower above the city, her arms extended wide in welcome toward those sailing home.

The iconographic evidence of Marian devotion in San Pedro is overwhelming, but I wonder about the assimilated second- and third-generation offspring of these early San Pedro immigrants. What of Marian devotion among them? I am thus glad to come across a recent study by pastoral theologian Mary Clark Moschella entitled *Living Devotions* that studies the religious *habitus* of the Italian and Sicilian population of this very San Pedro Catholic community. This ethnographical study affirms the importance of devotional practice, both as it enables first-generation immigrants to negotiate the cultural disruptions of dislocation, and as it creates patterns of religious sensibility among later generations whether or not they explicitly engage in devotional practice or continue church affiliation. A profoundly sacramental imagination, learned skills of visual and material piety that infuse the activities of daily life with a sense of the sacred, a capacity for healing and creative transformation: these are the legacies of devotional practice that Moschella finds infused in the stories of the second- and third-generation residents whose spiritual home-place is Mary Star of the Sea. Her pastoral insights linger as intimations to be later explored.

Mary Star of the Sea on Bell Tower, Mary Star of the Sea Church, San Pedro.
Mary Star of the Sea with Baldaquin, Mary Star of the Sea Church, San Pedro.
Marian Symbol Window (Arc of the Covenant, Lily of the Valley, Tower of David),
Mary Star of the Sea Church, San Pedro.

Her given name was Estelle, or Star, and her devotion to the Virgin was deep. Estelle Doheny, née Carrie Estelle Betzold, venerated Mary under many titles, most notably as Our Lady of the Miraculous Medal. I stand now before the astounding image of this Virgin at St. Vincent Church at the corner of West Adams and Figueroa, a jewel of a church situated not far from the Doheny mansion and designed in 1923 by architect Albert C. Martin to reflect the Andalusian architectural style that had captured Estelle's imagination. The Miraculous Medal image before which I stand is remarkable even in this remarkable spot. It is an image that Estelle Doheny herself not only underwrote but had a say in creating. The image is inset in an ornate golden altar niche amid swirling columns, trumpeting angels, and ornamental hearts. Standing alone on a globe of the earth in her blue overcloak, rays of light streaming from her upturned palms, she is identifiably the same one who appeared in 1830 to novice Catherine Labouré in the chapel at the Daughters of Charity motherhouse on Rue de Bac in Paris. But this L.A. version of the image is singular because the halo that frames her face and the rays that reach out and downward are fashioned of bright neon lights.

The story of Estelle, a grand dame of early twentieth-century Los Angeles Catholicism, is as strange and theatrical as the city in which she spent the majority of her eighty-three years. Standing in the glow of Our Lady's neon emanations, I am arrested by the fact that our lives in fact overlapped. Estelle Doheny, of an earlier generation, nonetheless inhabited this same urban landscape with me until my eleventh year. Yet her tale has the feel of a saga that might have occurred in a long-ago universe I could never count as part of my own history. Nonetheless, there we were and, in the ongoing spiritual narrative of the city of Our Lady of the Angels, here we both belong.

Most people know of Estelle as Mrs. Doheny, wife of the entrepreneurial oil tycoon Edward L. Doheny or through the name attached to the many Southern California institutions and causes she supported with the fortune her husband amassed. The two met when Edward, having risen from poor Irish Catholic immigrant origins to prospector to rough and scramble oilman, fell in love with the sassy voice of the girlish telephone operator who placed his calls at the Sunset Telephone and Telegraph Company. The forty-four-year-old Edward brought to his second marriage the legacy of a sad divorce, a young son, and endless

Our Lady of the Miraculous Medal, St. Vincent's Church, L.A.
Library, St. John's Seminary, Camarillo.

ambition to create a giant international petroleum empire. She, a twenty-five-year-old from modest middle-class Methodist beginnings, brought intelligence, a capacity for long-suffering, and a spiritual resiliency that she would plumb to the depths over the course of her lifetime.

That life was characterized by alternating success and tragedy. Edward was at the cusp of the burgeoning oil industry, and he used the risk-taking ingenuity that had taken him from poverty to success to become a multimillionaire. He drilled for black gold throughout the West and Mexico and insinuated himself into political circles in Washington to further his business interests. Estelle, meanwhile, raised Ned, the son left after Edward's first spouse committed suicide, attended to the grandchildren Ned produced, and gave herself to building and philanthropic projects. In 1918 her close study of Catholic teaching led her to convert, and the wealthy pair became important figures in the L.A. archdiocese: among other notable ecclesiastics, Archbishop John Cantwell (appointed to the see of Monterey–Los Angeles in 1917) was an intimate in the Doheny circle and guided the Doheny philanthropic efforts. Although his wealth and business connections gave Edward some visibility in East Coast government circles, his Catholicism and

the fact that he was a westerner acted against him. So the Doheny rise to social prominence took place primarily in the Catholic world. In 1925 Pope Pius XI conferred upon the couple the titles of Knight and Lady of the Equestrian Order of the Holy Sepulchre, and in 1935 Estelle was elevated to the rank of Papal Countess.

Estelle was blessed with a sense of generosity. The Doheny mansion at Chester Place (now on the campus of St. Mary's College), the magnificent St. Vincent Church, Fern Ranch in Santa Paula, the libraries at the University of Southern California, the (now dispersed) rare book collection at St. John's Seminary in Camarillo, buildings at Loyola Marymount University, a foundation for the treatment of eye disease at St. Vincent Medical Center all serve as evidence of Mrs. Doheny's philanthropic impulses.

Yet Estelle's generosity was generated as much by suffering as by a sense of *noblesse oblige*. Students of U.S. history may associate the Doheny name mainly with scandal and corruption. At the height of his influence, Edward reconnected with Albert Bacon Fall, a companion from his early mining days who was appointed Secretary of the Interior under President Warren G. Harding. Fall, Doheny, and oil operator Harry Sinclair were implicated in what became known as the Teapot Dome scandal. It was discovered that Fall, without competitive biding, had leased public government land to Doheny and Sinclair for drilling. The latter two were exposed as having "loaned" Fall vast amounts of interest-free money. The sensational events of the bribery trials were covered in the national news and went on for almost a decade. To deepen the tragedy, son Ned, who had carried the "loan" to Fall, was mysteriously murdered before he could testify. Ned's death and the public humiliation broke Edward physically and mentally and, although he was eventually acquitted, he died in 1935 a diminished man. Estelle tended him faithfully to the end. To add to her sorrows, late in her life she suffered an ocular hemorrhage which severely compromised her eyesight. She was supported through all this by the pastor of the West Adams church, Vincentian William Ward. The Vincentian charism of care for the poor became Estelle's own and directed her charitable giving.

Our Lady of the Miraculous Medal, the distinctive Vincentian Madonna, claimed Estelle Doheny's heart. Here in the magnificent baroque environment of St. Vincent's this Virgin, first seen by Catherine Labouré, holds iconographical sway. My guide to this spot is Vincentian Br. Tony Wiedemer, a parish pastoral associate. Br. Tony reminds me and my photographer of the important contributions made in the L.A. area by the extended Vincentian family: the Congregation of the Missions, founded by Vincent de Paul; the Daughters of Charity Servants of the Sick Poor, which de Paul founded with Louise de Marillac; and the Ladies of Charity, an auxiliary lay organization founded to mobilize the wealthy on behalf of the poor. We learn that Spanish and Irish Daughters of Charity came to the frontier L.A. diocese in 1856 with newly appointed Bishop Thaddeus Amat, himself a Vincentian, after the unwieldy Monterey–Los Angeles diocese was divided. Later, sisters of the American province of the same congregation tirelessly staffed hospitals, schools, and orphanages and provided disaster relief throughout the region.

Our tour of the elegant parish campus reveals, besides the neon Madonna, the stained-glass versions of the double hearts of Jesus and Mary surmounted by the letter "M" also seen by Sr. Catherine in one of her Marian visions. Framed by a curving phrase "O Mary, conceived without original sin, pray for us," another aspect of the visionary encounter, the Virgin looms in stone over the church entrance doors. Our Lady's message to the awestruck seventeenth-century novice was to have a medal struck with her distinctive image that, if worn, would confer divine graces. Estelle Doheny did more than wear the miraculous medal on her person; she had it erected for posterity in stone, glass, wood, metal, and neon. It is even recounted that she had diamond-studded medals of Our Lady of the Miraculous Medal struck for the Ladies of Charity in L.A.

On a December morning in the Santa Barbara pastoral region of the archdiocese, I am escorted about the Camarillo campus of St. John's Seminary where the results of some of Estelle Doheny's endowments are visible. Dr. Paul Ford of the seminary faculty has invited Rita Flanders, former curator of the Doheny library collection, to join us and we are whisked about the immaculately groomed grounds while my hosts warm to the task of sharing their formidable knowledge of the site. The stunning windows in the chapel are a 1939 gift of Estelle commissioned from the Tierney studios in New York. They make the Vincentian impress on the archdiocese vivid. I am informed as well that during a visit to the World's Fair held in Ireland at about the same time, Archbishop Cantwell admired a set of stained-glass windows fashioned by the Henry Clark Studios and that Mrs. Doheny promptly purchased them. The acquired windows filter striations of colored light today through their panes onto the pews of the adjacent priests' chapel.

The Papal Countess not only favored the Vincentian Virgin but retained an early devotion to Guadalupe and to Mexico. Rita Flanders shows me a small chrome Guadalupe statuette that Mrs. Doheny treasured and alerts me to the Countess's penchant for the baroque architectural style that dominated colonial New Spain. The syncretism of Estelle's loves becomes clearly visible on the front edifice of the seminary library: the towering beige stone portal is a copy of Mexico's Guadalupe shrine, only in place of the Mexican Madonna is the Lady of the Miraculous Medal flanked by a Celtic cross and the respective coats of arms of the archdiocese and the Doheny family.

I encounter devotion to the Miraculous Medal at various L.A. parishes including St. Louise de Marillac in Covina, named in 1963 as a tribute to Estelle by Cardinal McIntyre because of her patronage of the Daughters of Charity; at St. Catherine Labouré Church in Torrance; and as a monumental modern Piczek sisters mosaic and a hand-painted folk mural placed, respectively, above the church entrance and on a schoolyard wall at Our Lady of the Miraculous Medal in Montebello. The present-day imprint of the devotion testifies to the tireless Vincentian pastoral presence in the Los Angeles region. It also testifies to the generous patronage of Estelle Doheny and her intimacy with Our Lady, born out of the abundance and tragedy that characterized Estelle's life.

Weeks later, as I peruse the photographic proofs of the Miraculous Medal, I am struck by the ubiquitous image of light that so often accompanies the Virgin Mary. She is the morning star whose light first pierces the inky night sky. She is the steady light of the North Star that orients seafarers and those navigating rough seas. Rays of light—symbol of divine grace—stream from her outstretched palms. Light, she is surrounded by light.

Our Lady of the Miraculous Medal, Piczek Studios Mosaic, Our Lady of the Miraculous Medal Church, Montebello.

Our Lady of Lebanon Altar, Our Lady of Lebanon, St. Peter Maronite Catholic Cathedral, L.A.

Chapter 9

God-Bearer
Theotokos

Hail, O you who carry Him
Who Carries All!
Hail, O Star who manifests the Sun!
Hail, O Womb of the Divine Incarnation!
Hail, O you through whom
creation is renewed!
Hail, O you through whom the Creator becomes a Babe!
Hail, O Bride and Maiden ever-pure!

—From the Akathist Hymn, First Chant

Edward Doheny was not the only early industrialist whose fortune was directed to the benefit of the city of Los Angeles. His contemporary, Griffith J. Griffith, another man like Doheny whose story has its sad, seamy side (he served time for shooting and maiming his wife), made his wealth in silver. He bequeathed to the municipality a four thousand–acre parcel of land for use as a public park at the eastern edge of the Santa Monica Mountains. At the pinnacle of that parcel in the Los Feliz area on the south-facing slope of Mount Hollywood stands Griffith Observatory. It seems that Griffith, interested in the advances in astronomy taking place in California, was given the opportunity to gaze through the newly constructed telescope at Mount Wilson Observatory in the nearby San Gabriel Mountains. So awed by his stargazing was he and so convinced that if every person could be given a cosmic perspective that the world would be different, Griffith endowed the world's first public observatory.

I visit the stately structure with its classic Art Deco, Greek revival, and Beaux Arts architecture on one of my late pilgrimage rounds. Here it was in the rotunda during my elementary years that my friend Chris and I used to hang over the lip of the display that held Foucault's Pendulum and watch the truth of the earth's rotation be confirmed by the periodic toppling of upright metal pegs. Foucault's experiment is still there, although the Observatory has been reopened after a state-of-the-art renovation. Now a 152-by-20-foot panoramic wall display entitled the Big Picture, created of astronomical observational data collected through space exploration, takes the visitor much farther into the cosmos then Griffith was able to gaze. It allows a breathtaking view of a minute part of the night sky that contains over a million galaxies, stars, and other celestial objects, an immensity of which we are a miniscule portion.

Human beings have always looked to the skies, not merely to guide their safe passage on the oceans and on land, but to gauge their own significance in the universe. All the global religious traditions have sacred stories that situate the human experience in a cosmic context. My own college-age experiences of cosmic religiosity are linked to the Sikh Gurdwara on North Vermont Avenue, the white-domed Vedanta Society Temple in the Hollywood foothills, and the Vedanta Temple on Ladera Lane high on the mountainous ridges above Santa Barbara. But Christianity, of course, has its cosmic narrative. The familiar passage from the Gospel of John "In the beginning was the Word and the Word was with God and the Word was God" serves not only as a foundation for Christological speculation but situates the Good News in an unfathomably vast cosmic context. Equally striking are the Genesis creation narratives and select passages from Old Testament Wisdom literature. These latter passages are associated with the Virgin Mary and are read on her feast days. They point to the intuition that Mary has cosmic importance.

> The LORD created me at the beginning of his work,
>   the first of his acts of long ago.
> Ages ago I was set up,
>   at the first, before the beginning of the earth. . . .
>   [T]hen I was beside him, like a master worker;
> and I was daily his delight,
>   rejoicing before him always,
> rejoicing in his inhabited world
>   and delighting in the human race. (Prov 8:22-23, 30-31)

Centuries before the present-day scientific advances in astronomy that are reflected at Griffith Observatory, Christians were thinking about the big picture, not in the language of scientific method but in the language of sacred poetry and story. The ancient Christian churches especially found ways of speaking about Mary that emphasized her cosmic importance. Those Christians who belong to the branch of Christendom known as Eastern Orthodoxy or Byzantine Christianity continue to honor her primarily in this way. She is after all, *Theotokos*, God-Bearer, or Mother of God. The title, formally validated at the third ecumenical council held at Ephesus in 431, arose as the Christian community was sorting out the relationship between the human and divine natures of Christ. The title *Theotokos* refuses the idea that Mary was merely the mother of Jesus's human nature. She was as well mother of his divinity: Mother of God. The title underscores the theological assertion that Mary's son was fully God and fully human, and that his two natures (divine and human) unite in a single Person of the Trinity.

Both in the liturgy and in visual representation, *Theotokos* with her cosmic and salvific significance permeates Byzantine and Eastern Orthodoxy. One hears this in the famous Akathist Hymn sung during the Friday evening service of the first five weeks of the Great Lent. Composed in the sixth century, the Akathist Hymn is to this branch of Christianity what the rosary and the Litany of Loreto are to the Latin Rite church, only more so.

There is no better prayer to express love and veneration of the *Theotokos*. The majority of the hymn is made up of praises directed to the Mother of God, always beginning with the salutation of the Archangel Gabriel. Among the hundreds of breathtaking invocations with which she is addressed are these:

Hidden Sense of the Ineffable Plan
Celestial Ladder by whom God came down
Bridge leading earthly ones to heaven
You who gave birth to Light ineffably
Tendril whose Bud shall not wilt
Soil whose Fruit shall not perish
Gardener of the Gardener of Life
Earth who yielded abundant mercies
Space of the Spaceless God
Gate of the Sublime Mystery
Container of God's Wisdom

The list goes on and on. This mother is not the accessible Madonna of Renaissance art cradling her cunning infant. She is a woman of cosmic import. She is the one who bears God.

In 1962, on the eve of the opening of the Second Vatican Council, the image of the Virgin Mary chosen for prominence at the annual Los Angeles Mary's Hour was Our Lady of Perpetual Help, the Byzantine-styled icon popular in the Latin Church. The pastor of a Van Nuys Byzantine Rite Catholic Church was interviewed in the archdiocesan paper *The Tidings* about the choice. He was quoted as saying that the choice was appropriate as hopes were high that the impending council would bring about the unification of the separated brethren of Western and Eastern Christianity. That hoped for unification, while still not yet realized, has nevertheless made progress through ecumenical dialogue in the half century since the Vatican Council.

Long before this mid-twentieth-century event, however, there were Eastern Rite Catholic Churches that, through historical circumstance, blended spiritual, juridical, devotional, and liturgical elements of East and West, and these churches are today represented in the Los Angeles archdiocese. United in their acknowledgement of the primacy of the Bishop of Rome, these Eastern Catholics may practice intercommunion. They thus have a standing in the L.A. archdiocese, although each autonomous or "Particular Church" has its own episcopal authority.

On a busy weekday my photographer Dorothy and I wend our way through traffic-clogged San Vicente Boulevard to Our Lady of Mount Lebanon–St Peter, the elegant Maronite Cathedral under the jurisdiction of the Eparchy of Our Lady of Lebanon in the Western United States. The Maronite Church, whose liturgical language is Syriac, has a heritage reaching back to Maron, a fifth-century Syriac monk, and an unbroken communion with Rome: indeed the local parish bulletin lists regular Sunday Masses as alternately Maronite and Roman Catholic. Maronites fleeing from famine and persecution came to the United States from Lebanon in the early nineteenth century. This cathedral on the West Coast is a fairly recent foundation.

Iconostasis, Nativity of the Blessed Virgin Mary Ukrainian Catholic Church, L.A.

The aesthetic of Our Lady of Mount Lebanon identifies it as from a tradition born in a region that has long been a crossroad between East and West. To the right of the central altar is a pastel statue of a demure Our Lady touching an exposed heart on her breast. Above her a turquoise blue roundel with six stars supports a banner with words taken from the Song of Songs: "Come to me from Lebanon, My bride." In one startling illumined glass along the side aisle, Our Lady is a simple presence standing with arms spread in the gesture of grace. In another she is symbolized by a towering cedar, the tree often referred to in the Bible and native to Lebanese soil. Maronite Christians have a great devotion to Mary and claim special intimacy with her because according to legend Jesus and his mother visited the Lebanese cities of Tyre and Sidon during his public ministry. Although I visit Our Lady of Mount Lebanon–St. Peter in summertime, it is delightful to discover in the pamphlet rack a parish newsletter left over from spring. It features a story about the May Crowning that took place here on Our Lady of Mount Lebanon's feast on May 5 and contains parishioners' often touching testimonies in English and Lebanese about their devotion to their patroness.

Beside the Maronites, the archdiocese is home to twelve other Eastern Catholic Churches. With Dorothy I am able to visit several that strike us forcefully with their Byzantine aesthetic. The Ukrainian-Byzantine

Icon Wall, St. Andrew Russian Greek, St. Paul Melkite Greek Catholic Church, El Segundo.

Dormition Icon, St. Andrew Russian Greek, St. Paul Melkite Greek Catholic Church, El Segundo.

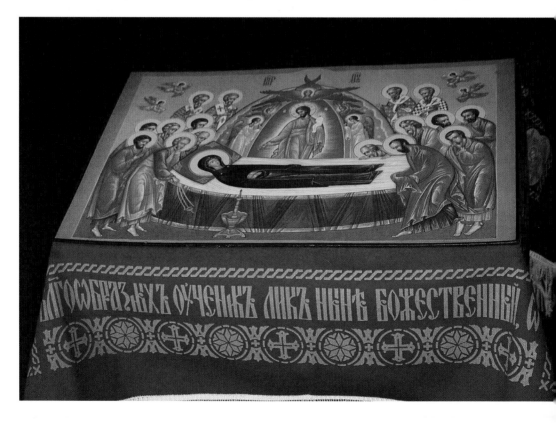

Nativity of Blessed Virgin Mary church on De Longpre Avenue in Hollywood is a case in point. The edifice with its domed roof surmounted by a cross arrests us as we approach the residential side street on which it is located. Inside the church is a jewel box of deep crimson, velvety midnight blues, and brilliant golds. The focal point of the light-filled interior is the majestic iconostasis that stretches across the entire width of the sanctuary. Here in this sacred space the shimmering, golden expanse of the ornate iconostasis frames traditional icons of the Virgin, John the Baptist, and other saints. Above them all, set off by a soaring arch and rising on the vivid cerulean east wall above the hidden chancel is *Theotokos*, her extended arms emerging from her blood-red cloak. In Byzantine style, all the images are two dimensional, meant to provide a window onto the sacred archetypes rather than to suggest realistic representations as do three-dimensional western images. A maroon-carpeted side altar presents Our Lady of Perpetual Help framed in golden splendor. A silver *Hodegetria* icon—in which the Virgin points to her child as the source of human salvation—is set out upon a draped pedestal and waits for those who venerate her to stoop and kiss her image.

Among Eastern Rite Catholic Churches, the Ukrainian branch is the largest—2 percent of Catholics across the world are members—and like many other Eastern Catholic particular churches, the community on De Longpre Avenue celebrates using the ancient Liturgy of St. John Chrysostom rather than the Roman rite. This practice they share with the St. Andrew Russian-Greek Catholic community in El Segundo on the Santa Monica bay. The building in which the Russian Greek Catholics meet is also known as St. Paul's because the Melkite Greek Catholic Mission gathers here as well. The group referred to as "Melkites" are generally Arabic-speaking Greek Catholics from the Middle East. The same person, Fr. Alexei Smith, is pastor and administrator of both communities. He celebrates services in English punctuated with a mixture of either Arabic and Greek or Russian. The afternoon Dorothy and I locate the unobtrusive structure in a quiet residential section of El Segundo Fr. Alexei is there to greet us. His is a fascinating story. A professional undertaker, he became a parishioner at the parish, then left to attend seminary and returned as a freshly minted priest. He has been here since 1987. He chats in a lively manner while he escorts us about the church interior.

St. Andrew–St. Paul is another wonder of a sacred space. Less light-filled and shimmering with gold than the Ukrainian church, it nevertheless is bathed in the sense of mystery that only a Byzantine aesthetic can convey. The small wooden structure was originally a Roman Catholic congregation that has since moved to a more spacious El Segundo

location. The low central room through which we move has at its east
end a handsome wood-paneled iconostasis covered with traditional
icons. The remainder of the irregular interior space, every wall and
pillar, corner and niche reveals *Theotokos* in one of her ancient forms
flanked by flickering candles. The approach to Mary here, Fr. Alexei
informs us, is more theological than devotional. Yes, she is much loved
but it is her cosmic role as God-Bearer that informs that love.

From Fr. Alexi we learn something of the history of those Russian
Christians who recognize the authority of the Western pontiff. In 1905
they were formally united with Rome but during the Soviet era were
forced underground. After the fall of communism, the community
emerged again. As of 2006, Russian Catholics have no hierarchy of
their own; their few parishes are served by priests ordained in other
Byzantine Catholic Churches, as in El Segundo, or by former Orthodox
priests or Roman Catholic priests with bi-ritual faculties.

The communities Fr. Alexi serves observe a cluster of feasts that
stress the august role of Mary in the plan of salvation. These relate to
familiar Western Marian observances in varying ways. Because it is
August and we are in the "small Lenten season" that precedes the ap-
proaching feast of the Dormition of the Virgin (in the West, the feast of
the Assumption), Fr. Alexei brings out an icon of that mystery fashioned
in subtle indigo, beige, and rose and lays it carefully on a lectern for us
to view. The Mother of Jesus, falling asleep at the end of her earthly life,
lies serenely upon a bed in the center of the composition surrounded by
angels and the twelve apostles. Behind her the risen Christ appears in
a convex *mandorla* and holds in one hand a small figure, his mother's
departing soul, to be taken up with him into heaven. The icon, which
celebrates the Virgin as the first fruit of the redeemed humanity, will
be carried at the head of the solemn procession that will wind through
the streets of El Segundo on the fifteenth of August.

Among the remaining Eastern Rite churches in the archdiocese, I am
afforded only an exterior glimpse of St. Mary's Byzantine-Ruthenian Cathedral in Sherman Oaks, the first Byzantine church in the Golden State.
Established in 1956, the structure with its two golden minarets honors
Our Lady of Perpetual Help with a stunning stained-glass window
and with a garden shrine. Originating from an area near the Carpath-
ian Mountains where the borders of Hungary, Slovakia, and Ukraine
meet, this particular church harkens back to Sts. Cyril and Methodius
who in the ninth century brought Christianity to the Slavic peoples.
Adherents arrived in the United States in the nineteenth century with
immigrants to coal-mining regions. Today Ruthenian Catholics celebrate

the divine mysteries with the ancient Byzantine liturgy of Constantinople (in Church Slavonic) but, like the Lebanese, observe the rhythms of the western liturgical year.

Dorothy and I have a much fuller view of St. Mary Coptic Catholic Church, one of only three such communities in the United States. It is difficult to locate the tiny church in its older residential enclave sandwiched among homes and small manufacturers under the shadow of a Glendale freeway trestle. But when we arrive, the resident priest, Fr. Francis, proves to be a generous host. Drawn out from the quiet of his rectory behind the church, he shares the remarkable story of this place. In 1991 the miniscule Egyptian Catholic community in the area took over what was originally a Mormon church, and St. Mary's was born. The Alexandrian rite, which here means the Mass of St. Gregory or St. Basil offered in Arabic and English, is one of the most ancient in Christendom, tracing its roots to the Apostle Mark. Coptic Catholics represent an eighteenth-century schism over papal primacy within

St. Mary and Angels behind Altar, St. Mary Coptic Catholic Church, L.A.

the Coptic Orthodox community. Today the patriarch of this particular church resides in Cairo. Fr. Francis himself hails from Egypt and came here by way of Australia where he served before being transferred to Los Angeles. I get the distinct sense that he feels he is a long way from anywhere: the parish is small in numbers, and most members live scattered about the huge metropolitan region and are not able to attend regularly. It certainly is quiet the weekday we visit.

Inside, St. Mary is another wonder of a sacred enclave. I never cease being amazed by the extent to which cultural identity is engraved so indelibly in these spaces. Everything here speaks artistically of the ancient region on the Nile that for centuries has been saturated by Arab culture. A low dark wooden ceiling shelters the nave, the central feature of which is a contemporary wood *iconostasis* whose featured icons strike one with their dark-rimmed almond-eyed beauty and bold two-dimensional design. Above the altar behind the *iconostasis,* a singular representation of a narrow-visaged *Theotokos* and her small kingly child looms from a velvety black backdrop. Flanked by two elongated angelic figures, they hover majestically in their deep black space. Around the nave are newly fabricated renderings of the mysteries of the Virgin's life.

Fr. Francis patiently explains to us the centrality of Marian veneration among Coptic Catholics that reflects a mixture of Eastern and Western practices: on Fridays a rosary to St. Mary is held followed by a Bible study; at each Mass one song to her is always sung; novenas are held before each of her feasts; and May is acknowledged with a prayer in her honor offered daily; and, as in most Eastern Rite communities, the Assumption is a liturgical highlight. The Virgin, Fr. Francis instructs us, is seen at St. Mary's Catholic Coptic community as the august mother of the community more than the purely scriptural Mary. She is, he says, Our Mother, the Mother of the Church, and the Mother of God.

In keeping with Fr. Francis's observations, it seems that, as devoted to the Virgin as they are in these Eastern Rite Catholic communities, there is little sense of her as a companionate sister and little of the domestic sentimentality of the Western Madonna cradling her child. Instead she is endowed with cosmic majesty. Even with the gracefulness of the ubiquitous Byzantine icon of the Virgin of Tenderness who lifts her child gently to her cheek, *Theotokos* is decidedly of the archetypal realm, the uncreated reality glimpsed by gazing through the icon, a reality that itself gazes upon this created realm through the medium of wood, paint, and gold.

Interestingly, in the West today and quite independent of Eastern Catholic influence, one strand of what might be termed third-wave feminist Marian speculation is moving decidedly in the direction of the cosmic. This speculation takes a number of surprising twists and turns. Scholar Charlene Spretnak, who describes herself as a feminist thinker, believes that while both Vatican II documents and liberal feminists offer important correctives to a patriarchal institution, they have "demoted Mary" to being merely an exemplary model of discipleship. Spretnak refuses to downplay Mary's regnant and divine attributes. She sees these traditional titles and attributes of the Madonna as corresponding to insights in the emerging scientific cosmology, especially contemporary reengagement with the cosmos as the fecund matrix or *quantum plenum* of all life. She finds in Mary more than human cosmological proportions and celebrates her as the mystical female body that embodies grace. In so doing Spretnak critiques our modern perceptual orientation that she thinks has led to the demotion of Mary and attempts to enthrone her once again with the help of postmodern cosmology. She goes on to explore the use of imagery in devotion and explains this ancient practice in fresh ways.

> The unbroken field of space-time is also relevant to the cross-cultural sense of participatory consciousness in the nonmodern engagement with figurative symbols, that is, statues. . . . The statues of Mary are not dolls. They are not even mere signs representing something to us, as the modern theory of semiotics would have. The concentrated symbolic power possessed by these "small bodies" of the Great Mother can best be understood in the premodern and postmodern sense of participatory consciousness: Our engagement with an expansive and multivalent symbol brings us into the unitive embrace of the sacred whole, into nonlinguistic awareness of the unbroken field of matter and energy arising and passing away trillions of times per second, constituting all things past and present. Mary is a gateway to our realization of that profound unity.

In less polemical but no less provocative fashion, British theologian Sarah Jane Boss feels that traditional theological Marian themes reveal truths about the larger cosmic reality of which we are a small part. Boss posits that the Blessed Virgin as the immaculate conception and the assumption and in her role in the mystery of the incarnation is comparable to the dark matter of science or prime matter: the chaos out of which creation emerges. Among the many Marian themes Boss explores, the Throne (or Seat) of Wisdom is particularly interesting for its cosmic implications. Mary, of course, has long been associated with the scriptural figure of Wisdom and her British interpreter waxes eloquent about this medieval image of Mary as the throne upon which her regnant son sits. From the symmetry of Mary and Jesus's majestic roles, Boss concludes that just as Christ is the Wisdom of God through which the world is created, so Mary is the Wisdom of God through which the world is renewed. This scholar's ultimate concern in her explorations is not devotional but ecological. Boss argues that the increasing trend toward the domination of nature and the female body that has occurred in Western culture is reflected in changing attitudes toward the Virgin Mary. Thus the human choice between wisdom and folly as set out in Scripture is, in her view, the choice between reverence for a God-bearing creation symbolized in the Virgin Mary or ecologically devastating contempt for creation's God.

Intimations of the cosmic, ecologically significant Virgin continue to swirl about in my mind on the December afternoon I visit Griffith Observatory. The city is uncharacteristically rain-drenched, and the usual view of the metropolitan basin from the observation decks is obscured by a thick blanket of low-lying fog. The astronomical devices set up for public use reflect merely a dark, shrouded atmosphere. Even with the fog, I am aware that since the turn of the twentieth century when Griffith J. Griffith stared in wonder at the luminous expanse of the night sky, the science of astronomy has opened up the heavens to a vista that completely dwarfs his. Beyond our world and our solar system lie innumerable planetary systems and innumerable galaxies, over a hundred billion of which are now technologically visible to us. Venerating the *Theotokos* is meant to be an analogous experience. The ancient archetypal iconography as found in L.A.'s Eastern Rite churches gives the one who prays intimate access to a reality so vast, and ultimately so mysterious, that it takes one's breath away. *Theotokos*, God-Bearer, is the gold-inflected Virgin whose presence, if we allow it, leads one to the limits of imagination and the intersection of the human and divine.

Lourdes Window, Our Lady of Lourdes Church, Tujunga.

Chapter 10

Perpetual Help
Perpetuo Socorro

¡Oh Madre del Perpetuo Socorro!
cuyo solo nombre inspira confianza
¡Madre de amor venid en mi Socorro!

—*Invocacion: Novena del Milagro a Nuestra Señora del Perpetuo Socorro*

On a Wednesday evening in August, I make my way off the main streets of Glendale to the older residential neighborhood in which Holy Family parish is nestled. With others, I make my way inside the vintage 1920 ornate structure to attend the weekly evening Mass that will be followed by a Novena to Our Lady of Perpetual Help. The novena, a nine-day prayer cycle that leads up to a liturgical feast or a weekly prayer done over a period of nine weeks, gained currency in the nineteenth- and twentieth-century church. One variant, the one taking place at Holy Family, is a Perpetual Novena, in which each nine-week cycle is followed by another. This practice still flourishes in the city of Our Lady of the Angels.

After the service, during which those of us gathered acknowledge Perpetual Help as maternal refuge, comfort in time of trial, and respondent to our petitions, I am plied with traditional hospitality in the form of Filipino-style chicken on the parish patio. Ernie, a spokesman for the Holy Family parish Filipino community, declares that his group is responsible for the reinstitution and popularity of the Wednesday novena, and the cookout celebrates the revival of the novena in the parish ten years before. Ernie explains the ritual I have just experienced as a practice that encourages community and continues the beloved religious practice brought from the homeland. In Baclaran, where the Philippine national shrine of Our Mother of Perpetual Help is located, the Wednesday evening devotion regularly attracts an estimated one hundred thousand devotees. This summer evening in Glendale the church held over three hundred worshipers. The many immigrants to the U.S., like Ernie, have reaffirmed here their national passion for the novena and their sense of the hovering benevolent presence of Our Lady of Perpetual Help.

As do all Marian images, Perpetual Help has her own complex backstory. This includes an early tale of her miraculous origins, several versions of a story about her adoption as a beloved Western Catholic Virgin, and a tale of her arrival in Southern California. A Byzantine-style image, she is reputed to have been painted in the thirteenth century. Clearer records from the fifteenth report that she was much venerated in Rome where miracles were attributed to her intercession. The stories about her arrival in the Eternal City vary, but a common one tells of a pious merchant who brought the image from his travels in the East and

Novena to Our Lady of Perpetual Help, Holy Family Church, Glendale.

requested in his will that she be venerated publically. Eventually the Re-demptorist order, founded in the mid-eighteenth century by Alphonsus Liguori, came to be responsible for the care of the image and promotion of the devotion. When Pope Pius IX, motivated by a deep personal ven-eration, had the image crowned, assigned a celebratory feast day, and established an archconfraternity to which privileges and indulgences were attached, the image was raised to worldwide importance.

The Redemptorists preached fiery missions widely in California throughout the nineteenth and early twentieth centuries and left the seared landscape behind them scattered with images of Our Lady of Per-petual Help. These missions flourished in an era in which the Catholic Church conceived of itself as being in conflict with a threatening modern world. The Redemptorist fathers brought a stirring evangelical message of rescue and refuge to those outside of or fallen away from the Catholic fold: Our Lady was key in their efforts. Perpetual Help is immediately recognizable no matter where she is located. Similar to many portraits of the Virgin with the infant Jesus found throughout Russia and the East, the genre of Perpetual Help's portrayal is known as the *Hodegetria* (literally "She who shows the way") which features the Virgin's hand pointing to her Son. Particular to the Perpetual Help icon are other de-tails: on either side of the mother and child are the Archangels Gabriel and Michael bearing the instruments of the passion and the infant Christ gazes upon the cross. His left sandal falls off his foot as if he has hur-riedly run back to the arms of his mother for her help and protection.

Today the Perpetual Help devotion is the most widely officially sponsored parish devotion in the L.A. archdiocese. Over seventy con-gregations hold novenas in her honor. In some locations the image is used as the focus of a healing ministry as at the architecturally stunning Spanish baroque Holy Family church in South Pasadena. More often, as at Glendale's Holy Family, she has had her special devotees. At times Perpetual Help is asked to carry the changing concerns of the Catholic world. On a damp Friday in February outside Our Lady of Perpetual Help parish in Santa Clarita I find an example of her carrying a concern often expressed in the contemporary ecclesial environment. A large mo-saic of the recognizable Byzantine-style icon fronts the church building while to the side, skirting the parking lot, is a modern sculpture of the Holy Family featuring a mother and father protectively cradling their infant child. It is dedicated as a "memorial to the unborn."

Among the many striking aspects of the medieval cult of the Virgin which first enthralled me during my early graduate studies at the University of California at Santa Barbara is the extent to which Mary has consistently been turned to in times of need. Theologically speaking, she functions not as the final resting place for the ardent petitions flung in her direction but rather the penultimate one. She, as it were, is supposed to pass them on to her son. Still, she is the one to whom generations of devotees have first turned for shelter and aid. You don't see the visual image often today, but one of my medieval favorites is Mary imaged as Mother of the Faithful. Also known as Mother of the Church, this Mary is an archetypal figure with ample cloak spread wide, under whose sheltering wings throngs of grateful believers cluster.

Although during my pilgrimage I had just about decided that this classic Marian representation had pretty much disappeared in L.A. (except on the upper segment of a modern stained-glass window at *La Purisima Concepcion* in Lompoc), she appeared as a twelve-inch-high modern bronze relief placed in my hands at a Monday evening reflection time with the Notre Dame Sisters in Thousand Oaks. Like any number of other teaching sisters, this group came to Los Angeles at the request of Archbishop Cantwell in 1925, after which they established schools in Huntington Park, Watts, South Gate, Downey, and Thousand Oaks.

Among the five religious women present this night in the upper room over the cafeteria of the all-girls' Regina High School in the renovated space which serves as their convent is Sr. Lisa, the institution's development director. Like her other U.S.-born community members in the German-founded Notre Dames, Lisa has spent a lifetime in active educational ministry. A self-reported "news junkie," she has strong views about global justice and links her activism on behalf of social causes to her devotion to Mary as Mother of the Church, a title that she appreciates was affirmed at the Second Vatican Council. Lisa, who I would guess is around my age, grew up in a strongly devotional Catholic household which she found too centered on "me and Jesus." She felt called instead to expand her awareness to others around the world. Mother of the Church was a Marian title that fit the bill and won her affection. Knowing of Lisa's fondness for the title, one of her superiors brought a modern metal version of this Mary back from a trip to Germany and gifted Lisa with it. It is placed now in my hands. The bronze Mary and her son in three-quarter relief are wrapped beneath her swinging cloak under the folds of which are gathered tiny figures of her faithful: one on crutches, one shepherding a small child, others peering up in expectation of her help. Lisa has named her "Mary of the

Folks" and she laughs when she says that it is to Mary of the Folks that she herself turns when "a thousand times a day" people come to her and hang on her skirts asking for help of all kinds.

Other images throughout the region certainly convey the message of Mary as perpetually available to help in all sorts of ways. In Altadena, at St. Elizabeth of Hungary Church, a historic baroque structure similar to the one at South Pasadena's Holy Family, I find more fascinating material evidence of devotion to Mary as healer of the sick. St. Elizabeth's is a large community with an active ministerial staff. Behind the church complex is a Marian grotto that for many years gave the church a reputation as the "Lourdes of the West." Before the rock grotto, the story of Lourdes once again comes alive. The tale began in the Pyrenees mountain range of southern France at a river near a damp cave called the Grotto of Massabielle. There in February of 1858 a fourteen-year-old girl named Bernadette Soubirous came to draw water for her mother. While

she was doing so a young woman dressed in white appeared. She carried a rosary of shining gold, and yellow roses rested upon her bare feet. Eighteen times during the next months the lovely woman, who identified herself as the Immaculate Conception, visited Bernadette. The child was asked to impart a message of penance and prayer for sinners. On one occasion, she was asked to dig in the ground. From that spot, a spring gushed forth which became famous for its healing properties. The shrine at Lourdes, with its huge basilica, consecrated in 1876, and its complex of ritual healing baths is, after the shrine of Our Lady of Guadalupe in

Prayer Altar for the Sick with Our Lady of Perpetual Help, Holy Family Church, South Pasadena.

Mexico, today the world's most visited Catholic shrine. Replicas of the Marian visitation, with the tiny figure of Bernadette kneeling among the rocks before the white-robed figure of the Virgin, are ubiquitous all over the global Catholic landscape.

The Lourdes grotto at St. Elizabeth's, one of a number of identical ones in the archdiocese, has a unique history. These towering grottos—in a 1940s photo on the St. Elizabeth parish website hundreds of gathered parishioners are dwarfed by the mountain of cantilevered volcanic rocks within which the life-sized apparition statue rests—were built by Japanese American Catholic Ryoko Fuso Kado. Kado, a convert who came to the U.S. in 1911 and ran a nursery, was imprisoned in the infamous California internment camps that marked U.S. citizens and immigrants of Japanese descent as dangerous persons of interest during World War II. Fuso vowed that when he was released he would build a grotto each year for as many years as he was granted freedom after his internment. He was able to complete over twenty replicas of Lourdes before his

Lourdes Grotto, St. Elizabeth of Hungary Church, Altadena.

death in 1982. His intent was to create these monuments so that "people who pass by and stop to say a prayer may reach up their hearts to God in a much troubled world and thereby gain solace and consolation."

Perhaps the most well-preserved of the grottos Mr. Kado created is located at St John's Seminary in Camarillo. It is situated at the base of a hilly incline on the spacious tree-shaded property, somewhat distant from the majestic Spanish baroque seminary itself. This imposing black volcanic stone canopy that enshrines a white-stone scale replica of Our Lady at the shrine at Lourdes appears as moist and generative as the mysterious spot in the Pyrenees where healing springs once gushed forth from the parched earth. Unlike the original shrine, which over the years has spawned a startlingly commercial industry of devotional paraphernalia and activity, this secluded seminary grotto, which draws students wrestling with life-altering vocational questions as well as with anxiety about exams is clearly a place of quiet prayer.

I find other images of the Virgin who heals amply displayed at the newly renovated suburban parish of Our Lady of Lourdes in North-ridge, one of a string of Marian-titled churches that spans the San Fernando Valley. Among the bold modern Marian window designs here that suggest a pierced heart, a lily opened to the Spirit, and a regnant victory is a realistic light-filled image of Mary as she appeared at Lourdes, the yellow flowers upon her bare feet prominently displayed. Nestled in the foothills further to the east of the metropolitan basin in Tujunga is another Lourdes parish. A tall modern bell tower alerts the visitor to the presence of the church tucked into the low hillside of this suburban enclave. Here the healing waters of Lourdes are the main focus of the décor. As I enter the sanctuary, I become aware of a water-filled rock grotto at ankle level to my right filled with green plants and floral offerings. It features white plaster statuettes of a kneeling Bernadette and Our Lady. Above me dominating one entire wall of the sanctuary is an extraordinary multicolored modern stained-glass tableau of the healing activity over which Our Lady of Lourdes now presides in France: infirm pilgrims enter bathing pools; a priest gestures toward a crucifix, altar, and banks of votive candles; and behind the Lady herself hang rows of crutches, symbolic of the cures that have taken place at this healing shrine.

Back in Thousand Oaks I have a smaller, personalized version of a Lourdes image placed in my hands by one of the Notre Dame sisters. This occurs during the same Monday evening reflection period that one of the lifelong grade-school teachers present refers to as "show and tell." The woman who passes me a ten-inch-tall white and aquamarine plaster statuette of Our Lady of Lourdes is Sr. Bernadette. Her devotion to the particular Marian presence is hers in part because of her name, but also because long ago, as an eighth grader, she sent letters to nuns in France and received back holy cards and copies of the personal journals of her namesake saint. The particular mass-produced statue Sr. Bernadette presents me has special significance for its owner. She first sighted it in a religious goods store in Simi Valley but did not feel she should acquire it for herself. The next time she was in the store was after the devastating 1994 Northridge earthquake. Most of the store inventory had been damaged or destroyed, and workers were attempting to piece together repairable fragments of religious art, the Lourdes statuette among them. They gave the statuette to her as a gift. The very brokenness of the shattered and restored statue speaks to Sr. Bernadette of the power of Our Lady to heal and to draw devotees to her son.

That healing might occur as a result of contact with a holy person, object, or site is an idea much older and more universal than Christianity, but it is an idea that is highlighted in the Gospels and associated with the reign of God that Jesus proclaimed. That the blind will see, the deaf hear, and the lame dance for joy is part and parcel of the Christian imagination. This is an imagination into which many modern Americans must either ease sideways with the aid of scientific deconstructive explanations or embrace with what philosopher Paul Ricoeur called a sort of mythic second naïveté. I suppose I can be counted among the latter group.

As an only child I had plenty of opportunities to cultivate a vivid imagination. In part, that imagination was fueled by female cultural expectations of the era. For years I moved about the school grounds in company with my nine imaginary and perfectly well-behaved stair-step children. Plus, my imagination was fueled by the pixie dust of Disney's Magic Kingdom that swirled through my waking awareness as a child of Southern California. After all, my given name was Wendy, the name coined by J. M. Barrie in his tale of Peter Pan, and on my fifth birthday a select group of girlfriends and I were treated to the opening of the new Disney film with Peter, Wendy, and Tinkerbell featured in Technicolor on the big screen. That enchanted Disney park was also the place where I landed my first young adult professional job in show business as a

Our Lady of Perpetual Help Altar, Nativity of the Blessed Virgin Mary Ukrainian
Catholic Church, L.A.

"Kid of the Kingdom," dancing and singing on the Tomorrow Land stage. This was the cultural stuff of my imaginative world. But there was another dimension to that world, one fueled not by films or little-girl dreams of growing up to be mommy, but one generated by an attentiveness to mystery. I'm not sure where it came from. Maybe some people are simply born with the "religion gene." Maybe it was the mythic world unconsciously instilled in me by Josephine, the grandmotherly African American nanny who was my constant daytime companion during my first several years. In any case, it was my experience that mystery lurked everywhere. I sensed that there was a God, or a goodness, or a presence of some sort beyond that could be quantifiably validated. It was there when I woke to the sun entering my bedroom window through the tangled filter of the trees outside and thus knew that I had been given a fresh start each particular day.

This imagination was expanded in my grade- and junior-high-school years by the lilt and lift of hymnody breathed forth with such joy at Hollywood First Presbyterian. Presence: It was very real. That contact with this presence, whether direct or mediated by a person, place, or object, can heal is not a strange thought, for in my own life such people and places have been springs of refreshment and healing. It has taken a sort of second naïveté to own this as an adult. But at this point I am not surprised or bemused by stories such as the one Sr. Leanne shares in the "show and tell" circle of the Notre Dame sisters in Thousand Oaks.

Leanne, younger than some of her Notre Dame sisters and, unlike most of them, a convert, grew up in a mobile family. As a nominal Protestant, Leanne did not grow up with the habituated Marian devotion common before Vatican II. While respecting her community members' experience, she finds that she relates best to Mary as Throne of Wisdom or perhaps as companion or sister. Her theology is updated, her general outlook modern and progressive, yet Leanne has a powerful story of healing to share. As a young woman, drawn to the Catholic Church and then to religious life almost to her own bafflement, she nonetheless embraced her call with gusto. Within a few months of her entry into the novitiate, a crisis of meaning and identity nearly derailed her. A mentor advised her to speak to Mary. What that might mean the younger woman could not imagine, but she began simply speaking to statues of the Virgin as she passed them in the hallways of the convent and school. She spoke, as it were, into the vacant ether of her misery and confusion. Then one night she had a striking dream. A beautiful woman of indeterminate ethnic identity appeared to her. Although the woman did not identify herself, Leanne knew that it was Mary and she found her presence consoling. The dream woman shared with her four penetrating truths of which the remembered content remains obscure. The effects, however, remain vivid and permanent. There is no doubt in Leanne's mind that in this nocturnal visitation the deepest stirrings of her heart, felt as confusion and loss, were answered. Healing came and the healer was Mary.

Chapter 11

Miraculous Virgin
Milagros

Remember, most loving Virgin Mary,
never was it heard
that anyone who turned to you for help
was left unaided.
Inspired by this confidence,
though burdened by my sins,
I run to your protection
for you are my mother.
Mother of the Word of God,
do not despise my words of pleading
but be merciful and hear my prayer.

—The *Memorare*, sixteenth century

From a distance, Catholicism may seem like a timeless, even eternal, verity and, depending on your perspective, as either a comforting bastion of unchanging tradition or as an institution irritatingly slow to evolve. But in truth it is not. Especially on the local level, the Catholic community reveals itself as dynamic, multidimensional, and in constant flux and flow. Take, for example, the fact that even in the short span of years that I have been making my Marian pilgrimage, many of the parishes in Our Lady's city not only have changed leadership or pastoral direction but have experienced change in the physical environment as well.

Vietnamese Our Lady of La Vang, Our Lady of Loretto Church, L.A.

Immaculate Heart of Mary on Santa Monica Boulevard and Alexandria Avenue was one of the first parishes I visited. In part this was because it was within easy striking distance of the guesthouse which I made my base of operations, but also because that area of town—Silver Lake, Echo Park, Los Feliz, and Griffith Park—was familiar to me from decades of early habitation. The parish, long before I knew to identify it, is just south and east from Los Angeles City College where for a number of years I pursued theatrical training, and just down the street is the Cahuenga branch of the public library that I often frequented as a young adult.

On my initial pilgrimage visit to Immaculate Heart of Mary I found the most arresting feature of the space to be the two glassed-in devotional shrines packed with exotic statuary situated in the narthex that separates the sanctuary from the front entrance doors. On my return visit Fr. Rodel Balagtas, an energetic young priest, is my host. He is of Filipino heritage, more precisely from the Luzon region, and is familiar with the Bicol area where the famed shrine to Our Lady of *Peñafrancia* draws scores of pilgrims each year. In the L.A. area, he tells me, the Bicol festivals have been reenacted, and here at Immaculate Heart Our Lady of *Peñafrancia* is highly venerated. On my initial solitary round of pilgrimage visitations, and before I could identify her, I had noted her in the glassed-in devotional: a stunning diminutive creature with a golden, spiky aureole framing her face and a gem-laden crown beneath a sunburst of jeweled stars, clothed in a gleaming pearl-encrusted, triangle-shaped robe spread over a silver-embossed underskirt. She was crowded between the Santo Niño, another glamorous Filipino Virgin that I later learned is Our Lady of Manaoag, and a gruesomely realistic Christ writhing on the cross in death throes. By the time I returned *Peñafrancia* had been moved to a spacious side altar where she alone resided in pearl-studded splendor.

Immaculate Heart of Mary, like most L.A. parishes, serves a diverse population. Although the highly participative Filipino parishioners had wanted *Peñafrancia* to be placed in a prominent location when the parish did some remodeling, Fr. Balagtas wanted to honor other parish groups as well. So a generous Guadalupe display is now visible in the side altar next to the Virgin from the Bicol region. This is not the first time in the parish history that ethnic diversity has been inscribed on the material environment. Vertical strips of stained glass that allow multicolored light into the building were commissioned in the 1980s by Monsignor Bell, a former pastor who believed that each branch of the global Catholic family present in the parish should be represented. Here in an angular stained-glass interpretation high above my normal range of vision and in statuary at eye level is evidence of the faith of Irish, Eastern European (especially Polish), Central and South American (notably Mexico, Peru, and El Salvador), and Filipino Catholics from all regions of the islands.

An earlier archeological layer of evidence, from the 1920s when the Immaculate Heart sisters staffed the parochial school, is seen in the niche to the right of the altar. Next to the ubiquitous Perpetual Help hovering above a candlelit shrine is a graceful, if rather conventional, European Virgin who is still honored. She is clad in an aquamarine blue cape and stands with head tilted down and finger pointing to a flaming, flower-ringed heart on her breast. Above the rows of deep red and blue candles set before her are fresh bouquets of vivid crimson and white blooms set amid dark green foliage, a sign that the parish flower committee is actively engaged.

So many of the archdiocesan churches I visit are similarly richly layered with architectural and deco-

Virgin of *Peñafancia*, Immaculate Heart Church, L.A.

rative artifacts from differing eras and populations. While these sorts of sites may be the bane of architectural purists and those responsible for liturgical environments, and while I appreciate the value of a church that is aesthetically coherent, I love these layered spaces, spaces that belong to and house the history of the people who have inhabited them. The Marys of this church on busy Santa Monica Boulevard may be many but it is to *Peñafrancia* and her miraculous sisters that my attention turns. Unlike her early modern European counterpart whose head is tilted humbly downward and who is first and foremost a model of interior virtue, the *Peñafrancia* and other miraculous virgins face their devotees directly. They convey frank familiarity with miraculous power.

The backstory of *Peñafrancia*'s power is as convoluted and contested as are most miraculous image tales. Version one can be summarized thus: *Peña de Francia* means "rocky hill of France," which is where she originated in the fifteenth century when the Virgin visited a boy named Simon and requested that he build a shrine to her on a nearby hill. The chronicles of his arduous journeys to find the spot are filled with stories of amazing coincidences and supernatural visitations. Version two: the devotion, also replete with miracle stories, can be traced to Spain in the region between the provinces of Cáceres and Salamanca from whence it traveled in the seventeenth century to the Philippines and became notable for the miraculous healing of, among others, a theology student named Miguel Robles de Cobarrubias. Eventually the Filipino image become patroness of Bicolandia. She was crowned in 1924, and *Peñafrancia* is now enshrined in splendor in the *Basilica Minore de Nuestra Señora de Peña de Francia* in the city of Naga. She arrived in Los Angeles with her devotees when they immigrated in large numbers to the United States in the latter half of the last century.

Dozens of miraculous virgins seem to have come to Los Angeles from the Philippine Islands as well as from the Caribbean and Central and South America. Each nation from these regions has its own virginal patroness whose cherished image is said to have appeared in an astonishing manner and to have the power to rescue, heal, and transform sorrow into rejoicing. Symbol of cultural particularity and national pride, Mary in these guises is the miraculous one, always accompanying her people.

Nor are L.A.'s miraculous virgins confined to this hemisphere or to the Pacific islands: Our Lady of La Vang from Vietnam makes her presence known in statuary scattered throughout the archdiocese. I discover this graceful image for the first time at Our Lady of Loreto parish near downtown where a sizable Vietnamese population is served. La Vang is distinctively Asian: she stands serenely clad in white silk overlaid with a turquoise-blue embroidered robe. Her black hair is pulled back under a golden arc, and both she and her rose-robed child gaze forward. His small hand extends in blessing. La Vang too has a backstory that confirms that Mary's protective mantle spreads itself generously over those entrusted to her care. Her first sighting occurred in 1798 deep in the jungle forests of *Quảng Trị* province where refugees had fled during an intense period of persecution of foreign faiths. She offered solace and brought healing to those who were sick. In the intervening centuries, suppression, persecution by competing feudal lords, and hostile governments of all stripes are the context in which the Vietnamese Catholic community has clung to Our Lady of La Vang. I have been told that, while Guadalupe is the Virgin of the poor, La Vang can rightly be called the Virgin of the afflicted.

St. Cecilia parish, a looming edifice of renaissance Italian architectural style, is south of downtown, near the University of Southern California campus. In the Catholic pantheon of saints, Cecilia is located among those of historically dubious legend who have been officially eliminated from the liturgical calendar. Nevertheless, because Cecilia has for centuries been honored as patroness of church musicians, she still retains a place in the Catholic imagination. I find the proximity of the parish to USC, with its legendary school of music, arresting. For it was there, during the academic year of 1965–66, that I briefly pursued a degree in music with an emphasis on opera repertoire.

The parish today stands as a record of the Los Angeles archdiocese's pastoral sensitivity and common sense. Fr. Joseph Forlani, a priest of the Comboni Missionaries of the Heart of Jesus who has been in residence for the past two years, meets Dorothy and me in the hallway that conjoins the cavernous church with the parish offices. We are told that the parish, soon to celebrate its centennial, was, until six years ago,

Nuestra Señora de Juquila, St. Cecilia Church, L.A.

Guatemalan *Nuestro Señor de Esquipulas* with Sorrowing Mother, St. Cecilia Church, L.A.

Marian Altar, St. Cecilia Church, L.A.

Nuestra Señora de la Soledad, St. Cecilia Church, L.A.

dying. The residential population had shrunk and there was talk of closing. Presently, St. Cecilia is vitally alive because it was designated as a home-place for the many specialized devotions that were not formally observed elsewhere in the diocese but were increasing in popularity as immigrants poured into the metropolitan basin.

As we enter the massive domed sanctuary of St. Cecilia, the older priest hands me a Spanish-language pamphlet detailing the story of the *Virgen de Juquila*. He orients us to her glass-encased, white-satin-robed image that dominates the Marian shrine to the left of the main altar. In fact, she obscures an older painting of Our Lady of Lourdes appearing to Bernadette that once was the focus of the space. Dark-skinned with spiky strands of straight black hair streaming over her shoulders, this folk image of *Juquila*, beloved by the *indios*, was carried to L.A. by immigrants from the mountains outside Oaxaca in southwestern Mexico. They asked the cardinal for a sacred place to house the statue and he agreed. Now she is alone in her own designated space from which to receive the veneration of her devotees. To *Juquila*'s left on a sidewall is an impressive shrine for *Nuestra Señora de la Soledad*, the patroness of the diocese of Oaxaca. Here the image of Soledad is foregrounded against a painted backdrop of Oaxaca's sunlit landscape replete with native dancers in plumed headdresses. According to her legend, her image was discovered in a chest along with an image of the risen Christ. Attached was a note which stated "I am the sorrowful mother at the foot of the cross."

Along the next wall segment is a massive painting of a sun-drenched, palm-shaded Nigerian village featuring an oversized depiction of Blessed Cyprian Michael Iwene Tansi, the native-born Trappist monk venerated by the Igbo people. Across the wide expanse of the nave the black-skinned Lord of *Esquipulas* from Guatemala hangs on a rough cross. At his feet two folk figurines, of the Virgin and Mary Magdalene, are draped in white mantles. *Salvador del Mundo*, patron of El Salvador is also present. Each of the communities that these figures represent gathers for Mass on designated Sundays and feast days. Fr. Joseph reports that the Guatemalan contingent mounts street processions that can last up to two hours and can involve as many as seven thousand participants.

Not all of the Marys represented at St. Cecilia are miraculous in origin and in wonder-working powers, although most are. How these miraculous Marys coexist in my consciousness with the trimmed-down, companionate sister of feminist reform, or the theological symbol of the fully realized human person, or the scriptural character subject to endless exegetical scrutiny, or the guardian of national and religious exclusivism is an interesting question. For she does quite comfortably coexist. Not that I am apt to accept the legends attached to the multiple *milagros* without some of the scholar's interpretive distancing. But on another, more primal, level, these miraculous stories bespeak a hope that haunts the human heart to which I am no stranger. It is the same hope that longs for springs to water dry lands, for the lame to leap, the blind to see, and for death to be no more, a hope that is heard in the plaintive cries of the Prophet Isaiah and is echoed in the kingdom that Jesus preached.

Virgins with miraculous powers not only are native in areas of colonial expansion but also have been present in the tradition from the earliest eras. In fact, much of the classic biography of the Virgin Mary comes not from the canonical Scriptures but from the apocryphal Gospel of James, known also as the Protevangelium of James (or as Hollywood might title it, the prequel to the Gospels). In this second-century text, we learn of Mary's parents, Joachim and Anne, who are visited with news of an impending birth. Then we are made privy to the sheltered childhood in the Jerusalem Temple of the girl whose is destined to bear the Savior. Her marriage to Joseph, whose flowering staff miraculously indentifies him as her future protector, is recounted as is her encounter with an angelic messenger and the birth of her child in a cave accompanied by midwives. The Christian story recorded in the proto-Gospel of James is rooted in the belief that with God all things are possible, including miracles. Mary is one flowering stalk springing from that root.

Throughout the medieval and early modern eras, Mary continued to perform the role of miracle worker. My L.A. pilgrimage leads me to a site named for one such classic medieval Virgin. Montecito is the wealthy residential enclave nestled in the foothills just south of Santa Barbara where old-wealth families, celebrities, and Saudi Arabian sheiks own estates; and large crews of gardeners, housekeepers, estate managers, and financial advisors find gainful employment. About a mile and a half off the Pacific Coast Highway, which ribbons the south coast, I follow the winding oak-lined lane to East Valley Road, turn right, and find myself once again at Our Lady of Mount Carmel Church. It was here, in this jeweled box of a faux mission-style church that, following graduate school and just before we left California for the East Coast, but long after the waning of my professional singing career, I was a liturgical cantor.

Our Lady of Mount Carmel and Simon Stock, Our Lady of Mount Carmel Church, Montecito.
Our Lady of Mount Carmel, Our Lady of Mount Carmel Church, Montecito.

Built in 1936, Mount Carmel combines the building patterns of Pueblo Indians with Spanish-colonial design. While the dominant aesthetic motif of the petite Montecito church is mission style, on the right-hand wall above the altar is a majestic oversized oil painting of Our Lady of Mount Carmel as she appeared in the mid-thirteenth century to Carmelite priest Simon Stock. With the glowing cheeks and sumptuous beneficence of a renaissance Madonna, the lavishly draped Lady holds her chubby child and reaches out from a pillow of clouds to dangle before the awestruck cleric a dark brown scapular, the distinctive brown "sacramental" worn to this day by Carmelite devotees. The Order of Carmel, including its lay branch, considers itself totally Marian, a privilege that it claims to have received from Mary herself and which is made visible through the brown scapular. The original significance of wearing this scapular implied that one was clothed with Mary's garment in the sense of being clothed with her attitudes and devotion to Christ. Today, devotees describe its meaning as being clothed in the garments of salvation.

Later during my sojourn I speak on the phone with Fr. Carol O'Sullivan, an English diocesan priest who serves as spiritual chaplain for the Third Order Carmelite group that meets at Mount Carmel every month, a group of about thirty from different parishes. In England a Carmelite priest convinced Fr. O'Sullivan that a framework for one's spiritual life was necessary in order for it to flourish. Hence his affiliation with the Carmelite spiritual tradition in which he has found such a structure. There is only one Our Lady, Fr. O'Sullivan assures me, but there are different approaches to her. The essence of the Carmelite approach is contemplative. A member of the Third Order (the first and second orders are, respectively, Carmelite priests and nuns), he and others like him must spend time each day in contemplative prayer. He describes this prayer as a conversation with God "à la Teresa of Avila." In addition, Third Order Carmelites participate in the church's Liturgy of the Hours. While the structure is loose, this is, Fr. O'Sullivan insists, a difficult vocation. They pray for the Body of Christ and for everyone, including those who do not pray and they "keep Our Lord company." They see themselves as leaven in the loaf of the wider Catholic community.

Despite her miracle-infused origins and her promises, perhaps the Lady of Mt. Carmel that is the focus of this Montecito group does not today quite fit the mold of a miraculous virgin in the way that *Peñafrancia* or La Vang might. Who is to say? There certainly is little evidence of the performative and emotive outpourings among Third Order Carmelites in the region, qualities that characterize some of the devotion to other *virgens milagros*. Rather, even with the talismanic protection of the brown scapular, Marian devotion among the Mt. Carmel set tends to be more sedate and focused on personal moral and spiritual development more than on the invocation of Mary as worker of miracles. Still, Our Lady of Mount Carmel is one of a long line of powerful miraculous Marian figures.

Deep into my pilgrimage journey, I visit the Cahuenga branch of the L.A. Public Library, a site familiar in my adolescent years. The library sits on Santa Monica Boulevard close by the Immaculate Heart parish with its Bicol Virgin. I find myself aghast at what seems to be the decay of a once pleasant neighborhood intellectual watering hole. The scarce holdings on the library shelves seem not to have been updated for decades. Instead, stacks of magazines and random videos proliferate.

How things change. The last time I was here was perhaps 1973 when I had begun to withdraw from the theater and film industry by returning to college, and my fledgling historical investigations had made me curious about the lives of obscure saints. In the religion section I had discovered an old Butler's *Lives of the Saints* and found myself reading an entry for St. Hubert. Now, one needs to understand that I was a student of history and accustomed to perusing narratives written in the manner of modern historiography. I was not familiar with hagiography, that particular ancient literary genre of saintly tales. The story of Hubert began innocently enough. His birth in what is now Belgium during the "dark ages" was chronicled, as were his education and ordination as priest. The pastoral activities he promoted as bishop of Maastricht were recounted. Then, seamlessly, the narrative began to describe Hubert's walking on water. I suddenly felt ill, so disoriented that I had to put the book down and my head on the table at which I was seated. It was as though tectonic plates had collided within me.

Our Lady of Grace overlooking Santa Barbara, Vincentian Retreat Center, Santa Barbara.

In retrospect, I am struck with amazement that I did not simply dismiss the story as a silly fantasy of a bygone age and never come back to it. But I didn't. Rather, here was my first initiatory step into one aspect of the sacramental Catholic imagination. In later years I learned more of the literary and historical reasons why Hubert and others might be clothed in miraculous deeds. But that is only part of what I began to understand that day in the Cahuenga public library. I began to get a sense of what it might mean to intuit the existence of parallel universes, to acknowledge, indeed to live close to, the thin places of which Celtic spirituality speaks so eloquently. It was not that I did not know of these places already. As a child, they were always close. But I needed to consciously thread together these intuitions with the adult and critical-thinking part of myself. Without this threading, I would find myself in a bifurcated world, either as a gullible literal believer in very strange happenings, or as a person fluent only in the language of what is empirically true, not one who has learned to read the cryptic markings of the soul.

Other scholars, more articulately than I, have wrestled with the seemingly impassable disjuncture between the religious cosmo-vision of devotional piety and the more common worldview of modernity. Among others, Latino theologian Roberto Goizueta has targeted the modern cosmo-vision that diverges significantly from an earlier one, as one cause of a dismissive attitude toward popular religion. Goizueta, referencing the popular piety of Mexico, describes what he calls the "sacramental realism" implicit in the devotional world I have been part of here in L.A.

> Popular religious practices embody an organic worldview, wherein the human person sees himself or herself as part of a relational network and a temporal continuum embracing all of reality, material and spiritual. This organic, holistic worldview is at odds with post-Enlightenment notions of time and space, of the material and the spiritual, and of the person's place within time and space, within the material and spiritual dimensions of reality.

Cuban Our Lady of Charity, Our Lady of Loretto Church, L.A.

This is, in fact, a perception in continuity with that of early Christianity as social historian Peter Brown has made amply clear. In his seminal study of the cult of saints in the Latin West, Brown shows that the genius of the new Christian faith's breaking in to the ancient world was its audacious claim of the conjoining of heaven and earth at the graves of the "special dead" who were at once present and invested with the transformative healing power of the divine realm. Those who thus straddled heaven and earth effected the ultimate reconciliation of the divided realms. Their bones and the gravesites where they were laid were likewise imbued with holy power. Although conceptions changed over the centuries, the persistent intuition that something had changed, that the transformative energy unleashed in the Resurrection was indeed available, continued. The martyrs and saints, with Mary as Queen of Saints and Martyrs, became, as it were, thin spaces through which divine energy flowed into the Body of Christ. That energy thus became available to all members of the Mystical Body.

But this insight still left unexplored for me the issue of devotional images and their surprising power. There has been intelligent study about the power of images and the ways in which they function within religious worlds. However, it is images that have most troubled detractors of devotion. The perennial question that haunts Christianity is about the appropriateness of images to depict the divine. Although the iconodules (lovers and defenders of images) triumphed over the iconoclasts (opponents or destroyers of images) during the Iconoclastic controversies of the seventh and eighth centuries, and Catholics of the early modern period reaffirmed and reformed the use of visual images in response their Protestant critics, the issue has not gone away. Charges of inappropriate "worship" of Mary and the saints are still leveled against Catholics. The question still persists, Do Catholics "worship" (the Latin is *latria*) images of the Virgin Mary? The answer is "No." Worship belongs only to God. The technical theological understanding is that devotional images are venerated (*dulia*). Images of Mary give rise to a separate technical term to describe the special honor afforded her: *hyperdulia*. Is this idolatry as has sometimes been claimed? "No," again.

Scholars have probed the issue of why human beings are in fact so drawn to images and are so affected by them. David Morgan, among others, has studied the ability of religious imagery to encourage interaction with believers who may wash, dress, address, and study it; to incorporate it into their emotional lives; and reduce the aesthetic distance between an object and a believer. Morgan states it well when he describes the "lure" of religious images as being always bound up with the quest for something better, as having the capacity to allow people to see their way to new possibilities of self and community: "The lure of images resides not only in their promise of continuity or renewal but also of transformation. In every case, the lure answers to a deep longing, which it is the underlying business of religious belief to engage." Scholars like Morgan and Goizueta have helped me to understand, at least to a degree, the process that had begun at the Cahuenga branch of the L.A. public library so many years ago.

Psychic transitions, like the laborious 360-degree maneuvers of great ocean liners, are gradual and accomplished only with the help of many small craft. So it was with the transition taking place in me. The small craft were varied: the return of religious longing, hard knocks, Jungian analysis, disenchantment, intellectual awakening, and the appearance of wise mentors. Along the way were several pivotal conceptual moments including that visit to the Cahuenga branch of the L.A. public library during which, out of historical interest, I picked up a volume of saints' lives and found in an entry on Hubert that typical hagiographic juxtaposition of the factual and miraculous, which prompted a disorientation that at the time was vertiginous but which was in fact a foreshadowing of a later seismic shift of conceptual awareness. I too have come to inhabit a sacramental worldview that can include the not uncritically perceived but nonetheless welcomed presence of miraculous virgins, figures who attest to the intermingling of the spiritual and the material, a worldview that, as Goizueta puts it, "rejects any clear separation between the symbolic and the real, or between the 'sign' and the 'signified'; for what the symbol represents is in fact experienced as truly present in and through the symbol."

OUR
LADY
OF

LA SAL ETTE
PRAY
FOR US

1846

Chapter 12

Lady of Victory
La Conquistadora

The fourth office which Our Lady renders to her children and faithful
servants is to protect
and defend them against their enemies. . . .
To secure them from the hawk and vulture,
she puts herself round about them, and accompanies them "like an
army in battle array" (Canticle 6:3). Shall a man who has an army
of a hundred thousand soldiers around him
fear his enemies? A faithful servant of Mary, surrounded by her protection and her imperial power, has still less to fear.

—Louis de Montfort, *True Devotion to Mary*, seventeenth century

Talk about parallel universes! My childhood experience of large-
capacity performance and sport arenas in Los Angeles is markedly
different from that of the hundreds of thousands of Southern California
Catholics of similar age. From 1950, when I was three, until at least 1970,
my twenty-third year, the archdiocese in concert with local Catholic
universities and colleges, sponsored a yearly Mary's Hour that at its
height drew one hundred thousand participants. The Hollywood Bowl
was the first venue where the popular devotional event was held. Later
it moved to Memorial Stadium and in recent years it has replayed at
various locales. A 2007 incarnation, known as the Rosary Bowl, filled

Our Lady of La Salette Window, Apparition Windows, Munich Studios of Franz Mayer,
1927–57, Immaculate Conception Church, Westlake/Downtown Los Angeles.

Pasadena's Rose Bowl with fifty thousand attendees. Two of these huge outdoor amphitheaters are mine in fond memory. My parents were symphony fans and on balmy summer nights we would picnic on the hillside near Hollywood Bowl and then enjoy the beatific multisensate experience of the strains of Tchaikovsky or Beethoven wafting out from the fabled shell. And, although sporting events were not on my parents' aesthetically focused radar, my mother did have a "thing" for USC football whenever they played for the championship in the Rose Bowl.

But for area Catholics, these venues came alive in Mary's month of May. On a Sunday one of these amphitheaters would fill with the Blessed Mother's faithful. The recitation of the rosary was a constant, but the archdiocesan *Tidings* archives reveal that these Mary's Hour programs adapted each year to changing times. For much of the 1950s, the specter of atheistic communism spread its shadow and Mary's Hour was given over to entreaties to Our Lady of Fatima. Fatima's messages to three Portuguese children in 1917, augmented over the years by Sr. Lucia, one of the surviving seers and given a particularly American twist by the Blue Army, warned of the "red threat" of communism. The gathered multitudes at Mary's Hour were entreated with words such as those of Cardinal Francis Spellman who, speaking before a crowd

Mary's Hour, L.A. Coliseum, 1954.

of one hundred thousand in 1954, proclaimed that there could be no coexistence between the United States and communist nations.

Parallel universes indeed. These highly visible Catholic events taking place in public spaces never entered my youthful consciousness. The city, of course, is huge and my frame of reference during my youth was personal. Yet even as a child I would no doubt have been perplexed by a fear-fueled stadium of souls praying for the conversion of Russia. Yes, I did have the terror of atomic warfare kinesthetically imprinted on me through the routine "drop drills" to which American school children were subjected during the Cold War era. But by family inheritance I had developed an alternative view of the Cold War that questioned the U.S. decision to unleash the Pandora's box of civilian-targeted atomic warfare. When, in junior high, I was assigned the role of debating the question "Should America have dropped the atom bomb?" my father eagerly supplied me with materials from the American Friends Service

Mary's Hour, L.A. Coliseum, 1964.

Committee which raised searching moral objections to the U.S.-initiated global precedent. Not being much of a debater, I lost. But the bone-deep uneasiness about ends and means never left me.

My recoiling from the easy cohabitation of spiritual communities with specific political causes was thus, in part, due to my father's influence. My mother, a former screenwriter, cast a dim eye on the witch hunts of the McCarthy era when the House Committee on Un-American Activities made a purge of the arts community. But my recoil was religious as well. A prime reason for my eventual defection from the choir programs at Hollywood First Presbyterian Church after a half-dozen happy years was the virulent church-sponsored anticommunist crusade which I could not, in my own preteen mind, reconcile with Sunday school studies about loving one's enemies. I, whose childhood experience included Ban the Bomb and Civil Rights marches, had no mental card file into which to deposit the entry: religion equals hate.

On an early December day I find myself at Our Lady of Loreto parish in the central city. It is a fog-shrouded Saturday just shy of seven a.m. and the largely Vietnamese congregation is embarking on their prayers to Our Lady of Fatima in the dimly lighted church. The Fatima devotion is very popular in Vietnam, I learned from Fr. Michel Hoang in our previous day's phone conversation. Why this specific Roman Catholic devotion originating in Portugal should have taken root half way across the world is something of an academic puzzle to me. In 1917, the year of great European import (World War I was raging and the Russian Tsar was overthrown, initiating the Russian Revolution), the Virgin Mary is reported to have appeared to three peasant children as they guarded sheep in the hills near the Portuguese village of Aljustrel. These children delivered to the world a message of an apocalypse that they claimed could be averted by following the Virgin's instructions. Those instructions quickly resonated across the globe.

The logic of this small Vietnamese congregation at Our Lady of Loreto in the city of Our Lady of the Angels raising their devout prayers under the aegis of Fatima on a Saturday morning nearly a century later comes clear to me when I pay an on-site visit to Fr. Hoang at the Vietnamese Catholic Center, out of the boundaries of the Los Angeles archdiocese in the city of Santa Ana, known mainly to those outside

Southern California as the site of the Magic Kingdom of Disneyland. But Orange County, in which Santa Ana is situated, is distinguished by another fact: it is home to the largest population of Vietnamese outside of Vietnam itself. As I round a busy intersection, an ornate pagoda-roofed structure is visible among the strip malls. Just outside the elaborately gated entrance, in a carefully maintained Asian-style garden, a gracious statue of Our Lady of La Vang, the patroness of Vietnam, presides at the edge of a still pond. Inside, a courtyard bordered by meeting rooms faces an elegant chapel dedicated to the Catholic martyrs of Vietnam. Once I have negotiated the maze of offices and am seated across from Fr. Hoang's ample desk, he informs me about Marian devotion among those to whom he ministers. Why, I inquire, should the appearances of the Virgin to three shepherd children in Portugal in the years of the First World War resonate clear across the globe?

The story of Fatima is well known in Catholic circles. Whatever one might think of apparitions (the Catholic Church itself is generally loath to give official sponsorship to such reported phenomena), there are a

Consecration to Our Lady of Fatima, St. Charles Parochial School, North Hollywood, 1948.

select few Marian sightings that have become the focus of official veneration. Fatima is one of them. In her first appearance to the Portuguese peasant children, the Virgin asked them to return on the thirteenth of each month and to pray the rosary to obtain world peace. During the subsequent apparitions, which by then had gained notoriety, the Virgin was reported to have prophesied the chastisement of the world and asked the faithful to make reparation to the Hearts of Jesus and Mary, dishonored by sin. To avert this, she asked for the consecration of Russia to her Immaculate Heart. The Fatima encounter gained a wide Catholic following and, as the Soviet Union emerged and anticommunist sentiment increased, the Virgin of Fatima became the image that expressed the church's anxiety about communism's atheism. In fact, the Catholic Church in the early twentieth century was in a defensive posture against many aspects of the modern world. Mary's pure, untouched heart became a cherished symbol par excellence of fidelity to the past.

Fr. Hoang reminds me that the faith first came to this Southeast Asian country through the missionary efforts of the Portuguese and Spanish, but that the French colonial enterprise came to dominate. With the encouragement of the colonial power, which hoped to counter Buddhist influence, Roman Catholicism established a solid position in Vietnamese culture. When in the 1950s communism gained control in the north, a mass exodus of Vietnamese Catholics into the southern regions took place. From that vantage point, the South Vietnamese church watched with growing concern at the expulsion of foreign priests and a campaign of harassment against their fellow religionists in the north. The election in the south of President Ngo Dinh Diem, a French-educated Catholic, gave further impetus to the anticommunist campaign that the southern church was now waging. Many of the large numbers of Vietnamese now living in southern California are refugees or offspring of refugees who fled from their native land during the upheavals of the 1950s and 60s. That they cleave to Our Lady of Fatima is a remnant of their country's history. Fr. Hoang confirms that devotion to Fatima still thrives in his population, although it is not clear that it is as focused on anticommunism as it once was. Rather, it seems a more general Marian veneration that affirms ethnic identity and facilitates social cohesion. At the Vietnamese Catholic Center every Saturday, an 8:00 a.m. devotion to Our Ladies of La Vang and Fatima precedes the Eucharist and attracts up to six hundred attendees.

For the most part, in the contemporary Anglo-American Catholic context, and especially in this archdiocese, Fatima's presence is now muted. In the mid-twentieth century, however, many Los Angeles Catholics, like their Vietnamese coreligionists, did urgently feel the lure of Fatima's call. A 1948 picture from St. Charles parochial school in North Hollywood, uncovered in my search of the archdiocesan archives at San Fernando Mission, captures students on their knees dedicating themselves to Our Lady under the title of Fatima. Twenty years later, according to a 1988 issue of *The Tidings*, forty-two L.A. parishes sponsored such Fatima devotions in the form of observance of the first Saturday on five consecutive months. This fervor is no longer so evident. At present, Fatima images are scattered about in various locales but there are no official Fatima devotions listed in the archdiocesan directory.

Any modern Anglo-American interest in Fatima that does flourish is generally associated with the Blue Army of Our Lady of Fatima, established in 1947 in New Jersey. Its founders, Monsignor Harold Colgan and layman John Haffert, established their apostolate specifically to oppose the Red Army of communism. The Blue Army understood itself as continuing to respond to the entreaties that the Virgin Mary was reported to have delivered in 1917 and which she continued to deliver for decades through Lucia, one of the original seers. As suggested, central to the Fatima message was the idea of consecration of the world to Mary's Immaculate Heart, a symbol that by the nineteenth century had taken on militant overtones.

There was a foreboding, apocalyptic feel to the Fatima cult that warned of dire consequences if the world did not return to God. Eventually, with the revelation of another of Lucia's encounters, the idea of praying for the conversion

Our Lady of Fatima and American Flag, Our Lady of Guadalupe Church, Guadalupe.

of atheistic Russia emerged. Clearly, Mary as Our Lady of Fatima was seen as operating at the interface where the God-heeding and the God-shirking worlds meet. The present day Blue Army, known now as the World Apostolate of Fatima, is no longer overtly anticommunist although it still represents itself as being in conflict with much of modern society in a variety of ways such as in its organized opposition to abortion.

Despite her somewhat faded popularity, on my L.A. journeys I do discover another vivid variant of contemporary Fatima enthusiasm in what might seem an unlikely quarter: intertwined with the life story of a former Hollywood screenwriter. One of my hosts at Holy Family in Glendale is Brad Thomas, an assistant to the pastor, to whom I am referred when I inquire about the state of Marian devotion among the congregants. Brad is a man of enormous energy who, I am informed as we whisper together in the back of the sanctuary before services begin, gave up a lucrative career in Hollywood to do his present pastoral work. The story is a bit sketchy in its whispered version, but the gist of it was that in 1979 Brad found himself unable to take his own son to a film for which he had written the script, so sleazy was the movie. Shamed, he took time off from work and while resting at his sister's house ran across a magazine devoted to the prophecies delivered at Fatima. His conversion to her message was complete. So deeply is he convinced by this apocalyptic message that he has written a TV miniseries based loosely on the teachings of the Blue Army. Presently, he told me, he is writing a novel entitled *Stephanie's Journey* in which an atheistic young journalist reporting from Bosnia is converted to the faith by the Virgin's intervention. A planned sequel, *Joey's Journey*, will feature Stephanie's son who is destined to become a cardinal.

Brad, like a small contingent of Fatima devotees (but at present not the official World Apostolate of Fatima), is convinced that the mysterious "third secret" of Fatima is yet to be revealed. This secret, in his mind and the mind of like believers, corresponds to the prophetic texts of the Book of Revelation. He is drawn to this idea despite the fact that in the year 2000 the Vatican released the contents of the sealed document in which the "third secret" was reportedly kept and declared that the events prophesized had already occurred. For Brad and those who share his perspective, however, devotion to Our Lady is the key to averting the terrible conflagrations warned of in the as-yet unsealed secret. For him, Mary is the spiritual warrior par excellence.

It is no secret that Mary has as many identities as the people who love and claim her. Some of those identities are less accessible to post–Vatican II American Catholics than others and may seem less beneficent than "mother" or "lady." Some, indeed, may cause dismay. I have to admit that this militant or even apocalyptic Mary I encounter in Glendale is for me a perplexing figure. The dualistic worldview out of which she seems to emerge is foreign. Scholars note that over the centuries Mary has served as a "Boundary Figure" in the religious imagination of the Catholic faithful. In differing eras the Virgin has defined the boundaries between Christians and non-Christians, between Catholics and other Christian churches, and between Catholics and the secular world. For example, the medieval rise of Islamic empires in the East and the gradual establishment of a high Islamic culture in Spain galvanized European Christians and made of Mary the guardian of Christendom and a warrior par excellence against non-Christian foes. The medieval legends of Santiago de Compostela, known as the Moor-slayer, are closely associated with the gradual reconquest of Muslim territories and in them the Virgin figures prominently. On the late medieval frontiers of Christendom the pattern was for a reconquered Muslim city to be renamed in the Virgin's honor and for the Christian ruler, after a triumphant procession into the town, to hear Mass in the converted mosque now dedicated to Mary.

At the dawn of the age of colonial discovery, the Catholic monarchs Ferdinand and Isabella who provisioned Columbus on his excursions into the New World were the same king and queen who had expelled both Moors and Jews from the Spanish peninsula in their campaign of reconquest. For Columbus, as for his royal patrons and others like Cortes and Pizarro who ventured across the waters, Mary was the foe of all outside the Catholic faith whether they were Muslim infidels or the "pagan" peoples of the New World. She came with colonial expansion not merely as a component of religious heritage but explicitly as the one under whose mantle the conversion of the indigenous was to be accomplished. She served as a link with the land these men left behind, but she also animated the devotees enlisted in her service as a warrior leading them against non-Christian forces.

To invoke one of her colonial titles associated with conquest, whether *Remedios* or *La Conquistadora* or others, was to invoke past Spanish victories accomplished under her aegis. In fact, the oldest statue of the Virgin in the U.S. to whom a constant devotion has been maintained is *La Conquistadora* enshrined now in the Cathedral in Santa Fe, New Mexico. She was brought to the colonial territory in 1624.

In the early modern era Mary was similarly invoked on the European continent as the guardian of orthodoxy against what was seen as the threat of the Protestant heresy. The newly minted Jesuit order in particular held up traditional (if reformed) veneration of the Mother of God as an identifying characteristic of loyalty to the Roman faith. The Jesuits also viewed her as an unfailing advocate in the confessional wars that ravaged early modern Christendom. When this vigorous new religious society embarked on its missionary exploits across the Atlantic it brought a militant Marian devotion to the unbaptized natives.

To turn to more recent cognate examples of this theme, American religious historian Anne Matter has analyzed the explosive late twentieth-century rise in the United States of what she calls the "tabloid cult" of Marian apparitions. Matter argues that the increasing appearances of the Virgin to a host of visionaries or in the form of weeping icons or as images discovered in the desert skies and on teapots cannot be accurately understood as a throw back to an earlier piety. These apparitions can only be viewed as a frankly modern and American version of Marian experience. Drawing on the work of cultural anthropologist Sandra Zimdars-Swartz and historian William Christian, Jr., as well as her own field research, Matter associates this "tabloid cult" with increased cultural stress. It borrows freely from American Protestant fundamentalist rhetoric that is suffused with apocalyptic imagery. Apparitions follow an identifiable pattern that features innocent seers of humble origin often pitted against those in power. Secrets, hidden revelations, and dire predictions are common. Matter identifies the 1917 Fatima sightings and their aftermath as the key to late twentieth-century appearances because it was at Fatima that a political element was added to previous apparitional formula. Earlier sightings, such as Lourdes in France or Knock in Ireland, found their raison d'être in healing and cures, but after Fatima subsequent sightings have become explicitly political and typically conjure up fearful end-time scenarios.

Well-publicized American apparitional movements with high visibility such as those in Conyers, Georgia, or Bayside, Massachusetts, are emphatically not endorsed by the official church. Yet they draw many Catholics. They exist at the fringes of American Catholic life. Janus-faced, on the one side they tend to face backward and idealize a type of devotion prominent before the council and the ecclesial modernizing of John XXIII and Paul VI, and on the other side they face fearfully forward in dreadful anticipation of the cataclysmic end times. For many, Mary stands at the head of the forces amassed against the principalities and powers.

Here in the archdiocese, historic iconographical evidence of Mary's status as warrior at the forefront of the "Catholic cause" comes in varied forms besides Fatima. Certainly Our Lady of Guadalupe has in the last two centuries carried revolutionary and messianic messages. Plus, ironically, she has legitimized colonial authority. In other words, she has been associated with both political and religious power and its continuation and with its usurpation in countless conflicts from the Mexican revolution to the United Farm Workers.

The militant face of Mary past and present is also evident today in other iconographic and ideological ways. On a weekday morning I arranged to visit Our Lady of Victory in Compton. My MapQuest directions took me off the freeway through a heavily industrialized corridor onto streets lined with graffiti-scrawled buildings. Our Lady of Victory is a small sacred oasis in this densely populated area. As I walked the perimeter of the earth-toned sanctuary on my first visit I was accompanied by the sound of a woman's voice coming from the adoration chapel singing an intimate Spanish hymn of love directed to the Divine Presence enshrined in the alcove. Later I become aware of the specificity of the church's Marian appellation. The 1911 parish boasts a number of classic images of Mary under her title Our Lady of Victory, the most arresting fashioned in multicolored tile above the entrance door and in stained glass on the sanctuary wall to the left of the altar.

Our Lady of Victory Window,
Our Lady of Victory Church, Compton.

This title is associated with the defeat of the Ottoman Turks at the 1571 naval victory at the Battle of Lepanto by coalition forces of the Christian Holy League. European Catholics viewed the conflict as a decisive victory for Christendom over its foes. To celebrate, Pope Pius V introduced a feast of the Blessed Virgin Mother of Victory to be celebrated on October 7. (Later this feast was renamed for Our Lady of the Rosary because a rosary procession for the success of the Holy League had been organized in Rome). The images in the church in Compton, whether its parishioners see her this way or not (which I suspect they do not), recall her in her guise as warrior and victor.

Another modern militant Mary encounter, this time without the anti-Muslim overtones, comes by way of a phone interview with Fr. Chris Troxell, an associate at Our Lady of the Rosary parish in Paramount. To my queries about Marian devotion in this congregation that he had shepherded for the last four years, Fr. Chris is forthcoming. Over twenty years before when ministering in Monterey, he was introduced to the Militia of the Immaculata, an international movement founded in 1917 by Franciscan Maximilian Kolbe (canonized in 1982 as a "martyr of charity") which is aimed at the spiritual renewal of self and society. As associate pastor, the priest has started an official militia group at Our Lady of the Holy Rosary where members do penance for the conversion of sinners, strive for personal holiness, and seek to bring others to Christ through Mary.

Recalling the man credited with reviving rosary devotion in the early modern era, Fr. Chris informs me that the teachings of Kolbe build on St. Louis de Montfort's but go further. While de Montfort revivified the practice of the rosary and emphasized personal consecration to the Virgin, the Franciscan's devotion goes beyond "enslavement" to become the "property" of Mary. There are various levels of consecration that are at the core of the militia's practice: individual consecration, group membership, or the lifetime devotion through which one becomes the "property" of Mary and utterly obedient to her direction. Fr. Chris's voice waxes enthusiastic as he expresses his delight that at the parish he has found others to share this intensive devotion to the Immaculate One and the battle she is waging against a sinful world. Mary seems to serve Fr. Chris as a powerful weapon against the disturbing world in which he finds himself.

Both Fr. Chris and Brad Thomas, despite their different perspectives, signal their sense that the faith is embattled and that the task of the Catholic is to take up arms in a spiritual war of vast proportions. As historian Kane points out, such "Marian movements are striving to recover the countercultural status of the Catholic Church in the contemporary world as an institution living in high tension with its environment." For these men, in quite distinct ways, the Virgin is clearly a "boundary figure," a guardian of a clear Catholic identity, a standard of moral and spiritual purity, and a warrior who strives in a cosmic battle against a fallen world.

Vietnamese devotion to Fatima, enslavement to Mary, consecration to the Immaculate Heart, belief in the unopened third secret of Fatima, and titles that recall anti-Muslim, anti-Protestant, and anti-pagan sentiments that fueled past Catholic fervor are, I admit, uneasily lumped together. Plus I hesitate to lump together all followers of the Militia of the Immaculata or the Blue Army or modern visionaries. Yet in each case there is an underlying sensibility: the church may be in the "world" but is in contrast to it. Indeed, the world is envisioned as a battleground upon which the forces of good and evil engage in combat. The preferred tactical approach is to amass spiritual weapons of great power. The Virgin is thus called upon to assume her place at the head of troops energized to take up the cosmic fight.

As I ponder the ethos of this part of the Catholic community, I am reminded of theologian James Alison's thoughts on the distinction he sees between the apocalyptic and the eschatological imaginations. The former imagination, this Englishman contends, sees dualisms everywhere, heaven vs. earth, this age vs. the age to come, the righteous vs. the impious, saved vs. damned. This is an imagination with the defeat of some and the vindication of others foreseen. In contrast, the eschatological imagination, which Alison views as Jesus's own, abandons dualisms and seeks to nurture and empower life in the midst of violence and contradictions. Jesus was, Alison affirms, fixed on the utterly effervescent goodness and vivaciousness of God who, in becoming human and aligning with the victim, allowed us to begin to live according to God who, with radical agapic love, neither judges nor condemns nor casts out.

I may have drawn this picture too starkly but I do think that there is an apocalyptic sensibility at the root of the sort of Marian piety that I encounter in Paramount, east L.A., and Glendale. Of course, it is not confined to these places nor to the Virgin but permeates entire sectors of Catholicism and American Protestant Christianity in general today as it has in the past. The enemies change, the times change, but the battle goes on.

Lest I leave Mary in her guise of Our Lady of Victory too easily and relegate her to historic or certain ecclesial elements, I must admit that there are times when I resonate with aspects of this sort of thinking. As a case in point, I find myself rereading a poem written by Thomas Merton, the Trappist monk who captured the imagination of American Catholics in the mid-twentieth century and who is associated most with a contemplative vision of the world. The poem harkens to another Marian apparition, one that took place in 1846 in the tiny village of La Salette in France. The cult of La Salette has over the years developed its own self-interpretation as predicting an apocalyptic collapse of the world due to the growing godlessness of society and has much in common with Fatima and other militant Marian apparitions. Yet while Thomas Merton drew upon that tradition he focused it in a very different direction, one with which I find myself in sympathy. Sensitized from a young age by my father's peacemaking witness as a conscientious objector in World War II and nurtured on such disquieting literature as nuclear scientist Leo Szilard's *The Voice of the Dolphins* I lived a mid-twentieth-century American childhood in which the unthinkable had become thinkable.

During that same period from the vantage point of his monastic cloister, yet alive to current world events, Merton the monk recalled the hundred-year-old prophecy of Our Lady of La Salette. He placed the apparition in a frame that makes of it something quite other than that generally made of Marian sightings. The timing of his composition was significant. On August 6, 1945, the United States had stunned the nations of the globe by dropping the first atomic bomb on the Japanese city of Hiroshima followed three days later by a second assault on the ancient city of Nagasaki. Merton's words elicit from me a deep nod of recognition.

>La Salette
>
>It is a hundred years since your shy feet
>Ventured to stand upon the pasture grass of the high
>Alps,
>Coming no deeper in our smoky atmosphere
>Than these blue skies, the mountain eyes
>Of the two shepherd children, young as flowers,
>Born to be dazzled by no mortal snow.
>
>Lady, it is a hundred years
>Since those fair, terrible tears
>Reproved, with their amazing grief
>All the proud candor of those altitudes:
>Crowning the flowers at your feet
>With diamonds, that seized upon, transfigured into
>nails of light
>The rays of the mountain sun!-
>
>And by their news,
>(Which came with cowbells to the evening village
>And to the world with church-bells
>After not too many days,)
>And by their news

We thought the walls of all hard hearts
Had broken down, and given in,
Poured out their dirty garrisons of sin,
And washed the streets with our own blood,
if need be-
-Only to have them clean!

And though we did not understand
The weight and import of so great a sorrow,
We never thought so soon to have seen
The loss of its undying memory,
Passing from the black world without a word,
Without a funeral!
For while our teeth were battling in the meat of
miracles and favors,
Your words, your prophecies, were all
    forgotten!

Now, one by one,
The things you said
Have come to be fulfilled.
John, in the might of his Apocalypse,
could not foretell
Half of the story of our monstrous
    century,
In which the arm of your inexorable
    Son,
Bound, by His Truth, to disavow your
    intercession
For this wolf-world, this craven zoo,
Has bombed the doors of hell clean
    off their hinges,
And burst the cage of antichrist,
And roused, with His first two great
    thunderbolts,
The chariots of Armageddon.

(Thomas Merton, 1946)

Our Lady of the Holy Rosary Window, Apparition
Windows, Munich Studios of Franz Mayer, 1927–57,
Immaculate Conception Church, Westlake/
Downtown Los Angeles.

Our Lady of Malibu, Our Lady of Malibu Church, Malibu. Artist: Renata Druks, 1956.

Chapter 13

Our Lady of Peace
Nuestra Señora de la Paz

Hail Mary, Mother of Peace,
sacred is your name.
Blest are you among all women
and blest is your child with whom
you redeemed the cosmos.
Holy Mary, hold us in prayer now
and at the hour of each dawn. Amen.

—Mary Lou Kownacki, OSB, *Mary the Peacemaker: A Novena*

Traces of Mary as warrior, boundary keeper, and harbinger of apocalypse are present in L.A. However, the metropolitan basin that contains the sprawling archdiocese is not Spain of the fifteenth-century *reconquista* nor is it Europe of the sixteenth-century ecclesial reform. Neither is it mid-twentieth-century America with its anticommunist rhetoric, although there is plenty of present angst about the contemporary world and plenty of cultural bleed-over from fundamentalist circles to fuel apocalyptic Catholic sentiment. Present-day Los Angeles, that polyglot, cultural hodgepodge is quite distinctive. In my mind, its ethos is best captured in the 2004 film *Crash*. Promotional clips for the film established the mood of the city as a volatile one:

> A Brentwood housewife and her D.A. husband. A Persian store owner. Two police detectives who are also lovers. An African-American director and his wife. A Mexican locksmith. Two carjackers. A rookie cop. A middle-aged Korean couple. They all live in Los Angeles and during the next thirty-six hours they will all collide.

The tone of the promo is perhaps overly melodramatic yet the reality to which it points and the accuracy with which the film portrays the uneasy coexistence of so many groups that fissure into class, gender, religious, ethnic, and racial conflicts rings true. The city of Our Lady of the Angels, and thus the archdiocese under her protection, is not a creamy melting pot, but a lumpy and often inedible stew. My question is: who is the Virgin becoming in this context? Or perhaps one might say, how is she newly responding to her people here and now? In fact in my peregrinations I have discovered that she is expressing herself in new ways. The daughter of a man of lifelong dedication to conflict resolution and peace work, I am touched by the Virgin's unheralded role as peacemaker.

My itinerary with my photographer on a late January day is westward through the San Fernando Valley corridor, my many planned stops assiduously charted on one of my dozens of AAA maps of the area. This is the route, much altered now, that my parents and I used to take

Our Lady of Peace, Our Lady of Peace Church, North Hills. Artist: Yvonne Seibel.

Our Lady of Peace, Our Lady of Peace Church, North Hills. Artist: Lalo Garcia.

on our annual Fourth of July visit to my uncle's home in the Valley. In those days the fragrant expanses of orange groves and pastoral scenes dominated, now the strings of contiguous suburban malls and traffic congestion provide what there is of scenery. Black dots on my maps mark my sequential destinations: Sun Valley, North Hills, Northridge, Canoga Park, and our last stop at ocean's edge at Malibu.

At Our Lady of the Valley, founded in 1921 and the mother church of the region's present six parishes, Fr. Aldon Sison, about to celebrate his twentieth anniversary of ordination with a Marian pilgrimage of Europe, directs us to the most distinctive of Marian images in the church sanctuary. Chief among these is a dramatic stained-glass window by the Pizcek sisters whose artwork adorns so many L.A. churches. Completed in 1967, the boldly colored, characteristically angular shapes of Pizcek design presents a kneeling King San Fernando offering the modern church to Our Lady of the Valley. She, orange cloak studded with symbols of her son's life and passion, hovers in the sky above the local landscape identified by citrus groves, grazing sheep, and rocky formations that suggest the Simi Hills, Santa Susana, Santa Monica, and San Gabriel mountain ranges that cradle the Valley on three sides.

Later in the day a visit to Sun Valley's Our Lady of the Holy Rosary is made informative by Scalabrian Fr. Richard Zanotti who ushers us about, explaining the varied images on a multiuse side altar on which rest representations of the sixteenth-century Filipino martyr Lorenzo Ruiz, an elaborately dressed Filipino Our Lady of Manaoag, Cuba's Our Lady of Charity of *El Cobre*, and a contemporary wooden bas relief of Mary facing her devotees with her outstretched hands offering an over-sized rosary.

But it is at Our Lady of Peace in North Hills that my first hint of a new Mary who is particular to L.A. emerges. Our host is Rosie Hernandez, an enthusiastic young pastoral associate who has been at the parish

Our Lady of the Valley Window, Our Lady of the Valley Church, Canoga Park, Piczek Studios.

for two years, who specializes in adult faith formation. She gives us a thumbnail sketch of the parish founded in 1944. This is a varied community of Spanish, English, Vietnamese, and Tagalog speakers with a recent influx of Africans added to the mix. Yes, Rosie tells us, we have Marian devotions here: a daily rosary, a May crowning for the children at the school, one held separately by the Filipino community, and the huge Guadalupe festivities so ubiquitous all over Southern California that occupy the congregants for days in December.

But there is more. It seems that the parish name, Our Lady of Peace, is unique in the archdiocese and so is the iconography that we are shown. In the reception area outside the church offices hangs a modern painting of a young Mary cradling a dove, the 1969 artwork of Yvonne Seibel, a deceased parishioner. In addition, both outside the school and in front of the church stand traditional white marble statues of the parish titular virgin and child with a dove and olive branch.

The name, Our Lady of Peace, does that have significance for the parish? I inquire. Yes! Rosie exclaims. Apparently for a while there was some thought among parishioners that the title was not specific enough. After all, if you are a devotee of Our Lady of Guadalupe or Immaculate Conception or Our Lady of Lourdes, your virgin has a recognizable feast day or a memorable story associated with her. But more parish members liked the idea of being unique. So the previous pastor did some research to find out about the image, research which did not reveal a great deal.

So the parish began a process of claiming this title as their own and letting her speak to their specific situation. That situation was and is their great diversity and the reality of a metropolitan ethos. The parishioners decided to create their own image of Our Lady of Peace by commissioning California artist Lalo Garcia to design an image that would express the desire they had to be a community of reconciliation. They wanted an image in which the different communities within the parish could see themselves reflected. The result was a large outdoor tile mural, recessed in a rock alcove in the inner courtyard behind the church, of a young Mary of unidentifiable native origins poised before a red-and-yellow sunburst who receives on her outstretched hand a dove in flight. The contemporary image is graceful, and she serves, our host informs us, as a symbol of unity in a diverse community for whom peace and reconciliation is crucial to Catholic-Christian identity.

Our San Fernando Valley foray yields one other, quite different, example of a way in which Mary may function as a bringer of peace. Our Lady of Malibu parish, named for the idyllic village situated along

Pacific Coast Highway, is nestled in a cul-de-sac not far from the edge of Pepperdine University. At the entrance to the airy, contemporary structure, a handsome natural wood statue of the Virgin with two sea gulls fluttering about her feet welcomes us as we approach. Dorothy and I are greeted by Mary, a Sister of St. Louis, who provides us with a sense of the local demographics that impact the parish and its school. She tells a tale of property values that are sky high on the luxury beach-front, thus inviting fewer families with children. Nevertheless, Sr. Mary tells us, many of the classic devotions such as a May crowning, rosaries, and *la posada* practiced when the parish was staffed by Carmelites are still intact.

Then a piece of oral history is passed down. I ask about a rather unusual modern card-sized image that had been given to me and that bore the title Our Lady of Malibu. Quickly, Sr. Mary leads us to the ranch-style rectory across from the church and shows us the original oil painting I have seen reproduced in black and white. She also hands us a small pamphlet describing this mysterious almond-eyed image's origins painted by Vienna-born Jewish artist, Renata Druks, in 1956. Feeling insecure and unprotected and living alone, the artist retrieved childhood memories of Viennese women who had faith in the Madonna's presence and resolved to create her own protective Virgin.

Praying to the spirit of the Madonna, Renata offered herself as a medium and began to paint. Contrary to the expected pose of praying hands, Renata was guided to paint Our Lady of Malibu with hands folded protectively around what she came to believe was the seed of faith. "After a while," the artist recalled, "her presence within the painting made me feel much safer than I had felt in a long time. Many people felt very strongly about the image and often

Mary with Seagulls, Our Lady of Malibu Church, Malibu.

mentioned that I had captured a spirit that seemed to breathe life. . . . Her sweet face affirms the existence of friendship, love, and protection, a reassuring image when the world seems cold and eerie." Like so many stories heard throughout the archdiocese, this story is held close in local hearts. It is their unique *in situ* experience of Mary's presence, in this case, as the one who has bestowed peace upon someone in their midst and thus upon them all.

After visiting the San Fernando Valley and Malibu, I did some sleuthing about the traditional title of Our Lady of Peace. What became clear to me was that Mary under this appellation is no newcomer to Southern California. Mary in the guise of Our Lady of Peace in fact first entered the region with the priests of the Congregation of the Sacred Hearts of Jesus and Mary, the so-called Picpus fathers, who had been welcomed into the frontier diocese of California after their expulsion from Hawaii in 1831. Those were turbulent times on the West Coast: Spain had ceded control of its Mexican colonial dominion to the newly formed Mexican government and the Franciscan California mission system was soon to be secularized by the new overseers. At the time, the small Catholic community around *La Iglesia de Nuestra Señora de los Angeles de Portiuncula* was the responsibility of the friars at San Gabriel Mission. With the arrival of the expelled Sacred Hearts Fathers *La Placita*, the little founding church of L.A., was put under their guidance. Its first resident pastor was French Fr. Alexis Bachelot. While the hearts of Jesus and his mother are clearly the titular focus of this community's devotion, Our Lady of Peace, whose feast day is July 9, is in fact patroness of their missions. Thus devotion to Our Lady of Peace came first to Southern California with these missionary priests from Europe by way of Hawaii.

Continuing research into the title reveals that the Pacific is not the only direction from which Our Lady of Peace has entered the archdiocese. She has also been carried on the waves of immigration coming from south of the U.S. border where she is patroness of the city of San Miguel in El Salvador. In the archdiocese *Nuestra Señora de la Paz* is displayed prominently above a bank of votive candles next to an image of *Nuestra Señora de Suyapa*, the Marian patroness of Honduras, at the parish of St. Thomas the Apostle in the Pico Union district between Hollywood and downtown. The district is recognizable by the lamppost banners that identify the "Byzantine-Latino Quarter" as home to many Central American immigrants. The Salvadoran image with her billowing white dress decorated with the national insignia is credited with bringing an end to the fratricidal violence that threatened the country at the time of its miraculous seventeenth-century appearance. As do many national Virgins, the Salvadoran Maria today serves in the United States as a symbol of cultural identity for a people exiled from their homeland as well as a theological symbol. Many of those who turn to her fled their country during the civil violence of the 1980s. She is thus a poignant reminder of the devotion of those who have journeyed northward in search of a place where peace might once again be possible.

Several days after my visit to the San Fernando Valley and Malibu, in early February, I run across another striking example of the way in which Mary is newly expressing herself in the multicultural archdiocese. Sacred Heart church in Altadena turns out to be an even more diverse community than expected, with a sizable Filipino population as well as any number of African American parishioners who hail from the New Orleans area. We arrive at the church late in the day as Altadena is at the far northwestern edge of the diocese where the populated foothills meet the San Gabriel Mountains and the end of suburban sprawl. The pastor, Fr. Robert Victoria, an ardent young Filipino, has contacted his secretary who informs us that he will be a bit late for our appointment, as he is caught in traffic coming in from a meeting downtown.

Dorothy and I have just come from a visit at the handsomely appointed St. Elizabeth's, another Altadena parish, where for many years Marian devotees flocked to the outdoor rock grotto which earned the parish the nickname "the Lourdes of the West." St. Elizabeth's is clearly a very lively, well-endowed suburban community with a large staff that sponsors multiple ministries. In contrast, Sacred Heart feels a bit removed from the busy bustle of central Altadena.

If Sacred Heart parish feels quiet on a late Thursday afternoon, when Fr. Robert arrives the energy level ratchets up. His enthusiasm is contagious while he responds to our queries about Marian devotion among his congregation. Yes, it is lively, he suggests. Furthermore, his personal devotion to Our Lady is ardent. When he came to Sacred Heart, he reminisces, the parishioners of different nationalities did not have much to do with each other. On the streets, the groups were always at odds and sometimes in open conflict with each other. But there was also a longing expressed related to the Christian hope that people espoused. They longed to know that love of enemies was realizable. They longed to feel that the liturgical greeting extended to those in nearby pews each

Eucharist—"Peace be with you"—was more than a formality. Fr. Robert heard the longing as a pastoral imperative and took it upon himself to bring together the factions dividing his parish.

He discerned that the common ground among them was a deep devotion to the Virgin. So he marshaled the community to hold a full-scale Marian Congress at this modest Catholic church on the outskirts of Altadena. The parish galvanized into action. A December novena was introduced with Our Lady of Guadalupe presented not simply as the symbol of Mexico, but as the Empress of the Americas, a role she officially acquired under John Paul II. Each of the nine nights of the novena a different cultural group sponsored a multilingual rosary modeled on the practice at the Shrine of Lourdes in France, each decade of the Marian prayer spoken in a different language. Speakers were invited to present on various aspects of Marian doctrine, and parishioners were invited to bring the various images of the Virgin that they cherished to

Parishioners' Images, Marian Congress, Sacred Heart Church, Altadena.

the parish center where they were displayed in all their variety: Bon Secours from New Orleans; Our Lady of Manaoag; Piat and Mediatrix of All Graces from various regions in the Philippines; the Asian Our Lady of the Bird; Vietnam's Our Lady of La Vang; *Nuestra Señora de San Juan de los Lagos* and *Rosario de Talpa* from Jalisco, Mexico; *Desatanudos* who comes to Argentina by way of Germany; the former Yugoslavia's Medjugorje; *Corazón de Maria*; Mary, Help of Christians; the Immaculate Conception; Guadalupe; Our Lady of Mount Carmel, and the list went on and on.

Sacred Heart's Marian Congress culminated in the consecration of the newly renovated parish center to the Immaculate Heart of Mary. "Because," Fr. Robert informs us knowingly, "we are the parish of the Sacred Heart of Jesus and you can't have one heart without the other." He goes on enthusiastically to share with us what he considers the most remarkable aspect of this celebration of reconciliation under the

Salvadoran *Nuestra Señora de la Paz*,
St. Thomas the Apostle Church, L.A.

patronage of the Virgin. Before the Congress had taken place, he had been on a walking tour of San Francisco when an image in a shop window caught his attention. This was a Virgin he had never encountered before: a majestic crowned figure swathed in white and gold drapery holding her regal gold-crowned son in the pose of a king standing on a star-studded globe of the world. It spoke to him, and so he negotiated with the proprietor to have it shipped south to Altadena. There she was set up between four Marian shrines, each representing one of the parish's main cultural groups.

During the Congress, a visitor came up to Fr. Robert. He believed he recognized this Virgin: she was Our Lady of All Nations. As the young pastor relays this story to us, his eyes shine and he lingers at the thought. Since the Congress, Sacred Heart parishioners have often returned to venerate the image they describe as Our Lady of All Nations. More recently, Fr. Robert proudly announces, a Forty Hours Devotion took place under Mary's patronage and in October a multilingual Living Rosary was held in the church parking lot. A parish rosary group flourishes, and a Legion of Mary chapter is active. Yes, Fr. Robert assures us, she continues to do her reconciling work at Sacred Heart.

Wood Bas Relief, Flight into Egypt, St. Vincent's Church, L.A.

Chapter 14

Queen
La Reina

Gloriosa Reina de Los Angeles:
Ante Ti, Patrona de nuestra pueblo
acudimos con devoción, con esa devoción sencilla,
pero sincera, que desde pequeños,
nos han enseñado e inculcado
nuestros padres y abuelos y a lo largo de esta novena,
te vamos a confiar la necesidades
de todos las familias de este pueblo:
la alegria delos niños, las ilusiones de los jovenes,
para que crezcan ante las dificultades
cada vez _ayors, que encuentran en su juventud,
los develos de los adultos que luchan cada día
por sacar adelante su familia y ajudan a sus hijos
a buscarse un porvenir, el dolor de los enfermos
y el sereno atardecer de los ancianos.

—Oracion Preparatoria para todos los dias,
   Mass-produced domestic altar diptych from gift shop at
   La Placita, San Francis Imprint Inc, Burbank, California

Several years after I had begun my graduate studies at Santa Barbara, Professor Capps sent me a postcard from Our Lady of the Redwoods, a Cistercian monastery in Northern California. Dated September

Our Lady of Lithuania, St. Casimir's Church, L.A.

8, it read: "Feast of the Birth of Mary—one red rose on the altar." My remarkable mentor had made singular arrangements for me to spend a winter academic quarter in residence in the monastery, and it was there I came more deeply to know Mary. Founded in the twelfth century, the order of the Cistercians was from the outset placed under the protection of the Virgin. Cistercian luminary Bernard of Clairvaux is said to have had a vision of the Virgin blessing the enterprise by anointing him with drops of her milk, thus each of the worldwide Cistercian monasteries bears one of her titles. Our Lady of the Redwoods is no exception. Nestled deep in the primeval forests a five-hour drive north of San Francisco, this community of cloistered women lives out in modern day the ancient Cistercian charism of communal prayer and manual work. Redwoods is an observant community but not hermetically sealed from contemporary ideas.

It was there that I was introduced to Our Lady of the Redwood's unique sung version of the *Salve Regina*, "Hail Holy Queen," that classic Marian antiphon dating from the eleventh century. Medieval Christendom venerated its Queen with poetry and melody of exquisite beauty. Theirs was a chivalric veneration, it is true, but the regal figure to whom medievals directed their invocations was the mirror of the longing for beauty etched on their own hearts. Over the centuries the Marian antiphons—*Alma Redemptoris Mater, Ave Regina Caelorum, Regina Caeli*, and *Salve Regina*—have threaded through the prayers of the daily Divine Office, each antiphon featured in a different liturgical season.

The grey light of February slanted through the immense glass wall of the monastery chapel interlaced with shadows of the giant redwoods as we gathered for late Saturday evening prayer. In my mind, this time of day belongs to her. Her canticle of joy, the *Magnificat*, is sung at vespers and, as is the monastic custom, the *Salve Regina* draws the day to a close. The contemporary, vaguely atonal Redwoods chant allowed the text to linger: syllable by syllable, phrase by evocative phrase.

> Hail holy Queen, Mother of mercy,
> our life, our sweetness, our hope.
> To you do we cry, poor banished children of Eve.
> To you do we send up our sighs,
> mourning and weeping in this valley of tears.
> Turn then most gracious advocate, your eyes of mercy toward us.
> And after this, our exile,
> show unto us the blessed fruit of your womb,
> Jesus.
> O clement, O loving, O sweet Virgin Mary.

Still today, whenever I turn to Mary, the spare rhythm of that Red-woods chant unites me with centuries of ardor and tender supplication. It was Western medieval Christendom that gave Mary her royal identity. That age of royalty fittingly paid homage to the mother of Christ by naming her their Queen. She thus is not merely Queen of all her devoted followers, but seen as exercising a vaster reign as Queen of Heaven, Queen of Angels, and Queen of Saints. It is true that she had been long venerated in the Eastern Christian world with a reverence that extols her divine maternity and bestows august titles upon her but it was the Western church that gave us Mary as Queen.

The royal Mary is not always depicted in Los Angeles today in a manner that might be recognizable to devotees of an earlier age, as clothed in the flowing garments of a medieval queen. Discovered throughout the archdiocese are some startlingly contemporary depictions of her queenship. A large hanging *Regina Caeli* tapestry in a palette of browns and greys that adorns a sidewall at Our Lady of the

Regina Caeli Tapestry, Our Lady of the Assumption, Claremont.

Assumption in Claremont where Msgr. Thomas Welbers pastors is a case in point. This suburban parish prides itself on its distinctive religious art. A polychrome wood Madonna created by Claremont artist Albert Stewart and a set of stained glass windows begun by the Barillet studios in Paris and completed by the Los Angeles Piczek sisters and the *Regina Caeli* tapestry are among the many images to which Fr. Thomas points. As has been the case with several of the suburban parishes I have visited, overt Marian devotion is not a prominent part of the community life in Claremont. The patronal feast (the Assumption) is the occasion for a parish festival, in December there is a Guadalupe display, and Our Lady of La Vang is brought out for the Vietnamese New Year. Yet for the most part, although Mary is close in the background of parish life, she is not explicitly acknowledged. She functions, Fr. Welbers explains, for parishioners more as a companion than as an object of veneration.

Mary as Queen lives more vividly in the imaginations of Our Lady of the Bright Mount church, an imposing and immaculately manicured

Black Madonna of Częstochowa, Our Lady of the Bright Mount Church, L.A.

compound on West Adams Boulevard that is historically home to L.A.'s Polish community. West Adams is a broad, lengthy thoroughfare seemingly devoid of restaurants and so, because Dorothy and I are early for the 7:30 evening service at Our Lady of the Bright Mount, we pull in at a tiny taco vendor's stall. We are the last customers, and it becomes clear that generally the family who operates the stall leaves before dusk. So we wolf down our burritos hurriedly and drive to the nearby church. Buzzing the sacristy elicits no response, so we wander about. Our Lady of the Bright Mount is one of the few parishes we have visited that keeps its sanctuary locked, although perhaps it was the late hour that made this so. Perhaps a half an hour after we buzzed the rectory, a young nun in a crisp starched habit emerges from the gated area where, we assume, the church offices are located. A parish secretary remembers overhearing the pastor speaking to us on the phone several days previous so permission is given and we work quickly not to intrude on the pre-Mass prayers of the arriving parishioners.

Bright Mount is an imposing place, cavernous and formal. A huge framed image of Pope John Paul II, Karol Josef Wojtyla as he is known in his native Poland, is situated to the left of the altar. To the right of that altar is the identifiable image of the Black Madonna of Czestochowa, bordered by a dark wooden frame and set against a vivid background of radiating red-orange, white, and midnight blue underscored with the inscription *Regina Poloniae Ora Pro Nobis* (Queen of Poland, Pray for Us). The antiquity as well as the mysterious aspect of the Queen of Poland compels. Legend has it that she can be traced to the Gospel writer Luke who painted her on a cypress tabletop taken from Jesus's natal home. What can be said for certain is that documents situate her in Poland by the mid-fourteenth century, and that three centuries later the image was credited with miraculously saving the Polish monastery of *Jasna Góra* (Bright Mount) from the ravages of a Swedish invasion, an event which led to her crowning.

The Madonna's aspect is venerable, her own dark face and the dark face of the child look out at the devotee with solemnity. Robed in deep-blue fabric dotted with fleur-de-lis, she directs attention away from herself toward her son who, with the Gospels held in one hand, extends a blessing with the other. Perhaps the most unusual feature of Czestochowa is the two prominent scars on her right cheek. Again, legends abound as to their origin: plundering Hussites stole and marred the image or robbers effaced it, causing the image to bleed and the robbers to flee in terror. The composition, I learn later, minus the scars, is familiar to Eastern Orthodox Christians as a *Hodegetria*: the One Who

Shows the Way. Poland's Queen, like Poland's pope, remains close to the hearts of the Polish faithful even on the far-flung California coast.

Across the city, an equally stunning queenly image of the Virgin is visible in a roundel above the entry door of St. Casimir Lithuanian Church. I am struck by the fact that a person (myself in this instance) can be in proximity to a religious image for years and never notice it. St. Casimir's sits on the corner of Griffith Park Boulevard and St. George Street, kitty-corner from the John Marshall High sports field where, for the fall of my senior high school year, I leapt and yelled as part of the cheerleading squad that urged a not altogether stellar football team on to the rare victory. But I had no reason to look beyond my blue-on-blue pompoms to the Lithuanian church across the street.

Today, as I visit the site attentively for the first time, I see all the centuries-old Catholic affection and tender attachment to the Queen of Heaven present on the face depicted in the gleaming roundel at Griffith Park and St. George. Emerging from a pinwheel starburst, this bust of Our Lady of Lithuania, that long beleaguered nation's queen, arms crossed upon her breast, inclines her head downward and gazes benevolently upon those who enter the portal below. Upon her head, whose incline seems supported by a tiny angel, rests a magnificent two-tiered crown.

To the east across the shallow Los Angeles River, a slight statue of an aqua-mantled Virgin enthroned in a white plaster grotto stands to your left as you mount the short flight of front steps to the old Armenian Catholic parish tucked away in a run-down residential area of Boyle Heights. She, of mass-produced origins, would not be memorable except for the brass plaque beneath her that reads:

> In memory of our
> ARMENIAN MARTYRS
> who gave their lives
> for the love of God,
> the Christian faith
> and high ideals.
> 1915–1918

Our Lady Queen of Martyrs is the older of two Armenian Catholic congregations in the archdiocese, having been established in 1915 long

Queen of Martyrs Altar, Our Lady Queen of Martyrs Armenian Catholic Church, L.A.

before the assimilated postwar community had fanned out west into the expanding suburbs. On my first visit I catch a Sunday Eucharist celebrated in a linguistic mixture of Armenian and English and find myself fascinated by the distinctiveness of the service. The elaborately vested priest and two deacons face the altar, a practice to which I, as a product of the Second Vatican Council, am unaccustomed. Nor am I used to having sheer white curtains drawn before the altar at the moment of consecration so that the divine mystery enacted there might remain as such. I am reminded that Our Lady Queen of Martyrs is indeed an Eastern Rite Catholic Church.

Notwithstanding this fact, the Catholic aspect of that Eastern Catholic equation is underscored when I return for an interview with Fr. Antoine Panossian who quotes appreciatively from Pope Benedict's recent encyclical on love (*Caritas in veritate*) and assures me that his

congregation is very Catholic. As for Marian devotion here, he reports that the rosary is well attended, that the feasts of the Nativity of Mary, the Presentation of the Lord, the Assumption, and the Annunciation are more than cursorily observed and that May devotion is alive and well. This is more than I can say for the majority of Catholic parishes in the United States today. With the possible exception of the feast of the Assumption, these Marian celebrations, while present on the liturgical calendar are rarely given much attention. Armenian Catholics thus clearly mirror their Armenian Orthodox neighbors in faithfully observing this cluster of Marian festivals.

The interior of the sanctuary of this parish is bright with pastel hues: pink and rose predominate. The crowned Queen of Martyrs herself is regally situated above the altar in a niche wreathed in bowers of flower-studded greenery, golden rays of light pouring from her outstretched palms. Fr. Panossian shares with me a lively sense of his congregation along with a more complex history of Chaldean, Syrian, Catholic, and Apostolic Orthodox Armenians than I can assimilate but I do conclude that Mary is recognized here especially as Mother of God and as Queen.

It is as Queen of Martyrs (a venerable title enshrined in the Litany of Loreto since the sixteenth century) that she is most present for the memory of the forced deportation, expropriation, abduction, starvation, and torture of an estimated one and a half million Armenians living under the Ottoman Empire during the First World War—a genocide that has not lost its terrible power for this community. It is not the witness of early Christians persecuted by Emperors of Rome, nor the determination of Renaissance English Recusants who refused to abandon their inherited faith, nor the courage of Jesuit missionaries in New France, nor the heroism of sixteenth-century Japanese Catholics who died defying the Imperial government of whom this congregation thinks when it proclaims Mary Queen of Martyrs. Rather it is martyred sons and uncles, sisters and grandmothers, fellow Armenians who are vividly alive in collective memory.

Europe may still have ceremonial vestiges of its historic royalty, little American girls may still imagine themselves as frilly-skirted princesses, and kings and queens of high school homecomings seem not yet to have been dethroned, but, in progressive theological circles across the denominational divides, the dominant and subordinate relationships implied in the language of royalty tend to be shunned. Images of Jesus as brother, companion, or liberator and Mary as sister and *compañera* proliferate. Kinship replaces kingship, kin-dom rather than kingdom is preferred. These relational images for many suggest a more integral, responsible, and collaborative model of discipleship. They reflect the current sense that the Christian is one who participates in the world-transforming action of the divine. Across the archdiocese of L.A. there is ample of evidence of the preference for Mary as one with whom one might enjoy intimacy as with a sister or friend. There is also a widespread and touching sense of her as present as a nurturing mother. Yet everywhere are striking visual reminders of her vaunted role as queen, and in churches distinguished by their cultural identity, such as St. Casimir, Our Lady of the Bright Mount, or Queen of Martyrs, she continues to reign.

Close to downtown on James Wood Boulevard and a stone's throw from the campus of Loyola Law School is a parish where the Virgin's regal status is unabashedly on display. Immaculate Conception, founded in 1909 as Our Lady of Guadalupe and renamed in 1926, has a large Coronation Chapel that attracts a stream of devotees. It is located to the right of the main sanctuary and accessible through an outer door leading from a sheltered garden. I suspect that the people who kneel and pray here are not necessarily drawn because of the specific theme of the Virgin's crowning in heaven but because this a quiet set-aside world hallowed by decades of veneration where, whatever one's relationship to Mary and however you name her, she can be found.

The central visual element of the chapel—a mural that covers the entire dome above an altar—is chiefly notable for the way it underscores the regal role that Mary has played in the Catholic imagination. Billowing banks of cotton-candy clouds in an aqua sky upon which crowded swarms of angels and roly-poly cherubs surround a cloud-perched Christ and his mother. She inclines gracefully to receive the crown he offers while a bearded God the Father and a seraphic white dove, completing the Trinity, hover above.

It might be noted that this visual personification of the Trinity as a bird, an older man, and a younger man does not conform to official iconographical standards. Nor is the coronation of the Blessed Virgin an event that can be traced to Scripture but one, like others in the tradition about Mary, born of centuries-long cumulative prayerful reflection. To the objection that the event of the coronation is "made up," I point to the Christian gospels themselves that are the work, albeit inspired, of human hearts and minds as ultimate issues are pondered. Not that tradition has the same authoritative weight as Scripture; it does not. But tradition fleshes out, sometimes simply as poetic or metaphoric intimation, the truths to which Scripture points. The rich symbolic matrix of the Marian stories and images is a case in point. Of course, the line between validated or accepted belief and a wide-ranging exploration, refocusing, expansion, or contraction of a tradition's shared symbolism is indeed fine. Such business is at the root of religious "traditioning" that goes on across the globe and in every era. It is also one out of which schisms and sacred wars are born.

Be that as it may, the coronation of Mary has long persisted in the Catholic imagination. It is one of the Glorious Mysteries of the tradi-

Coronation Chapel, Immaculate Conception Church, Westlake/Downtown Los Angeles.

tional rosary and is visible across the archdiocese in stained glass and bas-reliefs wherever those Glorious Mysteries are portrayed. But it is not official dogma, unlike the immaculate conception of Mary and her assumption into heaven, which were so designated in 1854 and 1954, respectively. Yet, Mary's coronation, symbol of the enthroned place she occupies in the hearts and minds of generations of Catholics, continues to resonate. Here, in the silent chapel at Immaculate Conception, where throughout a weekday a steady stream of men and women come to kneel, implore, offer thanks, or to request her interceding aid beneath a painted cotton-candy clouded sky, Mary is, without a doubt, the reigning queen.

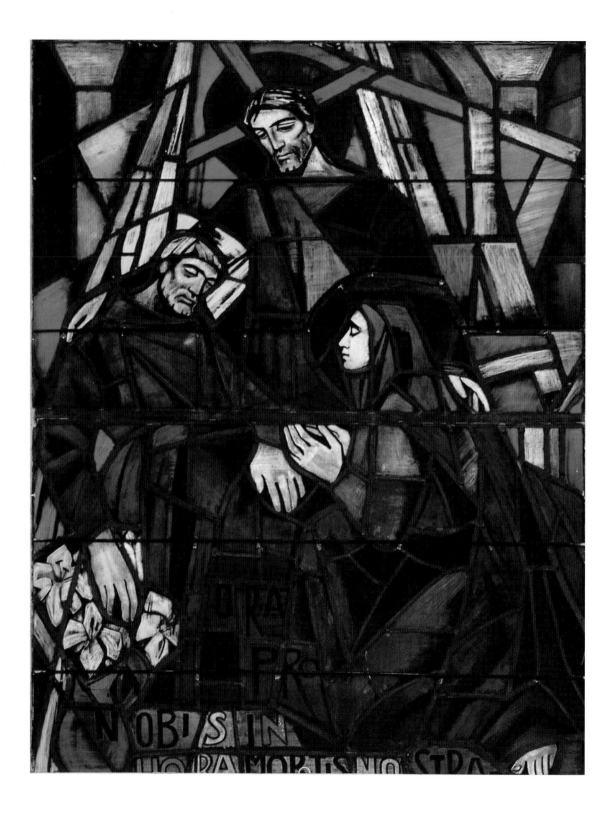

Chapter 15

Our Lady of Sorrows
Dolores

And the child's father and mother were amazed at what was being said about him. Then Simeon blessed them and said to his mother Mary, "This child is destined for the falling and the rising of many in Israel, and to be a sign that will be opposed so that the inner thoughts of many will be revealed—and a sword will pierce your own soul too."

—Luke 2:33-35

Perhaps it was a sort of late Victorian gentility or a reflexive response to having entered adulthood during the difficult years of the Great Depression. Perhaps it might even have been a product of some mid-twentieth-century child-rearing philosophy. Whatever the cause, I am struck in retrospect by how consistently my parents sought to shield me from life's sorrowful side. Even then, I found their reticence perplexing. A vivid childhood memory finds me standing outside my bedroom door at the top of a stairwell watching my parents depart for my paternal uncle's funeral and wondering why I was left behind. Nor was the secrecy around my maternal grandmother's last days ever broken: my guess is that discussion of nervous or mental collapse was off limits at the time.

Apparently there were topics deemed at midcentury inappropriate to acknowledge. Grief, loss, and sorrow, whether tragic or commonplace, were not subjects of conversation. Yet sorrow, deep and penetrating

Death of Joseph Window, Our Lady of the Assumption Church, Claremont.

sorrow, is necessarily part of human life and the prayer form most associated with sorrow, the lament, is as ancient a cry as any. A glance at the rich psalmody that makes up our heritage underscores the point. Lament, however, tends to be edged out of our shared contemporary awareness by prayers of praise, adoration, thanksgiving, petition, expiation, or intercession that are today featured in American common worship.

Yet lament is alive and well on the ground in the city of Our Lady of the Angels. I pause midday in one of my exploratory Marian pilgrimages in the newly gentrified "Old Town" of Monrovia for lunch and spread out my San Gabriel region maps on the patio table next to my sushi special. Fashionably attired young professionals conversing with business associates through their in-ear phone devices pass into the trendy shop opposite and emerge with steaming cups of double macchiato lattes, anxious to arrive at their next assignations. Two immaculately groomed matrons laden with purchases pause at the table next to mine. This is the America of the TV ads, of sleek new airport concourses, opulent malls, and affluent comfort, the consumer's America that is most represented in L.A.'s Westwood and Brentwood districts.

My anticipated next stop, in a morning spent traversing barrios, industrial enclaves, and upscale suburban neighborhoods, is, according to my map, close by. The light blue–tiled edifice of Immaculate Conception is, in fact, a few short blocks from bustling, affluent Old Town. Arriving, I discover a side door and slip into the church's darkened interior to find the sanctuary draped for Lent, a purple cloth looped over the life-sized wooden corpus above the altar. As is usual, I do not find myself alone. Los Angeles area churches, even during these early nonliturgical afternoon hours, are havens for people who pray; sometimes in a common rosary or novena, more often as solitaries. For the most part, it is not the well-heeled matrons or the young professionals sipping their lattes who are found, but members of that vast army of workers who daily travel into neighborhoods like this to wash the restaurant dishes, change the hotel sheets, and collect the accumulated trash of an affluent, acquisitive society. Sometimes they move between the sacred statuary touching rows of plaster-of-paris feet or kneel and offer a whispered petition. Sometimes they are seated quietly with heads bowed.

This day my fellow pray-ers are a man, possibly in his midthirties, who kneels at the crossarm of the transept, his back erect and face turned upward, a profound attentiveness claiming him as he waits before his Lord. The man's posture bespeaks a deep resolve and enraptured adoration. Farther back a middle-aged woman also turns her gaze to the wooden crucifix but she is choked with tears, hunched over in what can only be a grief so raw it cannot express itself in any other posture. His almost military alertness and her ragged sobs are offered up wordlessly to the figure above the altar in this Marian sanctuary of the Immaculate Conception. A few short blocks away is the relentless bustling productivity of affluent urban America. But here in this substrata of urban life, the thin veil that separates human and divine is torn apart by the raw power of anguish and intimate longing.

Lament has been called a cry of hope. In that crying out is the affirmation of a God who hears that cry. I weigh this remembered claim against the presence of this man and woman offering up their ardent prayers in this hushed Monrovia sanctuary. I weigh the claim against other memories as well: the graffiti-scrawled neighborhood of Compton and a woman hidden somewhere inside Our Lady of Victory's adoration chapel softly intoning a Spanish song of praise; a young mother at Epiphany Church in South El Monte tenderly lifting her toddler daughter to the base of the plaster statue of *Sagrado Corazon;* two young gang members with tight-gripped fists crouching in the back pews of Our Lady of Lourdes in the barrio of East L.A. while a mortuary hearse idles outside; the wallet-sized photos lining the framed images of Guadalupe at Our Lady of the Rosary in Sun Valley or at Lompoc's *La Purisima Concepcion*, talismans invoking protection upon young military personnel exiled half across the world; hundreds of dog-eared photographs at El Monte's *Nuestra Señora de*

Photos of Loved Ones Tucked in Guadalupe Poster, Our Lady of the Holy Rosary Church, Sun Valley.

Crucifix with Sorrowing Mother and Photos, *Nuestra Señora de Guadalupe* Church, El Monte.

Guadalupe thrust into the shrine of the Sorrowing Mother and her Crucified Son, photographs of children lost to jail or drugs or violence fluttering in the breeze like prayer flags.

Devotion to Our Lady of Sorrows is an ancient one that gained popularity in the Western church of the fifteenth century. Fashioned from generations of communal reflection upon the fabric of the biblical narrative threaded together with the anguished sighs of the faithful, the devotion is focused on seven discrete moments in the life of Mary as recorded in Scripture. The young mother brings her first born to the temple with an offering where the priest prophesies that her child has a fated role to play in Israel's life and that a sword of sorrow will pierce her heart as well (Luke 2:25–35). Next, she flees with her child to far-away Egypt, her spouse being warned in a dream that King Herod seeks to destroy the boy (Matthew 2:13–15). When her son is twelve, the family travels to Jerusalem for the Passover festival and on the return trip she loses him (Luke 2:41–50). Her son has been arrested, tried, and convicted as a criminal. His final humiliation is to be forced to drag the

Presentation Window, Chapel,
Holy Family Church, Glendale.

Finding in the Temple Window,
St. Gregory Nazianzen Church, L.A.

The Fourth Sorrow: Jesus Meets His Mother:
Mater Dolorosa Retreat Center, Sierra Madre.
Artist: Humberto Maestas.

cross on which he will be crucified through the streets. There he meets his mother (Luke 23:27–29). On the hill under the ominous shadow of the instrument of her son's torture and death, the mother stands (John 19:25–30). When his lifeless body is taken down from the cross, she receives it, cradling him in her arms (Psalm 130). Her son's broken body is laid it in a cold tomb while his shaken mother attends (Luke 23:50–56). These are the seven sorrows of Mary as mother, the one who carried Jesus under her heart for nine months, followed him throughout his life, and continues to carry him still. Devotion to her sorrows signals the community's recognition that she is privy to the fathomless wells of human sorrowing. Her heart, pierced, broken, and intimate with her son's great heart, is the earthen vessel into which all the sorrow of the world can be poured.

I move reflectively among modern visual representations of Mary's sorrows on the grounds of Mater Dolorosa, the Passionist order's retreat center in Sierra Madre in the foothills of the San Gabriel Mountains. The order, established mid-eighteenth century in Italy by Paul of the Cross, has as its special founding charism the remembrance of the passion of Jesus which the founder believed had the power to change people's lives. Here that remembrance is refracted through the gaze of Jesus's

mother. A circular garden a bit removed from the retreat facility creates a meditative space through which I walk guided by a pamphlet of contemporary prayers. Shallow beds of bright summer flowers and greenery frame the contemporary mosaic depictions of six of the Virgin's sorrows. The "fourth sorrow," Mary's meeting with her son on the road to Calvary, is represented by two striking life-sized bronze figures crafted by sculptor Humberto Maestas that dominate the garden. The anguished mother extends her outstretched hand across the space that separates her from her child, just missing the crossbeams of the cruciform implement of his imminent execution. I pause for a moment before the image of this unimaginable scene.

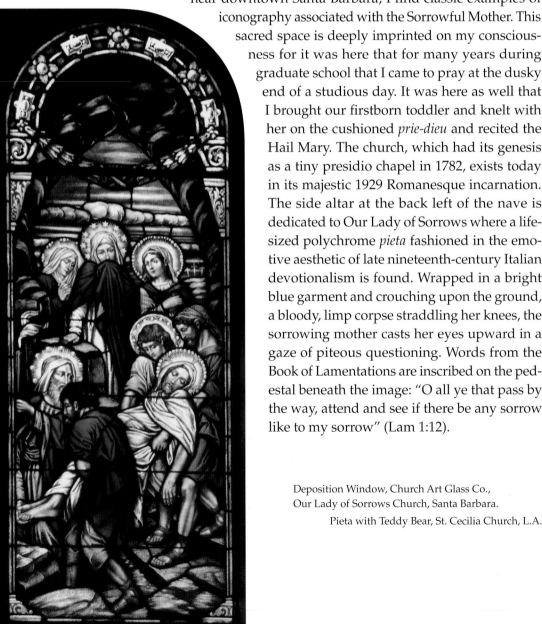

Further up the coast at the Jesuit parish of Our Lady of Sorrows near downtown Santa Barbara, I find classic examples of iconography associated with the Sorrowful Mother. This sacred space is deeply imprinted on my consciousness for it was here that for many years during graduate school that I came to pray at the dusky end of a studious day. It was here as well that I brought our firstborn toddler and knelt with her on the cushioned *prie-dieu* and recited the Hail Mary. The church, which had its genesis as a tiny presidio chapel in 1782, exists today in its majestic 1929 Romanesque incarnation. The side altar at the back left of the nave is dedicated to Our Lady of Sorrows where a life-sized polychrome *pieta* fashioned in the emotive aesthetic of late nineteenth-century Italian devotionalism is found. Wrapped in a bright blue garment and crouching upon the ground, a bloody, limp corpse straddling her knees, the sorrowing mother casts her eyes upward in a gaze of piteous questioning. Words from the Book of Lamentations are inscribed on the pedestal beneath the image: "O all ye that pass by the way, attend and see if there be any sorrow like to my sorrow" (Lam 1:12).

Deposition Window, Church Art Glass Co.,
Our Lady of Sorrows Church, Santa Barbara.

Pieta with Teddy Bear, St. Cecilia Church, L.A.

It is, however, a stained-glass window in the central position above the *pieta*, one of a series created by the Church Art Glass Company in 1929, that most arrests me today. The windows are finely wrought, the artisans have captured not only the theological import of this scene—Jesus's body being laid in the tomb—but the human drama as well. The demeanors of the characters are delicately shaped, especially the expression of the Virgin. She is the central member of a triad of female figures that rise slightly above a hunched group of four men burdened with the effort of lowering Jesus's corpse into a tomb partly visible at the tableau's bottom edge. Mary Magdalene, identifiable by her flowing hair and purple-red cloak, is on the Virgin's left and on her right, one presumes, is Mary the wife of Clopas, whom the Gospel of John identifies as also present at the foot of the cross (John 19:25). The Virgin stands between them, her frame upright but slightly swayed, as if pulled into herself through an inhalation of breath. One stabilizing hand reaches out to touch a nearby balustrade; the other draws her ultramarine cloak up to cover her mouth. Her eyes have none of the wild pathos of the *pieta* grouping below; instead they look down upon the scene with a tenderness possibly only achieved through the exhaustion of deep and realized grief. An azure halo circles her face, lit from the daylight behind, and it is flecked with a crown of white stars. Here, I feel, is an image that reaches

Soledad, Our Lady of Solitude Church, L.A.

out to all who sorrow and identify with this heartbroken woman staring into the tomb that swallows up the one dearest to her in all the world.

It is not present at the Mater Dolorosa garden nor the Jesuit parish I visit today but I hold fast to another title of the sorrowing Virgin, one familiar to devotees in Spanish-speaking countries: *Soledad* or Our Lady of Solitude. Twice in the archdiocese I encounter this Marian title; at St. Cecilia parish near USC where as *Soledad*, Mary is the focus of veneration of parishioners from Oaxaca, and at *La Soledad* parish in East L.A.'s Belvedere district. At the latter site in 1940 local artist Rodolfo Vargas carved a famous wooden statue of the Sorrowful Mother clothed in black velvet and holding the implements of her son's passion.

Under the name *Soledad*, Mary has over the centuries been honored on Holy Saturday, that temporal space in the liturgical year between Good Friday and Easter Sunday, between the death and resurrection of her son. The title *Soledad*, introduced by Queen Juana of Spain after the 1506 death of her beloved husband, Philip I, acknowledges Mary's profound solitude in that liminal time when all has been lost and no new vision or hope is yet offered. That soul space is perhaps the most difficult moment in any instance of loss. Yet solitude, the experience of being alone, is the dark passage into which one must enter before light can dawn. *Soledad* is this painful, poignant moment's name.

Reminders of Mary's sorrows and her role as the one who embraces all human grief and suffering is not, however, limited to statuary or only experienced in personal meditation. The performative character of the Catholic devotional imagination gives rise to dramatic communal reenactments of Mary's sorrow, especially during Holy Week. Midmorning on Good Friday at Our Lady of the Valley in Canoga Park, the *Pabasa ng Pasyon* (the Tagalog chant reading of the Passion) has ended and parishioners assemble for the inaugurating prayer of the Divine Mercy Novena that will culminate on Saturday of the Easter Octave. In the screened-in adoration area behind the main altar several women kneel in private prayer while two of the parish men take responsibility for preparing the statue of the entombed Christ for the evening liturgical celebrations.

"*Santo Entiero*" ("Holy Corpse"), Our Lady of the Valley Church, Canoga Park.
Sorrowing Mother, Dolores Mission, Boyle Heights, East Los Angeles.

On my previous visit that prone polychrome corpse was visible in a glass coffin in the front vestibule under a mournful image of the Sorrowing Mother. Now, in this solemn time of the Triduum, he has been brought to a place of prominence; the tender ministrations of the two men washing the statue recall the long ago vigilant women who swaddled the body of their crucified friend for burial. Throughout the church, slow reverential movements are observed as individuals circle around the Stations of the Cross or press a kiss or fingertip upon a saint's toes peeking out under purple Lenten shrouds.

My husband and college-aged son are with me this Holy Week, neither of whom has visited the new downtown Cathedral of Our Lady of the Angels. Following the morning *Pabasa ng Pasyon*, we drive across town to attend the Good Friday service at three p.m. In keeping with the aesthetic elegance of the building, the afternoon liturgy is beautifully rendered, the homily thoughtful, the music sensitively performed, and the mood appropriately solemn. We intone the words of Psalm 22, "My God, my God, why have you foresaken me," words that direct our thoughts toward the mystery presently before us. This is a similar, if more polished, version of the Catholic liturgy I might attend in any one of thousands of parish churches throughout the country. Here, however, there is no blood-stained corpse and little of the random unscheduled devotional milling so evident at Canoga Park in the morning, cer-

Crucifixion, Stations of the Cross, St. Bridget's Chinese Catholic Community Chinatown, L.A.

Deposition, Stations of the Cross, St. Bridget's Chinese Catholic Community, Chinatown, L.A.

tainly no black-veiled Madonna through whose eyes the momentous event of the resurrection will be refracted.

Later in the evening of Good Friday, my two men and I venture across the river to Dolores Mission, the Jesuit-run parish in the barrio of East L.A. It has been difficult to determine if a *Pesame* service is going to take place tonight or not. Fortunately, a college friend of my son's has been in the barrio recently and remembers overhearing someone mention that such a service would indeed occur, so we make the eastward trek across the bridge over the dry bed of the Los Angeles River and park in the darkened side street down the block from the tiny mission church. Indeed, a community is gathered and already packed closely in the dimly lit interior—women, children, teens, men young and old, none exhibiting any signs of affluence or authority, only a few Anglos like ourselves. I mark once more the simplicity and functionality of the place. Tonight a large cardboard poster designed for a recent immigrant's rights rally is temporarily propped up and hides my favorite

Mexican *Stabat Mater*, Capilla, Immaculate High School, L.A.
Filipino Sorrowing Mother, Sacred Heart Church, Altadena.

Southern California Mary image, a barefoot Latina Madonna who carries her serape-wrapped child through the mean streets of L.A.

Up front, the altar has been removed and a life-sized polychrome statue of Dolores herself, the doleful Sorrowing Mother, stands in a pool of light, eyes up-cast and hands clasped in anguished prayer, an empty wooden cross and a presider's chair to her left. We arrive as a recitation of the Sorrowful Mysteries of the rosary is in progress interspersed with Spanish songs that express the suffering of the Mother as her heart is pierced by her son's death.

Soon the young Jesuit pastor seats himself in the presider's chair and begins his meditation on the weight of sorrow that Mary carries. The lights in the room are low, the air close, the mood of the crowd heavy. The priest draws us into the Virgin's grief with a first person narrative, "*Mi'ijo, mi'ijo,* [my son, my son]," he repeats soulfully. An antiquated projection screen furls down from the ceiling, and we view a brief emotive clip from a black-and-white European film featuring a wordless wild-eyed Madonna weeping as she clings to the foot of the cross under a stormy sky.

The meditation completed, we are passed sheets of paper and pencil stubs, and we invited to reflect on the burdens that weigh upon us. We inscribe them on our papers to present to the compassionate mother whose pondering heart alone can carry such grief. To the soft strumming of guitars we make our way up the center aisle, picking up carnations that we then lay tenderly at the feet of Dolores along with our intimate sufferings. The language of this service at Dolores Mission may not be my native tongue, the intense veneration, emotionality and cultural inflection may be foreign, yet motherhood has led me here in my own idiosyncratic way and I find myself at home.

As the *pesame* service concludes, community members are invited to share with the assembly what they have laid before the Sorrowing Virgin. My Spanish is insufficient, and my son must periodically lean over and provide a clue as to the drift of the evening but the deep affect in the voices of the women who rise needs no translation: "My boy has fallen in with bad men;" "My daughter is very sick and dying;" "I go to the prison to visit my son and I don't know if he will come home;" "The drugs find our children even on the playground." Here there is no pain that is isolated, no sorrow that breaks the heart held alone, mine included. There is no grief so stinging that it is not already known and borne here in this humble shelter in the barrio of East Los Angeles, borne in the wisdom of those present and, most generously, by the Sorrowing Mother herself.

Polychrome plaque, Seven Sorrows, Mater Dolorosa Retreat Center, Sierra Madre.

"M" and Two Hearts Window, Rectory, St. Vincent's Church, L.A.

Chapter 16

Jesus and Mary
Dos Corazónes

[T]he Blessed Virgin is totally related to Christ, the foundation of faith and ecclesial experience, and she leads to him. That is why, in obedience to Jesus, who reserved a very special role for his Mother in the economy of salvation, Christians have venerated, loved and prayed to Mary in a most particular and fervent way. They have attributed to her an important place in faith and piety, recognizing her as the privileged way to Christ, the supreme Mediator.

—Pope John Paul II, *L'Osservatore Romano*,
  November 22,1995

Dorothy, my photographer, and I are early for our scheduled appointment at the Assumption of the Blessed Virgin Mary parish in Pasadena. This is the preservation-conscious city famous for its Rose Bowl, New Year's Rose Parade, the California Institute of Technology, and the Norton Simon Museum of Art. From genealogical research I know that this is where my maternal Canadian ancestors settled and where, during the depression, my mother and father first met on a blind date at the Pasadena Playhouse. I have made previous arrangements with Assumption's pastor Fr. Gerald O'Brien (an Irishman it turns out), to meet with parishioners who participate in the rosary after daily Mass. While we wait, Dorothy and I circle outside the modern brick edifice, then scan the interior of the high-ceilinged, irregularly configured church. On the church exterior, a larger-than-life contemporary mosaic depicts the assumption—the mystery of Mary's being taken up, body and soul, into heaven at the time of her death. An angular, barefoot figure fairly flies up the side of the building, her arms outstretched to reach a giant hand, a lamb, a white dove that make a Trinitarian frame for her joyous rise.

Inside the church is a gorgeous polished wooden assumption statue that was transported to the new building from the original parish structure. Tucked away in a side ambulatory are four vertical stained-glass panels. Fr. O'Brien has already alerted us to the existence of these unusual "Blessed Be" windows. These prayers are taken from the "Divine Praises" traditionally recited at Benediction of the Blessed Sacrament. The Marian figures are sweetly representational but are framed with a bold checkerboard of small colored glass squares.

> Blessed be the great Mother of God, Mary most holy
> Blessed be the name of Mary, virgin and mother
> Blessed be her glorious assumption
> Blessed be her holy and immaculate conception

The focus in these colorful light-pierced panels suggests the ecclesial moment in which they were ostensibly created when the Roman Catholic Church had recently proclaimed the assumption of Mary to be dogma and was reaffirming the dogma of Mary's immaculate conception proclaimed just short of a century prior. I am most struck, however, in this richly Marian environment, by the three stone roundels placed prominently on the front of the church's massive stone altar. One, in the shape of a dove, descends between two others each containing a heart, the first of which is wreathed by a crown of thorns, the second studded with three rosebuds and pierced through with a cross-shaped sword: the inseparable hearts of Jesus and Mary.

That the two hearts of the mother and son have for long been seen so conjoined is indisputable. The biblical roots of the idea are clear. The Gospel of Luke (1:26–38) depicts Mary as a girl who is told that she will bear a child. When the child is born, shepherds came with news that the child will be Messiah and Lord. These mysterious tidings Mary "treasured" or "pondered" in her heart (Luke 2:15–20). When she brings her child to the Jerusalem temple, the temple priest prophesies that the child will fulfill the hopes of all but that in the process she will share his sorrow—"a sword will pierce your own soul too" (Luke 2:22–38). Further on, Scripture shows her as "pondering" the mysterious destiny of her adolescent child when she loses him on a family journey to Jerusalem. Mary "treasured all these things in her heart" (Luke 2:51). Tradition has understood these strange words to refer to the deep heartfelt identity between Mary and her son.

Over the centuries the idea of the intimacy between Jesus and his mother, symbolized in the twinned hearts, has evolved. In the seventeenth century John Eudes, drawing upon medieval writers Bernard of Clairvaux and Bernardine of Siena, revived an interest in the quality of Mary's heart and wrote compellingly about the identity of the two hearts. In the centuries following, devotion to Jesus's Sacred Heart and the Immaculate Heart of Mary, as well as the Two Hearts, grew in importance. Any number of nineteenth-century religious congregations took the paired hearts as their identifying emblem. During my travels

Hearts of Jesus and Mary and Holy Spirit, altar at Assumption of the Blessed Virgin Mary, Pasadena.

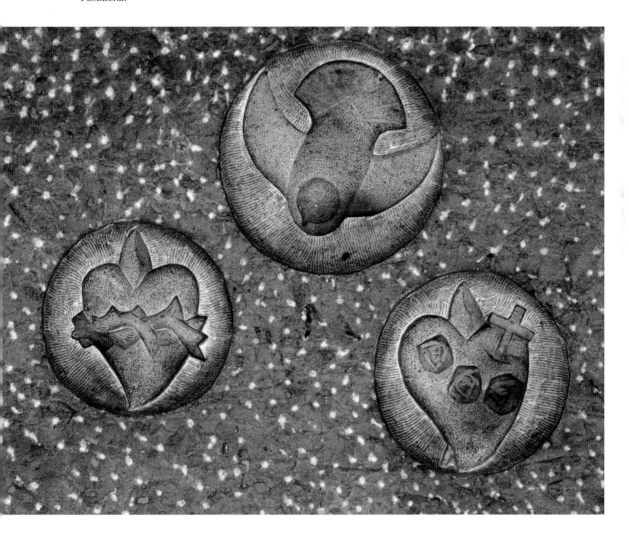

earlier this same week I had stopped by Holy Name of Mary parish, the handsomely appointed church in San Dimas in the pastoral charge of the Congregation of the Sacred Hearts of Mary and Jesus. There in the front courtyard I discovered the overlapping hearts of Jesus and his mother—the flower-encircled one with its protruding sword situated shyly behind its foregrounded thorn-encircled twin—emblazoned upon the cassock of a statue of St. Damien of Molokai, the congregation's canonized notable.

In several different locations the image of Our Lady of the Sacred Heart of Jesus, identifiable as a freestanding Madonna who hoists her young son up on one arm and cups in her other hand his Sacred Heart, is visible. This particular image, so explicit in depicting the intimate identity of mother and child, originated with the French Missionaries of the Sacred Heart founded by Fr. Jules Chevalier. He wrote of Mary's singular knowledge of the riches of Christ's heart and encouraged his followers to follow her as she would direct them to her son. The heart, of course, in both its biblical and classic theological articulations, stands for the whole of the human person not simply for feelings or emotions. The symbolic conjoining of hearts of mother and son speaks to the extent to which their deepest identities are perceived in the developing tradition to be one.

Despite the intimacy between Mary and Jesus that the tradition has imagined, the space that she occupies beside him has, however, not been uncontested. In fact, over the centuries it has been vigorously contested. A case in point is the early modern period when the Catholic Church, responding to its internal reforming instincts and prodded by the stinging critiques issuing from Protestant quarters, instigated pastoral reforms that assured that the cult of the Virgin would be theologically clarified to appropriately situate Mary in relation to her son. He was the source of salvation. She, for all her significance (and she was absolutely significant for the Catholic reform), was not to take his place. Her importance lay in her proximity to Jesus, and her role was to point the devotee toward him. For all the appeals to her under august titles, she was by ecclesial mandate emphasized as the model of the ideal human person.

Another massive wave of reorientation and reform that impacted all things Marian swept over the church following the Second Vatican Council in the 1960s. The nineteenth was a century of nearly universal Catholic devotional practice: at the century's close Pope Leo XIII consecrated the entire world to the Sacred Heart of Jesus and the branch of theology known as Mariology flourished. The religious engagement of

scores of lay Catholics took devotional form. Apostolic religious communities were named in a manner that reflected the current devotionalism.

But the liturgical and Biblical renewal movements of the early twentieth century that were accelerated by the Second Vatican Council began
to shift the ecclesial ground under which Mary sat. While devotions and
popular piety were not entirely dismissed, in seminaries and parishes
they were de-emphasized. Clergy and pastoral ministers emphasized
instead the Bible, the common liturgy, and the centrality of the person
of Christ. Devotions tended to fade back from central ecclesial focus.
In 1963 *Sacrosanctum Concilium*, the Constitution on the Sacred Liturgy,
offered to the church a Mary conceived primarily as "the most excellent fruit of the redemption" and "a faultless image" of that which
the church herself desires to be. Mary retired to her supportive place
behind her son.

Bronze statue of
St. Damien of Molokai,
Holy Name Church,
San Dimas.

The modest town of Guadalupe, at the far northern edge of the archdiocese (only New Cuyama, an hour's drive inland across the dry rangeland is farther) is the end point of my sojourn this day. Primarily a Spanish-speaking community of approximately fifteen hundred inhabitants, Guadalupe is recommended to travelers headed up Highway One as the home of the Far Western Tavern. Here the local rodeo queen's picture hangs in the window and prime sirloin, bull's-eye steak, and filet mignon from local ranches come in eight-, fourteen-, and twenty-ounce portions. My goal on this outing is to locate Our Lady of Guadalupe parish.

When I spy the church on the outskirts of town, I know I have found a treasure. The building is not large, but the entire side of the structure facing the street is decorated with an enormous hand-painted mural of a radiant Guadalupe and her supplicant Juan Diego. Roses cascade about the two figures and are mirrored by a live profusion of rose blooms in the garden beneath the mural. Inside I find a plethora of Marian images with one or two Fatimas surrounded by candles and an American flag, but mostly Our Lady of Guadalupe: on silk banners, in tile squares, in silver frames, with the Mexican flag, surrounded by *ex votos*, placed on lacey linen, tucked in her own side altar, enshrined in her own small chapel space. This, I realize, is *her* church.

I return two years later with Dorothy, eager to capture on film the arresting sight that had greeted me. To my dismay, the outside mural has been painted over: a clean coat of beige replaces what had been a technicolor mirage in the dry coastal desert. In contrast, inside the church there is a feast not only for the eyes but for all the senses, for we are here in December during the octave of Guadalupe's feast when Southern California's Catholic landscape is transformed into a lush floral extravaganza. Roses cascade down the steps of the altar, press into the side chapels, and festoon each of the dozens of images throughout the nave. Behind the church a hill of Tepeyac surmounted by a white plaster version of *la Virgen* is covered in blooms. But still I miss the folkart mural that greeted me on my first visit, the visual and unabashed public proclamation that this is her church. Of course, I am reading into this my own sensibilities. Still, whether this is the case here or not, it is true that the pastoral reorientation away from Mary toward her son continues to take place in the archdiocese. Indeed, it takes place all over the Catholic world with differing motivations prompting the efforts in different times and places.

At times the refocusing has been facilitated by the vision of a prelate. For example, Bishop Thaddeus Amat, the region's third bishop, felt that much of the style of California Catholicism was too tinged with the cultural remnant of its indigenous or Spanish-speaking populations. His sights were set on Rome, and he sought to bring his diocese into line with the aesthetic of the eternal city. Amat's concerns may have had less to do with the relationship between Christ and his mother than the relationship between colonial subjects and the colonizers but he was not alone in his era. He and other bishops focused on the way that the faith was actually practiced: the devotional, performative faith of this part of the world was in his view too local.

Of course, the process of what has been called the "enculturation" of the Gospel in the colonial New World has a long history. Thick are the Catholic annals that attest to the ongoing condemnation, suspicion of, theological argument about, or merely tolerance of devotionalism in colonial lands. This would include Marian devotion. Especially is this true of the varieties of popular religion that emerged in Latin America, Asia, and Africa, all areas of European colonization. For centuries, when the Catholic faith was exported along with European culture to non-Christian cultures, the concern has been to "inculturate" the Gospel. For centuries, from the European point of view, the early modern European form of Catholicism was the measuring stick by which one determined how much the Gospel really had "taken" in a foreign land.

Some added cultural flavor and some linguistic translation have always been assumed necessary to the process of moving from one culture to another. But there were limits to the extent to which adaptations were officially tolerated. Many popular devotions emerge from cultures in which European Catholicism was brought to an existing culture and an ensuing "appropriation" of the colonizing religious culture occurred. The result—often called "popular religion"—has frequently been viewed from the vantage point of the dominant colonial culture as a failure of evangelization or as much-too-syncretistic and, thus, a lesser version of the true faith.

I have to admit that during my L.A. study I have tended to conflate what are, from an official perspective, different categories of devotion. The current official Roman Catholic position on the varieties of practices I have encountered is discovered in documents promulgated by the Vatican itself. The 2001 *Directory on Popular Piety and the Liturgy: Principles and Guidelines* makes a distinction between what are termed "devotions" (defined as "various external practices, e.g., prayers, hymns, observances attached to particular times or places, insignia, medals, habits or customs") and "popular religiosity," "pious exercises," or "popular piety." The former—"devotions"—are favored and officially promoted. Examples of these include the Sacred Heart of Jesus, the

Angelus, First Fridays, the Immaculate Heart of Mary, the Miraculous Medal, Stations of the Cross, the rosary, novenas, relics, pilgrimage, adoration of the Blessed Sacrament, and veneration of the saints and the Holy Family.

The latter—"popular religiosity or piety"—which makes up much of what I find in Southern California's ethnic communities—is tolerated or sometimes discouraged for pastoral reasons. It is not however always clear to me where the difference lies except in history, origin, and perhaps official oversight. In other words, the practices that have been and are still officially promoted, theologically clarified, and authorized, most of which are the cumulative product of Western European religiosity, have official approval and are termed "devotions," while many of those that emerged from colonized lands have not received the same ecclesial support, and are labeled "popular religion."

It is a foggy midday in the oceanside city of Oxnard, the largest municipality in Ventura County, center of a thriving agricultural economy, major transit hub for Amtrak and Union Pacific railroad, home of two naval bases (Hueneme and Point Mugu), and a commercially important port. It takes an inordinate amount of time for Dorothy and me to thread our way down the congested, main thoroughfares south to Mary Star of the Sea parish. A modern building constructed in the shape of a star and flanked with glass windows etched to suggest the undulating waves of the ocean, Mary Star is presently staffed by the Augustinian Recollect Fathers. While we wait inside the sanctuary for Fr. Antonio Zabala of that community to cross the short distance between the rectory and the church itself, we note the small colorful wooden statuette mounted on a pedestal: a standing crowned Anglo Mary perches on a wave upon which rocks a small boat; her child faces the viewer while one hand holds an anchor and the other cups his mother's neck.

Fr. Zabala, originally from the Philippines, is a gracious host and answers my queries about the title, Star of the Sea, and Marian devotion in Oxnard. It has already been obvious that Guadalupe looms large in this region where Spanish is the language most commonly heard on the street. Not surprisingly, we have earlier this day discovered one of the most effusive of flower- and candle-rich feast day displays that I have encountered outside Our Lady of Guadalupe parish on Juanita Avenue farther inland from the port. The parish here at Mary Star of the Sea is about 40 percent Hispanic. It is 50 percent Filipino and just 10 percent "other." Reflecting this cultural makeup, the church sponsors three novenas: one for Guadalupe, beginning on December 3 and culminating on her feast on December 12; a nine-day celebration of *Simbang Gabi* during Advent (these are the popular dawn "Rooster Masses" from the Philippines that commemorate the pregnant Mary and Joseph's search for an inn in which to birth their child); and one every Wednesday in honor of Our Lady of Perpetual Help, again a Filipino favorite.

There is ample devotion to Mary in Oxnard. But all year, our host sighs, people want to be near her. The Protestants who criticize us certainly have ample ammunition in Marian devotion. Sometimes, he muses, she does seem like a goddess. People are constantly knocking at the rectory door, asking us to open the church so they can bring their offerings to her. I tell them that the Eucharistic Adoration Chapel is always open for them. He nods toward the enclosed space visible from the main sanctuary through the undulating glass. They should go there first. That is where I tell them they should go.

This Augustinian Recollect from the Philippines to whom I speak at Oxnard's Mary Star of the Sea worries that his parishioners have not got the theology right. He is not alone in his guarded opinion of popular devotion for that reason. His seminary training is in part responsible for this. I applaud the ongoing theological reflection that asks important questions about the assumptions that lie behind people's religious acts; and I am the first to cringe when, for example, it is reported that in the cathedral parish in Omaha votive candles are frequently lit to secure a Saturday Nebraska football game victory. Granted, on game day Husker football might aptly be described as the dominant religion of my adopted state. Be that as it may, it is incumbent on those in positions of responsibility to indicate the perimeters within which a given tradition sees itself as normatively functioning. At the same time, they might well examine those very perimeters and explore whether they accurately outline the tradition's deepest wisdom.

Pastoral reluctance to let Marian and other sorts of "popular religiosity" go unchecked is understandable from the perspective of the primary narrative of the Christian faith. It is Jesus the Christ in whom the believer finds atonement or "at-one-ment" with God. Theologians of all stripes from the most traditional to the most progressive would agree. That Mary should be divorced from that narrative and stand alone as a sort of archetypal goddess figure is theologically heterodox. If differing "Marys" associated with nations or movements or agendas fail to find their common identity in the scriptural young woman, Mary of Nazareth, this too would fall outside the integrity of normative doctrine. I have respect for this way of going about the common task of being church together. Yet I am loathe to be too quick to tidy up people's devotional instincts.

The pastoral approach I discover at Our Lady of the Valley in Canoga Park is somewhat different than the one at Oxnard's Mary Star of the Sea. Rather than focusing away from Marian piety, the attempt in this parish in the San Fernando Valley is to fold popular devotions, to which parishioners are much attached, into proximity with liturgy and communal prayer. In our conversation, Pastor Fr. Aldon Sison shares his opinion that the devotionally oriented community is best served by incorporating their devotional practices into parish life. I am invited to the 5:00 a.m. *Salubong* that will be enacted on Easter dawn at Our Lady of the Valley during which, in Filipino fashion, processions of men and women carrying life-sized statues of the risen Christ and his long-suffering mother will meet to the peals of Alleluia!

Arriving at the Canoga park parish early on the morning of the *Salubong*, I find mothers hovering over their children who are gussied up in angel outfits. There is much stirring around with lights and costumes. Fathers with video cameras wait nearby. When the sanctuary lights dim, the positioned spotlights come on and the drama begins: miniature angels file up the center aisle to the choir loft to the sung strains of Alleluia. A narrator reads aloud the biblical story of the three women coming to the tomb of Jesus after his crucifixion. All the while, a fellow who appears to be an organizer rushes in and out, motioning to people about when they are to enter, and parents keep popping up with cameras to photograph their haloed offspring. Eventually a young man wearing a black beard and wig appears as the risen Jesus and the crucial scene of the ceremony unfolds. Two life-sized statues, one of the risen Christ and one of his mother, are wheeled up parallel aisles onto the altar area. The black veil that has covered Mary's head during the long Lenten season is removed and replaced by a white veil. The children burst out in song.

This event, which at Our Lady of the Valley is clearly part cultural heritage and part religious devotion, is the prelude to the Easter Eucharistic celebration. Even with all the parental hovering and the chaos that accompanies children's theatricals, I am touched by the symbolism of the exchange of black and white veils, a touch that lends an intimacy to the resurrection narrative. The Eucharist that follows is delivered in English and Tagalog, and the homilist imparts a message that stresses the classic themes of the season. He reminds us that this Mass is held at dawn because Christ is the light in the darkness and tells a story of a wise man who, when asked when do we know when dark has turned to dawn? answers that it has become dawn when we can see one another as brothers and sisters.

This linking of popular devotion and liturgical ritual, this folding in of what might be deemed extra-liturgical practice into the common life of the parish is not unusual. A Eucharistic celebration generally follows the ubiquitous predawn *Las Mañanitas*, the devotion that wakes *la Virgen* with mariachi music in hundreds of sites all over the archdiocese on Guadalupe's feast day on December 12. And the devotional Holy Hours of the myriad Marian groups that flourish here, whether or not they are identifiably ethnic or culturally specific, are similarly linked. The very fact that the devotions do not stand alone attests to the ongoing theological and pastoral concern about what is to be considered central in the tradition.

Recent academic studies—historical, theological, sociological, catechetical—of the cult of Guadalupe and other forms of popular religiosity have wrestled anew with the question of the relationship between established theology and popular religiosity, especially in its expressions in the Mexican American, Tejano, Latino/a, and *"Nepantla"* communities. At the root of many of these is the insistence that Anglo-European expressions of Catholicism should not be considered "normative." Nor must other expressions be thought of as simply charming or exotic cultural kitsch best left to those originating communities. Instead, these heretofore "minority" forms of the faith are being mined for the rich insights that they contribute to the entire global Catholic enterprise. This idea is articulated forcefully by Latina theologian Ivone Gebara, among others, who makes the point that "normative" Western Catholicism, often understood as identical with the Gospel, is itself a product of centuries of European "inculturation."

Reacting against deep-seated prejudices about the theological validity of devotional practice, other scholars have focused upon popular religiosity's compatibility with or contributions to mainstream Eurocentric theology. Roberto Goizueta holds up the symbolic world encoded in *metizaje* that offers a relational theological anthropology that subverts the dualism that plague Western theologies—i.e., life vs. death, public vs. private, individual vs. communal. Goizueta simultaneously deplores the tendency of systematic theology to deprecate popular Catholicism and similarly critiques classic liberation theology's dismissal of the faith of the people as "otherworldly." He stresses instead popular Catholicism's capacity to affirm life and express the hope that is fundamental to any struggle for justice.

In a parallel move, Anita de Luna focuses on *religiosidad popular* among Tejanos (Texans of Mexican descent), and critiques catechetical methods that do not take seriously the distinctive, yet profoundly Catholic, Tejano religious synthesis. Rooted in a sense of Divine Providence, Tejano religiosity makes the crucified and vanquished Jesus central, sees Guadalupe as the Mother of the Dispossessed, celebrates hope in the midst of struggle, and is pervaded with a sense of intimacy with the saints. De Luna suggests that catechetical materials that are rooted in a more Eurocentric theological vision need to be rethought for use in Tejano communities.

Among Latino scholars, perhaps Orlando Espín has been most influential in arguing for the importance of doing theology "from the ground up." He notes that the ordinary way that doctrine has developed has been in and through popular religious practice. For Espín the disjunction between "official" and popular religion is a false one and, although he affirms that academic theology and the magisterium should play a hermeneutical role in doctrinal development, he believes that the entire church is in fact charged with the task of transmitting the Gospel. The intuition of the people moved by the Spirit thus must be a primary resource for theology.

There is a complicated dialectic in the tradition between the spontaneous outpourings of many hearts and the careful distinctions, caveats, and definitions of official stewards who try to pinpoint one center around which the many may become one. All of this is part of Mary's story. The scriptural witness and the cumulative theological formulations of her identity surely must be pivotal. At the same time, my own experience of her does not always so neatly conform to this theological ideal. Nor do the moving testimonies of some of those devotees who entrust me with their stories. Not that I want to abandon my equally strong sense of Mary as the *point vierge*, the still point of convergence in the bewildering diversity of experiences, peoples, cultures, rituals, languages, philosophies, spiritualities, and aesthetic orientations that make up this global Catholic communion. She is, for me, the utterly single-hearted, and simple (in the truest sense of that term) place where irreconcilable opposites are held in delicate and fruitful tension. She is at one and the same time properly perceived in her relationship to her son and yet also independent of him.

As I muse on Mary and Jesus, their intimacy as well as their contested relatedness (rather, I think, like many mothers and sons), I am taken back to another conversation, held on a weekday morning at St. Francis of Assisi in the Silver Lake district due west of downtown. The conversation brought to the fore my sense that Mary, and the devotional practices that enshrine her, do not necessarily divert attention away from the central foci of faith. Instead, they may reach into a place in the human heart where deep truths abide, a place where our common humanity and our grounding in divinity is intuited. The symbolism that proclaims that the hearts of Jesus and his mother are intertwined expresses this intuition.

My partner in Silver Lake that day was Fr. Richard, a well-read Franciscan of about my own vintage. As we chatted over mugs of hot coffee in the small latticed patio behind the rectory, he expressed impatience with some of the devotions that his ethnically diverse congregation persisted in practicing. These were, in his eyes, often not grounded in Scripture and doctrine, and he referred me to the eighth chapter of the Constitution on the Church in which Mary is described as the instrument of incarnation through her openness to God and thus model for the church. (This was, I was duly informed, an idea grounded in Franciscan/Scotist teaching). But at St. Francis, he continued, the Marian devotion was "too cultural," too "possessive," with too much emphasis put on national or ethnic Madonnas. Even though the church had tried to make Guadalupe universal, Fr. Richard bemoaned the fact that she was not. Instead she was identified in most people's minds with Mexico. As my conversation partner rolled his eyes, he opined that devotions were often so sentimental, and sometimes gruesome. "Goodness, the things I have been asked to bless!" he exclaimed.

But then his demeanor slowly changed as he began to recount the story of a young Latino man who came to him during the First Gulf War and asked for a blessing. When the fellow opened his shirt a full-sized image of *Nuestra Señora de Guadalupe* was revealed. "Why do you have Guadalupe on your chest?" the Franciscan queried. "Because I am being deployed to Desert Storm and I want her always to be close to me" came the response. My priest companion paused and stared into his coffee cup, lost in the remembered moment. "I blessed the tattoo," he said quietly.

December 12 Guadalupe Display, Our Lady of Guadalupe Church, Guadalupe.

Chapter 17

New Creation
Nuestra Señora de Guadalupe

Then I saw a new heaven and a new earth; for the first heaven and the first earth had passed away, and the sea was no more. And I saw the holy city, the new Jerusalem, coming down out of heaven from God, prepared as a bride adorned for her husband.

—Revelation 21:1–2

On Sunday, December 8, 2009, my itinerary takes me into East Los Angeles and the area known as Belvedere. This is the same area that *The Tidings* in March of 1954 designated "Mary's Land" because its largely Latino population had such intense veneration for the Virgin of Guadalupe. The region is more culturally diverse now but still is chosen for the annual archdiocesan Guadalupe procession that occurs on the weekend closest to her feast on December 12. This year, for the third year in a row, it is a Torch Procession: representatives from Los Angeles have traveled to Mexico City and received a torch lit at the famous Guadalupe shrine which has been carried overland back to the archdiocese along with two huge painted pilgrim images of Juan Diego and the Lady of Guadalupe. These have been peregrinating for the last month from one selected parish to another for the veneration of the faithful. Today the pilgrim images, along with the still brightly shining torch, will lead the festive parade along Caesar Chavez Boulevard east to the sports stadium of East Los Angeles College where Cardinal Roger Mahony will preside over the annual Eucharistic celebration.

I arrive early enough to park my rental car in a parking garage on campus and walk back up the parade route to be present at its beginning. The skies are uncharacteristically cloudy with threatened rain but participation is not at all inhibited by this fact. People are clustered on the sidewalks along the parade route, and costumed participants mill about in the adjoining streets waiting for the signal to turn the corner and take their place in line. Eventually the milling morphs into an actual procession, and the long parade of colorful floats and devotional groups moves by my curbside station at an erratic pace: there are mounted-horse cavalries; troops of Aztec dancers performing intricate steps to the pulse of drums; flags representing the nations of Central, South, and North America (for as much as Guadalupe is identified with Mexico, Pope John Paul II's proclamation of her as Empress of the Americas extended her patronage); billowing incense; costumes trembling with feathers and glittering with sequins and sunlit mirrors; parish confirmation classes and *Guadalupana* groups; young women dressed as *la Virgen* riding past on the beds of pickup trucks; amplified rosary prayers; Mexican flags; sombreros; family clusters in indigenous Guatemalan dress; and banners welcoming *La Paloma Blanca*. At the head of the festive chain a wheelchair-bound devotee carries the flaming torch followed by heavily festooned vehicles bearing the pilgrim images. As the elegant framed painting of Guadalupe passes, the bells of La Soledad Church begin to peel.

Unlike the well-oiled production of the annual Rose Parade that will be broadcast on national television one month from now from Pasadena, this Guadalupe procession betrays its nature as essentially a religious festival lovingly managed by volunteers. It is deeply moving precisely for that reason. It takes almost two hours for the straggling crowds to gather from the parade route into the college stadium and for the various groups to circle the stadium and settle into their assigned spots. This year's theme echoes the words spoken to the Aztec convert Juan Diego by the beautiful lady who appeared to him at the sacred hill of Tepeyac, words that echo those recorded in Scripture as spoken by the Angel Gabriel to a young Jewish girl: "Be not afraid"; "*No tengas miedo*"; "Do not fear." The homilist addresses the thousands of Catholics seated in the banked bleachers and weaves the Advent and Guadalupe messages together while alluding to the economic downturn, the vicissitudes of life, the shadow of deportation, and the severing of families occasioned by recent immigration raids. Do not fear. Be not afraid.

If Los Angeles is the city of the Virgin, it is even more emphatically the city where the Virgin of Guadalupe reigns supreme. For days before the official December feast, innumerable observances are in progress: novenas, triduums, rosaries, and processions are held in every corner of the archdiocese. On the day itself the metropolitan basin is awash in roses, millions and millions of roses. Even the smallest parish is fragrant with the sweet scent of the bouquets that Guadalupe's people bring to her and lovingly place at her feet. Rows of tall glass votive candles flicker amid the blooms, and Mylar balloons bob above.

Massive processions like the East Los Angeles one are not the only large-scale Guadalupe parades that take place in the archdiocese. I love the story shared with me about the origins of the one that occurs annually in Santa Barbara. That picturesque seaside town is famous as a tourist destination and for its wealthy residents. Apparently a number of years ago a local procession was proposed to the regional bishop who was skeptical about whether it would attract the area's particular constituents. He gave approval nonetheless. The route was planned to process from one of the city parks up State Street, the central business thoroughfare, to Our Lady of Sorrows parish. State Street consists of a several-mile-long tile-roofed concentration of trendy bistros, bookstores,

December Guadalupe Procession, Santa Barbara.

art galleries, banks, and boutiques. The Guadalupe procession led by Aztec dancers commenced on the appointed evening and as it wound its way up the thoroughfare, people gradually came from the side streets and joined the gathering throng. Even more strikingly, scores of devotees emerged from the kitchens and back rooms of the bistros and shops and knelt on the ground as images of their beloved Virgin passed by. The public street had become a place of prayer.

In fact, the entire archdiocese during the first weeks of each December is a place of living prayer. From agricultural New Cuyama to the high deserts of Palmdale to the shipping and oil economies of Long Beach, to suburban San Fernando Valley, to the central-city garment industry districts with their dense hives of immigrant workers, to the "Platinum Triangle" of Beverly Hills, Bel Air, and Holmby Hills, to the crowded barrios of East L.A., the archdiocese is at prayer. Guadalupe's feast day invariably begins with the celebration of *Las Mañanitas*, the ritual of song that wakes the Virgin on her special day. By four or five o'clock in the morning every mariachi band in the region is costumed and strumming away. To her devotees the music is as familiar as the Christmas carols that the rest of the Catholic population will lift up in a few weeks. The numerous times I have attended *Las Mañanitas* in different parishes throughout the basin I have always been struck with the astonishing beauty of the lyrics of the songs and with the affectionate manner in which *la Virgen de Guadalupe* is addressed.

> *Que linda esta la mañana en que vengo saludarte,*
> *venimos todos con gusto y placer a felicitarte*
> *El dia en que tú naciste nacieron todas las flores,*
> *y en la pila de bautismo cantaron los ruiseñores.*

She is *paloma, morenita, dulce madre, bonita indita, bella flore, la duena, virgencita*. Entering her presence through the imaginations of those who love her is like entering a paradisiacal garden. Always the story of her appearance, preferably referred to as an encounter, is retold. The narrative is familiar to most Catholics, at least in outline: Juan Diego, an Aztec peasant recently converted to the imported faith, was hurrying down Tepeyac hill to hear Mass in Mexico City on Saturday, December 9, in the year 1531. Bird song alerted him to the presence of a beautiful woman who asked him to go to Bishop Juan de Zumárraga in the city and request that a temple be built where she stood. Although Juan Diego demurred, feeling unworthy of such a task, she insisted so he completed his errand. The bishop was skeptical, but after being visited several times by the insistent peasant, himself prompted by the lady who kept appearing, Zumárraga finally demanded that Juan Diego ask a sign of the lady who had said she was the mother of the true God. The peasant, however, was distracted in these efforts because his uncle had become critically ill.

On Tuesday, December 12, the worried nephew was concerned enough to get a priest for his dying uncle, and, in order to bypass the insistent lady, avoided the Tepeyac hill. Despite this, she intercepted him, assured him that his uncle was cured, and calling herself "Holy Mary of Guadalupe" asked him once again to go to the bishop. Convinced of her words, he asked her for the requested sign. Although this was neither the season nor the place where roses grew, she directed him to a spot where in fact fresh roses were blooming. Gathering them into the lap of his rough *tilma,* he returned to Zumárraga. As Juan Diego unfolded his cloak, the roses fell out and he was startled to see the bishop and his attendants kneeling before him: the life-sized figure of the Virgin Mother, just as he had described her, was glowing on the cloth of the *tilma*. The bishop agreed to build her a temple and led a procession to the site to honor the Mother of God.

Guadalupe Story Textile, Our Lady of Guadalupe Parish, Santa Paula.

Scholars proceeding from every imaginable disciplinary angle have mined the rich lode of popular devotion in ways that illuminate the piety that surrounds the Guadalupe story. Timothy Matovina, in his study that concerns the Guadalupan devotion in San Fernando Cathedral in Texas, insists that the adherence to Guadalupe is much more than an expression of Marian piety. It is a complex reality that can either be transformational or conversely validate the social, political, ecclesial, or gender status quo. In his view it encompasses "patriotism, political protest, divine retribution and covenant renewal, ethnic solidarity and reinforcement of social hierarchy." In terms of women's roles, Matovina's research reveals that *la Virgen* serves contradictorily as "a model of female domesticity and virginity" as well as "an inspiration for women to be active in the public arena and demand equality, a plea for miraculous intervention and an inducement for greater participation in the church's sacramental life." Such devotion also provides a ritual arena for Mexicans and Mexican Americans to forge and celebrate an alternative world, one in which powerful realities like exile and racism could be defined and reimagined.

Other scholars have considered the function that religious devotion plays in the lives of displaced or marginalized persons in ways that illuminate the Guadalupe experience. Thomas Tweed's *Our Lady in Exile* focuses on the Miami shrine of *Nuestra Señora Caridad del Cobre* where Cuban Americans flock to express their "diasporic nationalism" and make sense of themselves as displaced people. Tweed emphasizes the importance of place (i.e., the shrine) in which groups vie with one another in constructing and inhabiting worlds of meaning. Cuban exiles who visit the shrine express their attachment to their natal landscape and culture through narrative theologizing, institution building, and ritual practices in which our Lady of Charity has become the leading mythic character. Tweed's observations translate well to an understanding of the Guadalupan devotion of hundreds of thousands of Mexican immigrants living in the L.A. basin.

Themes of justice and liberation and the inbreaking of God's reign that upends the status quo are the focus of other scholarly inquiries. Mujerista theologian Jeanette Rodriguez stresses Guadalupe's power to sustain and fortify Mexican American women. Nancy Pineda-Madrid, while warning that the Guadalupe can have detrimental effects for women if used to subjugate and silence, avers that she is also liberative in allowing women the space to speak as subjects in cultures that generally deny them such space. Lara Medina and Gilbert Cadina, who consider the Day of the Dead rituals, and Karen Mary Davalas who studies the long-practiced performance of the *Via Crucis* pageant in Chicago's Pilsen neighborhood, contend that rituals such as these are the vehicles through which Mexicanos/as react against and transform the oppressive realities of their experience as a minority group and publicly bring to awareness their own condition of suffering. Again, these observations shed light on what happens in December in Los Angeles.

Insights such as these can illuminate the Guadalupe experience from anthropological, sociological, and theological perspectives. But I am as much struck by the experience of simply being in the presence of this most revered of images. While I am aware of the possible limitations of Guadalupan piety, I find her people and her presence have a resonance well beyond these functional or sociological consequences to which most of these studies point. Latino theologian Virgil Elizondo enables me to articulate this sensibility in a compelling way. The earliest text of the numinous encounter between the beautiful lady and the Aztec convert is recorded in the Nahuatl language in the *Nican Mopohua*. Elizondo has rendered a translation of this text and a commentary that captures some of the deep abiding devotion that Guadalupe elicits. He makes much of the new emergent culture symbolized in Guadalupe, a *mestiza*, who is neither an Indian goddess nor a European Madonna. She is something new. On the one hand she reflects the Madonna of the conquerors but her iconography was also easily read by the Aztec people. The eyes, face, hands, the stars on her cloak, the sun in front of which she stands, the moon under her feet, the black band of pregnancy that girds her waist, the bird song and flowers in her tale: all these were symbols that spoke to the indigenous of a divine visitation and of a new creation, a new harmony between cultures that gave hope to the natives (Juan Diegos all) who were both "most abandoned and most beloved." Guadalupe is for Elizondo the first truly American person. As such, she is the mother of the generations to come who will synthesize the richness from their parent cultures and construct a society in which the barriers between peoples are broken. She is in this sense a harbinger of the new creation.

Although the region around Los Angeles was under Spanish and then Mexican rule well before it became part of the United States, once it was incorporated the Mexican Catholic population, both those who were in residence and those who continued to arrive from the south, tended to be ministered to in separate congregations. The result was the creation of Mexican chapels, small set-apart communities that served the Spanish-speaking populations of a larger parish. In part this was a pragmatic solution to linguistic realities but it was also a sign of the cultural distain of the European church hierarchy and the latent racism of the American settlers who came to dominate California politics.

Guadalupe Sanctuary, a gem of a sacred enclave hidden away in a maze of one-way and interrupted streets in East Los Angeles, has a somewhat different origin. In the 1930s the Belvedere area became a center for Mexican refugees fleeing religious persecution in their homeland. Msgr. Vincente Guzman was the founder of this remarkable place that opened in 1929. His dream was to create a sanctuary similar to the Basilica of Guadalupe in Tepeyac. A modest version of the Mexican shrine was completed in 1941. Today it may not rival that gigantic sanctuary in size but in sheer beauty the Guadalupe Sanctuary has few equals. Spanish was, and remains, the sole language in use here.

Our Lady of Guadalupe and Juan Diego,
Guadalupe Sanctuary, East L.A.

I speak on the phone to Fr. Delgado who has been in residence at the sanctuary since 1984 and is responsible for much of the interior decoration. He is a bit cautious when I ask permission to photograph and relents only when I identify myself as a practicing Catholic. I am actually touched by his attitude in the sense that in his mind this place is sacred, a space not merely of architectural or ornamental interest, but meant to be set aside for worship. To photograph it in any other spirit would be to violate its integrity. The sanctuary is in fact filled with palpable presence, even more than most churches I have visited. It is a space saturated with prayer. Upon entering I am greeted by a soft light that shimmers off all surfaces: the ornate gold-and-white textured walls reminiscent of Southwestern decorative tin ceilings reflect the daylight filtered through boldly hued clearstory windows. Stained-glass biblical scenes and images of the Virgin favored by Mexican Catholics are here: *Nuestra Señora del Sagrado Corazón, Sagrado Familia, Nuestra Señora del Carmen, Nuestra Señora del Perpetuo Socorro, Nuestra Señora de los Dolores, la Madre de la Luz.* Guadalupe herself is enshrined in statuary as well as on murals, and a large gilt-framed painting of her familiar iconic form is featured behind the main altar. Side chapels contain clusters of *ex votos*; in one a random collection of crutches, small silver replicas

Sanctuary, Guadalupe Sanctuary, East L.A.

December Guadalupe Display, Our Lady of Guadalupe Church, Oxnard.
Candles, Our Lady of Guadalupe Church, Oxnard.

of legs, curled photos, and dried flowers attest to gratitude felt for answered prayers.

The Guadalupe Sanctuary is constantly bustling with nine weekend and two weekday Masses, plus additional services on Holy Days. But this is not the only site where constant devotional activity occurs or where Our Lady of Guadalupe dominates the scene. During our December trip to coastal Oxnard, Dorothy and I stop by the spacious parish named for Guadalupe. In this hallowed space several men kneel in adoration before the Blessed Sacrament while a woman hobbles the length of the center aisle on her knees. This parish is under the ministerial auspices of the Missionaries of the Holy Spirit, and oversized posters featuring photos of founder Fr. Felix Rougier and mystical authoress Concepcion Cabrera de Armida, the spiritual mother of the Mexican congregation, are on display in the narthex. Everywhere else *la virgen morena* is evident: painted larger than life and framed by folk-design flowers and birds above the altar, appearing to Juan Diego on the right wall, revealed on his *tilma* to the bishop on the left, featured as a free-standing statuette on the altar steps and as a three-dimensional display surrounded by banks of votive candles outside the church.

Poignant and powerful Guadalupana stories abound in the city named for the Lady of the Angels. I hear them wherever I go. In Sun Valley, Fr. Richard Zanotti, a Scalabrian priest, takes the time to visit in one of the anterooms of his parish office before accompanying me about the grounds of Our Lady of the Holy Rosary, one of the string of Marian parishes threading through the San Fernando valley corridor. The parish over which he presides is at this point perhaps 80 percent Hispanic: mainly Mexican, Salvadoran, Costa Rican, and Honduran. He smiles as he speaks of the fervor of devotion that will, he admits, have to change some of his pastoral practice. This past year he had gone to bed after the scheduled December 12 festivities but was kept awake by the thirty or so singers and a ten-piece *banda* that continued to play well into the night. As the evening was cold, he rose and let them into the church where they continued their devotions. Next year, he informed me, the church would stay open all night.

Among the sights Fr. Richard shows me at Our Lady of the Holy Rosary is a reproduction of the Guadalupe image in a side chapel into whose frame parishioners have tucked wallet-sized photos of their loved ones, primarily young men and women in uniform. He tells us that he first hung the picture as a permanent display when, following a Guadalupana celebration, he provided a young man with a ride home. During their conversation, the fellow showed him a Guadalupe holy

card given to him by his mother along with a prayer for his safe journey as he left Mexico. The priest soon discovered that the young man's
present home was a freeway underpass. Luckily he was able to provide
help for the boy, but it left him shaken. The picture in the chapel stands
as a reminder of all the sons and mothers whose slender hopes are held
in the heart of *la Virgen Morena*.

These and dozens of stories that I hear stay with me. They are only
a minute percentage of the stories that people carry in their hearts and
share with their neighbors, stories that bring them back into the presence
of *la Virgin Morena*. Elizondo wants to point to this *Virgen* as a symbol of
the new creation, a new *mestizaje*. Classic theological statements about
Mary also hint about her symbolic function as the new creation: as the
human person fully realized through redemption in Christ. I would not
disagree with either of these insights. I discover, however, that there is
something experienced in the presence of Guadalupe that transcends
even these ways of viewing her. To be in the presence of *la Virgin Morena*
is not to be transported to some ethereal afterworld nor solely empow-
ered in the struggle for justice. It is to be brought—through the paradisiacal allusions, the multisensory evocations of beauty, floral profusions,
sweet strains of song, tender invocations, and maternal warmth—into
the presence of an exquisite beauty that allows all that is most human,
most earthly, and most cherished to bloom to its fullest potential and to
expand even beyond its fullest potential. To be with her is to truly grasp
the depth of what has been spoken: "*No tengas miedo;*" "do not fear."

It is December 12 at Dolores Mission in east Los Angeles. The mission is diminutive, and on a day as popular as this the pews are crowded.
Pressed in between two family groups waiting for the festive Mass that
follows the vigil to begin, I find myself looking about at the blooms
enveloping the Guadalupe shrine and the loopy ribbons of green and
red paper cutouts that hang from the rafters. There is, however, one odd
item that I cannot explain: a lump of folded fabric placed on the low step
before the altar. During the homily Jesuit Michael Kennedy identifies
the mysterious object. These were the sole possessions of a young man
found dead in the barrio just days before. Undocumented, he apparently arrived from south of the border not long before in search of work.
No one could identify him. Having no papers and no history here, he
now had no name. Like so many impoverished and desperate young
people he had run afoul of someone or something in the gang- and
drug-infected neighborhood. The staff at Dolores Mission is not completely unaccustomed to bodies being picked up on the streets of east
L.A., but this one has a special resonance. The tiny bundle on display

contains everything that was found with the body: a limp sweatshirt, a pair of worn jeans, scuffed sneakers. These items are placed before the altar in part to honor this boy, with his dreams and hopes common to any boy and with his dignity as a child of God. Kennedy gives him the name Juan Diego because the Juan Diego of the Guadalupe story was like him a poor man, marginalized by the colonial society that had co-opted his native land and faith. The peasant Juan Diego was to all appearances a "nobody," and yet the Guadalupe narrative puts him at the center of the story. The young man whose memory is held before us in the shape of the slight, folded fabric bundle, whose relatives from his native land will probably never know what happened to him, is for those of us gathered, Juan Diego. And perhaps more importantly, it is understood in this troubled yet blessed barrio neighborhood where we gather on this cool December morning that we are the ones that the Virgin of Guadalupe holds up and calls her own.

Guadalupe Display, December 12, Our Lady of Guadalupe Church, Guadalupe.

Chapter 18

First Fruits
Asunción

Come, O faithful, let us approach the tomb
of the Mother of God, and let us embrace it,
touching it sincerely
with the lips and eyes and forehead of the heart.
Let us draw abundant gifts of healing grace
from this ever-flowing fount.

—The Orthodox Feast of the Dormition,
  Vespers Orthros, *Ode 9*

As someone who has understood her conversion to the heritage-rich Catholic faith as in part a search for spiritual familial roots in a rootless modern culture, my family of origin is surprisingly rooted in the geographical space of Southern California. A meander over the grassy knolls of Inglewood Memorial Park, one of L.A.'s largest and earliest cemeteries, brings this truth home. It was here, during the fourth year into my Marian pilgrimage that my husband, our young adult children and I, plus a cluster of extended family members, stood at this gravesite in the Utopia parcel and watched as the slight rectangular box that held my mother's ashes was placed in the upturned ground next to the site where my father lay. On either side of her, the markers revealed the long-time California presence of the various members of the McFadden and

Santa Maria del Camino, Fernando Aritze, SJ, artist, Dolores Mission, Boyle Heights, East Los Angeles.

Hyde families, my maternal Canadian-born ancestors who purchased this family plot in the 1920s.

Interestingly, just across the narrow road in the parkland is the Hildale parcel, purchased in 1924 by my paternal great-grandmother for the use of the Somers/Wright clan. At the time of the purchases, neither family was aware of the other's existence. In fact, it was not until my parents met and married in 1937 that the two lines intertwined. Nor, that I am aware of, did any of them have much contact after standing for a formal photo at the time of the wedding. Yet here they all rest, a few hundred yards apart.

The Virgin Mary, I am often reminded in the course of these past six years, is many things to many people. Yet perhaps she is most enduringly a presence who speaks to the universal human concern about living and dying well. After all, her most familiar prayer begins with a greeting—Hail Mary—and ends with a plea for her presence at the moment of our passage into the mysterious realm beyond death.

> Holy Mary, Mother of God,
> pray for us sinners
> now and the hour of our death.

She is thus invoked, not because she is perceived as a powerful intercessor, although for many she is certainly that. Rather she is called upon because she is the one human being to whom tradition has perennially looked to see a human life lived in correspondance with the promise of the Good News. Two Marian dogmas, the immaculate conception and the assumption, carry in them the seeds of this hope. These are the mysteries, explored through the often opaque language of theology, that bracket the beginning and end of the life of the woman known as Mary.

The immaculate conception was not an idea imposed by the ecclesial hierarchy but one gestated within the womb of the Christian community for a long time before its final dogmatic definition in 1854. The ancient icon entitled the "Kiss at the Golden Gate" is a visual artifact that hints of the early church's intimation of Mary's special place in the mystery of salvation. The icon depicts Mary's long-barren parents Joachim and Anne at their moment of meeting after they have been told of the impending birth of a child. The icon anticipates by centuries the medieval controversies between the Franciscans (pro) and Dominicans (con) that swirled around the idea of a special dispensation at the time of Mary's conception. Popular opinion supported the Franciscans. During the Catholic Reformation, this idea became a rallying cry against the Protestant reduction of the Virgin to a mere scriptural referent. She was of course always understood to be conceived by ordinary means but, to use the rather formal language of Pius IX's 1854 dogmatic announcement, Mary was preserved from original sin by a "singular grace and privilege" given her by God "in view of the merits of Jesus Christ" as Redeemer of the human race. Like every other human being, Mary needed the redemptive benefits of Christ; but in anticipation of what God did for all through Christ, she alone was preserved from original sin "from the first moment of her conception."

Western visual expressions of this dogma have changed over the centuries. If the "Kiss at the Golden Gate" places Mary's unique conception in the context of human relationality, representations allowed after the reforms of the early modern period show Mary standing alone. She is generally depicted as in heaven in the form of a young woman who either looks up in awe at or bows her head to God. The moon rests beneath her feet and a halo of twelve stars surrounds her head, a reference to the woman clothed with the sun from the Book of Revelation (12:1–2).

The assumption of the Blessed Virgin, which like the immaculate conception had a long popular history before its formal definition, is the Western variant of the beloved Eastern teaching on the Dormition (Falling Asleep) of the Virgin. The popular development of the idea in the early church generated several narrative arcs that include the announcement of Mary's death, the apostles bidding her farewell, her dormition or falling asleep (*koimesis*—which remains the Eastern Orthodox iconographic version), her funeral, her assumption into heaven, and her coronation by the Trinity.

In the Western church, the assumption became the doctrinal focus. This dogma is summarized in the claim that, having completed the course of her earthly life, Mary was assumed body and soul into heavenly glory. Popular Western artistic expressions of this mystery tend to mirror early modern representations that show the Virgin lofted heavenward on billowing clouds. Again, the spiritual significance for us is not simply that we might admire the unique privileges that the Virgin Mother received through her son, but that we too might hope for an end, a completion that, whatever its specifics, is like being enfolded in familiar arms, lifted in joy, coming home.

It is true that these official Marian dogmas and their insertion into the liturgical calendar as feasts of obligation leave some American Catholics either bemused or cold; such dogmas are felt to distance her from us. As tastes in holy exemplars have changed, sizable segments of the population look for models other than the Virgin, certainly not a woman characterized as "perfect" or "sinless," to define their faith lives. As I am fond of telling my spirituality students at the university, we Americans like our saints and hero/ines "warty," we like them imitable rather than unimitable, and we want to know how they struggled with their own human quirks and shortcomings. This makes them companions rather than wonderworkers. With Marian devotion downplayed in some pastoral quarters in favor of her companionate role, honoring

Mary as immaculately conceived and assumed into heaven may place her outside people's frame of reference. Certainly it can put her outside the reach of immediate identification.

There has never been a time at a pastoral conference or workshop when, showing Dorothy's photos of Los Angeles Marys to participants, that the out-and-out favorite has not been *Santa Maria del Camino* found at Dolores Mission. The painting depicts Mary as a young Latina with her serape-slung infant as she walks barefoot along a road, the skyline of downtown Los Angeles, seen from the vantage point of the barrio, looming in the background. The preference for this Mary speaks of the desire that our models be earthy and human scale.

It is true as well that there is an uncomfortable legacy, still felt acutely among many women of the pre–Vatican II era, of the immaculate Mary as the ultimate good girl: the one who never speaks up, never makes waves, always obeys, who would never slow dance with boys or wear patent-leather shoes, the unattainable and ultimately oppressive, symbol of unquestioning female compliance. A generation of feminist scholars have mounted a critique against this Mary. Marina Warner became famous for puncturing the image of the virginal and set-apart Mary, who is "alone of all her sex," because she disparaged the real experience of women. Rosemary Radford Ruether and Elizabeth Schussler Fiorenza struggled to liberate Catholic theology and biblical studies, respectively, from the cultural patriarchal stranglehold that they saw as distorting the Gospel, thus liberating Mary from that prison. Other scholars have raised searching questions about the cult of the Virgin and its possible misogynist uses: how Mary's virginity been been misused to denigrate ordinary human sexuality and to characterize marriage as a lesser vocation than celibacy; how the priggish Mary supported ideas of female inferiority and social subordination; how long-standing dualistic thinking pitted Mary and Eve against one another as representatives of the pure transcendent feminine vs. the sexually carnal female.

Critiques such as these have encouraged Latina scholars to look closely at the way in which female dualisms function in Latin American cultures. Nancy Pineda-Madrid, building on the ideas of Chicana feminist scholar Norma Alarcón, observes that the beloved Guadalupe theophany so often identified with peace, hope, and consolation, is routinely contrasted in the Mexican/Chicano cultural tradition with Malinche who represents the evil, subversive woman. Pineda-Madrid points out that these two binary symbols have been used to judge women and exert control

Assumption Mural, Assumption of the Blessed Virgin Mary, Pasadena.

over their lives. By encouraging women to follow "Marianismo" (this pairs with "machismo") which extols the self-sacrificing, submissive, and self-subordinating Mary, Mexican American women are encouraged to be vicarious martyrs. Women can ignore only with peril such critiques of the abuses of the symbol of Mary. As with any theological construct, multiple interpretations are possible, and the temptation is very real for cultural, national, political, sexist, racist, or classist ideologies and prejudices to co-opt what at root should be a redemptive vision.

Yet for all that Mary has been interpreted in ways that subjugate or belittle, other contemporary scholars have plumbed the deep archetypal wisdom encoded in her personhood. Elizabeth Johnson, Rosemary Radford Ruether, Sally Cunneen, and others have reclaimed Mary for a new egalitarian world and church. It is especially Mary of the *Magnificat* (Luke 1:46–55) who excites these scholars to pick up their pens because she anticipates her son's ministry and, in continuity with the great prophets, proclaims the reversal of entrenched social and political relationships. American theologian Aurelie Hagstrom has explored the figure of Mary in terms of Christian hospitality, and Brazilians Ivone Gebara and María Clara Bingemer have proposed an understanding of Mary that seeks to reconcile her human significance as Mary of Nazareth with her transcendent universality as the Mother of God. Their compatriot Lina Boff has explored Mary as the feminine of God, the image of total and radical divine love expressed in human relationships in either masculine or feminine modalities, love that creates the possibility of radical openness to the Spirit and solidarity with the poor.

Additionally, recent European feminist commentary opens new vistas upon ancient ideas like the immaculate conception. English theologian Tina Beattie conceptualizes Mary as the missing feminine dimension of the incarnation and argues that the fertile, corporeal, and maternal aspects of the Christian story have been neglected in favor of a life-denying religion based on the sacrificial relationship between a Father God and his crucified son. Drawing and expanding on French psycholinguistic theorists, she develops a theological narrative that accommodates sexual difference within its vision of redemption and thus has significance for women. Beattie sees the possibility of the recreation of the world in Mary who is the necessary middle ground between heaven and earth where the human and divine embodied in Christ is born. This English theologian looks to a "parousia in which woman's redeemed personhood is revealed as the one who bears the image of God in a way that is different from but equal to the godlike persona in man." The immaculate conception figures prominently in her vision.

I love these new reflections which expand our sense of the mystery at the heart of the figure of Mary. While I do not intend to minimize the significance of official Mariological formulations that are designed to keep the fragile paradoxes of Christian faith in balance, the Virgin, both as she is experienced in the sprawling city under the mantle of her protection and as she emerges in the thoughts of contemporary theologians, is more generous than any carefully constructed definition could suggest. With all her splendor, power, and humility, earthiness and sublimity, subversive intercession, capacious embrace of the lost and forgotten, her bold maternal sheltering, profound attentiveness to the recesses of the heart where the Word is spoken, her almost reckless generosity, great dignity and even greater simplicity, her knowledge of all that is most searingly painful and most soaringly joyful in life—this Mary is the mirror of our most expansive selves. If she is the first fruit of the abundant harvest, so thus are we.

Artistic representations of the immaculate conception and the assumption are visible throughout the archdiocese. Among my favorite of the former are two found at *La Purisima Concepcion* parish in Lompoc. Founded in 1787 by Fray Fermin Francisco de Lasuen as *Mission*

Adam and Eve and Mary as Second Eve Window,
La Purisima Concepcion Church, Lompoc.

La Purisima Concepcion de Maria Santisima, the historic parish is a link in the chain of Franciscan missions that snake up the Pacific coastline. By 1845 the church had lost control of its mission lands which were eventually turned over to the U.S. Park Service as historical sites. The parish continued to function and was built at the present site in 1910. This was followed by the erection of another church building directly across the street in 1955. The two defining images of the immaculate conception that appear on each of these structures are fascinating.

Hoping to photograph the interior of the older one, Dorothy and I find ourselves in conversation with a young woman from the parish office. We ask about the advertised parish Triduum for the feast of Guadalupe and she admits that she is just learning about this Virgin. She hails from Guatemala where Guadalupe is not the Virgin of choice, and the American culture in which she now finds herself is primarily Mexican American. The girl unlocks for us the fabulously decorated older structure with its turquoise and rose striped design. Inside, the space has been fashioned into an auditorium. High up on the east wall is a remnant from this space's former life as a liturgical space. Within

Immaculate Conception,
La Purisima Concepcion
Church, Lompoc.

an ornate arched stained-glass window is an ecstatic looking Mary, an indigo cape swirling about her as she is hoisted aloft on cumulous billows by a trio of pudgy cherubs.

The *Purisima Concepcion* that announces her patronage as a bas-relief on the front face of the newer brick building across the street is quite different. The artists of the mid-twentieth century fashioned a more accessible yet less realistic Mary here. This immaculate one's posture, emphasized by the angular drape of her red underdress and the oval of her blue cape, is straight. She stands barefoot, hands pressed in prayer, upon a crescent moon perfectly balanced by two mirror-image cartoon figure angels. Behind her on a field of baby blue tiles shine a circular gold-tile nimbus and symmetrically arranged golden stars. The two contrasting depictions reveal changing aesthetic tastes and artistic styles. They may also say something about the shifting theological landscape of the twentieth century. From an exalted height above the human condition, Mary is shown to descend to meet us as companion and model for our emulation.

The Assumption of Our Lady was the name first given by Franciscan fathers Crespi and Gomez to the region along the scenic southernmost part of California's Central coast just a day's horseback ride north of the site later deemed *El Pueblo de Nuestra Señora de los Angeles del Rio Porciúncula*. The two padres were traveling with the 1769 expedition of Gaspar de Portola when they arrived at the picturesque site nestled between the Pacific and the Transverse Mountains coastal range. There they celebrated the Eucharist in the company of expedition soldiers and local natives. So when in 1954 a new Catholic church was built in the region's chief city, by then known as San Buenaventura, it was natural that the parish should be named for Our Lady of the Assumption.

On a sunny weekday Dorothy and I exit one of the Ventura offramps from Coast Highway/101 and pull into the parking lot of the rectangular modern church with its monumental exterior mural that commemorates the 1769 Mass. The interior of Our Lady of the Assumption reveals itself as high-ceilinged and light-filled; shafts of refracted color filter through a set of angular stained-glass windows. However, it is the twenty-eight-foot-high mural of the assumption towering above the altar that commands attention. Created by Millard Sheets of Claremont College for the 1954 structure, the mural is unlike any I have seen before. Although she echoes the traditional cloud-lofted image, this assumption feels different, less an abstract idea and more a gossamer vision. Here she appears as an elongated greenish-blue and reddish-orange draped figure, hands clasped in prayer and head cast slightly downward with a wistful gaze. She is held aloft by at least a dozen airy angelic figures, the pointy edges of whose filmy wings seem to strike the air and propel her upward in flight.

The two theological mysteries that bracket Mary's life—the immaculate conception and assumption—can be decoded. They need not spiritualize her out of her humanity nor place her on a lofty pedestal too high for mere mortals. These Marian mysteries speak to the primal hope of the human heart. As an idea that concerns our own spiritual reality, the immaculate conception speaks to the potential human capacity to bear divine life into the world, to be Mothers of God. It also speaks of the preparation necessary for such a task. We must be engaged in the conscious process of becoming spacious and attentive enough so that the Divine Word that longs to be born through us can be. Mary, the immaculate one, signals our human capacity for such a thrilling possibility. The assumption is an affirmation of our divinely originated creature-hood, of the goodness of the created beings that we are. It is an idea that gathers up the whole of us, and tells us that, fragile bodies and searching spirits alike, we may be welcomed back into the hidden ground of love from which we once came.

I am brought back in the midst of these reflections to the memory of my parents' gravesites at Inglewood Memorial Park. I am not often able to visit the Utopia and Hildale family plots to wonder again at the strange coincidence of both my father's and mother's relatives purchasing plots across the road from one another in the mid-1920s. But when I am, I find myself grateful for the meditation it affords: grateful that I, fashioned of the material elements of this earth home, will someday be returned to the sweet soil itself. Grateful that I will be in a sense mingled with those dear people from whom I come and to whom I belong. Grateful too that love is stronger than death, that this little human life I have been given is not simply the zero sum of its various parts, but, even with my personal shortcomings, it is in fact much, much more. It is Mary who has shown me so.

Assumption, Our Lady of the Assumption Church, Ventura. Artist: Millard Sheets.

Marian Altar (Cuban Our Lady of Charity, Our Lady of Perpetual Help, *Nuestra Señora de San Juan de los Lagos*, Our Lady of Fatima), *Nuestra Señora de Guadalupe* Church, El Monte.

Epilogue

Return

I pack up after a marathon last-chance Los Angeles visit. The Mary manuscript is close to being a first draft. Sunday morning I head down to the western section of the city to a Eucharist a colleague has suggested I attend. St. Agatha's Parish Family (that is the name they give themselves) is just off the Santa Monica Freeway near La Brea. The direction in which my car is headed brings back vague childhood memories of family visits to my maternal grandfather's home on the south side where my mother grew up and her parents produced a neighborhood newspaper. The area today is largely African American, a fitting neighborhood for the Gospel Mass that I anticipate.

The functional rectangular church that serves a Spanish-speaking as a well as an African American congregation is especially festive as decorations are still up from yesterday's Guadalupe festivities. A papier maché hill of Tepeyac with a Guadalupe statuette atop is swallowed in bouquets of bright flowers. To the left of the altar and beside an image of the Peruvian mulatto saint Martin de Porres, patron of social justice, hangs a painting of a black Madonna and child.

If I wanted an extroverted liturgy to engage me on this overcast morning, I have come to the right place. St Agatha's is alive with arriving parishioners hailing friends. In fact the first organized event is a full five-minute meet-and-greet in which the parish family mingles. As a guest I am not left out of the welcoming fray. A leader of the choir, wearing a purple satin stole over a black robe, makes mention of the decorations and comments that Guadalupe's message is a simple one applicable to any day: God is the God of all people. And, he adds, that is what St Agatha's is all about. The progressive Black and Anglo congregation affirms his sentiment.

The readings for the third week of Advent, known as Rejoice Sunday, set the tone, but it is clear that rejoicing is nothing new at St Agatha's.

The Gospel choir launches into a jazz version of "O Come, O Come Emmanuel" and to the wail of a saxophone riff the Mass commences. Fr. Joe, the charismatic preacher with a recognizably Nigerian accent, responds to the assembly's applause with a message of rejoicing. God is always good! Don't accent the negative! Don't be afraid! God has got your back! I leave St. Agatha's having been hand-clasped by dozens, including the gregarious woman on my left sporting a black velvet tam and saucer-sized rhinestone earrings, and the somewhat less extroverted woman on my right draped in traditional African dress.

What has it meant, this homeward leaning pilgrimage, this late midlife return to origins, this "trip to Bountiful?" What of this sprawling metropolis, this sun-drenched, car-clogged maze of asphalt and steel spread out upon adobe soil, creosote-covered hills, tar-flecked beaches, low wetlands, and arid deserts? A place at once tougher and more economically troubled than the place in which I grew up, perhaps no longer the utopia of frontier dreams that drew my forebears from Canada and Massachusetts. And who is she who presides over this city: this miraculous Virgin, model of virtue and the reflective life, symbol of the ecclesial community, maternal comfort, sister, mother, queen, protector, reconciler who inclines to the littlest and least, who offers consolation and aid, who marks off boundaries, or who gathers all under her sheltering cloak?

When I stand at a slight distance from her in the company of systematic and pastoral theologians, historians, anthropologists and sociologists, art and architectural scholars, theorists of all types, I see her as a remarkable cultural artifact, a religious symbol of great significance. At somewhat closer proximity, with pastors, pastoral associates, ministerial staffs, catechists, and religious educators, she reveals herself as a fount of faith and a pastoral conundrum with which to wrestle. She raises all the questions which the American Catholic Church is bringing into consciousness: What is our place in the vast multicultural Catholic world? How do we think about "popular devotion"? Do "ethnic" celebrations that at present are often compartmentalized belong to all of us as members of a global tradition? What are contemporary Latino/a theologians and other non-Eurocentric theologians suggesting about this? What is the relationship between the vivid, deeply rooted faith of people expressed primarily in a devotional mode and our common worship? Is the "cosmo-vision" of the Hispanic and Filipino faithful different from that held by most post–Vatican II Americanized Catholics? How does one relate to the apocalyptic Virgin of Fatima if one relates primarily to a Mary who is "always our sister"? Will second-generation immigrants "assimilate" or will they shape U.S. Catholicism into something other than what is it has become since Vatican II? What does pastoral ministry look like in this context? What prejudices might exist in the dominant church's leadership that privilege some forms of faith expression and suspect others? Why is this? What is the role of para-liturgical observance in parish, diocesan, and personal faith? These questions linger with the memory of my many conversations.

Closer still, with those who look to her as model of the Christian life or who find her a companion on the journey, sister and friend, I find both inspiration and welcome. Standing among the fingerers of beads, the bearers of flowers, and those who entrust to her their keenest hopes, I find myself, simply, at home. There is something about the way my conversation partners describe their relationship to Mary, no matter what their perspectives on her or on life generally. There is a poignant tenderness, a palpable hopefulness that they communicate. There was no real reason why my interviewees should have been so forthcoming, so revealing of the depths of their love in my presence except that their relationship to her was one of deep affection and in me they recognized a similar love. They spoke not in a catechetical mode nor to impress or inform me but out of their deepest longing and most audacious hopes.

She seems to represent, or even more provocatively, to be present at, some deep resilient space in the human heart in which newness and possibility germinate. She thus is the ecclesial *point vierge*, the virgin point beneath our fears and views and ego-driven ideologies, a virgin space not in the sense of absence of ambiguity nor pure because it denies the vagaries of the human heart with its cruel capabilities, but a space so deep and poised at the edge of unknowing and the un-sayable, that what remains is silence. This is the point where strangers are encountered in the full mystery of their otherness; a point where tensions meet and, while not resolved, still create new possibilities. This is the threshold where the divine Other invites. At this point the heart breaks open and what remains is mercy, grace, forgiveness, reconciliation, hope, and beauty.

These thoughts rattle around in my head as I wedge my suitcase into the trunk of my rental car next to the plastic bags of trinkets from Olvera Street I will carry home for Christmas. Pulling out of the driveway of my Silver Lake lodgings, on impulse I decide to swing by the Cathedral of Our Lady of the Angels one more time en route to the Burbank airport. When I arrive, it is mid-afternoon and I enter the sanctuary through the great bronze doors above which that barefoot, mixed-race girl in a simple shift, her hair pulled back into a plait at the nape of her neck, extends her arms in generous welcome. As usual hush-voiced tourists are wandering about the perimeter of the elegant interior. I have heard this structure caustically referred to as "Taj Mahony" or as "Our Lady of the Angles" by detractors critical of the cardinal for the expense of the construction or by those whose aesthetic tastes lean to the medieval rather than the modern. But I love this hospitable expanse, love the way I have seen so many diverse groups of people drawn in to inhabit it comfortably yet reverentially. The space itself seems an invitation, as openhearted and welcoming as the young girl cantilevered above the bronze doors.

I seat myself in one of the blond wood pews just beneath the larger-than-life tapestry image of St. Francis de Sales who, along with dozens of other saintly figures on either side of the aisles (whose visages are in fact those of local residents), faces forward toward the altar space gathering me and the curious visitor alike into the embrace of a communion much greater than ourselves. I breathe in the sense of the place. Lofty diagonal panes of alabaster filter light into the sanctuary and direct my eye to the six-paneled hanging halfway up the face of the wall before me. The patterned mélange of tans, browns, and grays at first glance are recognizable only as an abstract design. Viewed more intently, the designs gradually reveal themselves as the outlines of a vast street map. In fact, I see now, these are the streets of the present day *Pueblo de Nuestra Señora de los Angeles*, Mary's own city, that spread like an intricate web behind the cardinal's chair and swirl together into concentric circles around a subtle graphic. I peer forward and gradually make out the words the graphic spells: God will dwell with them.

Sources and Suggested Reading

Chapter 1: The Pilgrimage Road

Franciscan Herald Press published a multivolume set in honor of the first Marian Year: *The Marian Era: World Annual of the Queen of the Universe*, 10 vols. (1960–1970). The final volume features a selection from earlier volumes. Historical treatments of the figure of the Virgin Mary are readily available. These include the standard by Hilda Graef, *Mary: A History of Doctrine and Devotion* (reissued: Ave Maria Press, 2009). Newer studies include the three-volume one by Bertrand Buby, SM, *Mary of Galilee* (New York: Alba House, 1994–1996), and Miri Rubin, *Mother of God: A History of the Virgin Mary* (New Haven: Yale University Press, 2009). Sally Cunneen, *In Search of Mary: The Woman and the Symbol* (New York: Ballantine Books, 1997) and George H. Tavard, *The Thousand Faces of the Virgin Mary* (Collegeville, MN: Liturgical Press, 1996) provide additional insight into the Marian phenomenon. See also the elegantly produced book by Caroline Ebertshäuser, Herbert Haag, Joe H. Kirchberger, and Dorothee Sölle, *Mary: Art, Culture and Religion through the Ages*, translated by Peter Heinegg (NY: Crossroad Herder, 1997) as well as the equally elegantly produced *Divine Mirrors: The Virgin Mary in the Visual Arts*, ed. Melissa R. Katz (Oxford: Oxford University Press, 2001). Both have informative essays by noted scholars.

A useful resource for recent magisterial statements about the Virgin Mary is *Mary in the Church: A Selection of Teaching Documents* (Washington, DC: USCCB Publishing, 2003). It includes the 1973 statement by the U.S. bishops, Pope Paul VI's 1974 exhortation, Pope John Paul II's 1987 encyclical, and his 2002 apostolic letter. For a historical discussion of Catholic devotion in America that includes Marian practices, see *Habits of Devotion: Catholic Religious Practice in Twentieth-Century America*, ed. James M. O'Toole (Ithaca, NY: Cornell University Press, 2004). J. D. Crichton, *Our Lady in the Liturgy* (Collegeville, MN: Liturgical Press, 1997) is a handy guide to the official liturgical place of the Virgin Mary, the primary way many Catholics encounter her. Terrence J. McNally, *What Every Catholic Should Know About Mary: Dogmas, Doctrines and Devotions* (Xlibris, 2009) is a layperson's handbook with common critiques of the Marian tradition guiding its exposition. Mary Ann Zimmer, ND, has written a readable survey of Mary in Catholicism, *Mary 101: Tradition and Influence* (Liguori, 2010). On the revival of interest in traditional devotion, see *Awake My Soul: Contemporary Catholics on Traditional Devotions*, ed. James Martin, SJ, (Chicago: Loyola Press, 2004). For a modern Marian conversion story, see Beverly Donofrio, *Looking for Mary, or, The Blessed Mother and Me* (Penguin Books, 2000).

The journal *Marian Studies*, which is the annual publication of the Mariological Society of America, produced at the Marian Library at the University of Dayton, is an excellent source for scholarly articles on the topic. For all things Marian online, one can always be referred to the Mary Page run by the Marianists at the University of Dayton. It is available at http://campus.udayton.edu/mary//marypage21.html.

I have explored the concept of Mary as *le point vierge* more fully in my Madeleva Lecture of 2010. This is published under the title *Mary and the Catholic Imagination: Le Point Vierge* (Mahwah, NJ: Paulist Press, 2010).

Chapter 2: Our Lady of Refuge

Segments of this narrative previously appeared in a monograph entitled *Refuge, Warrior and Peacemaker: Faces of Mary in Los Angeles* published by Friends of the Santa Barbara Mission Archives in 2007.

Historical information in this section is taken from the small monograph by Arthur D. Spearman, SJ, *Our Lady: Patroness of the Californias* (Santa Clara, CA: Santa Clara University, 1966); *Art and Faith in Mexico: The Nineteenth-Century Retablo Tradition*, eds. Elizabeth Netto, Calil Zarur, and Charles Muir Lovell (Albuquerque: University of New Mexico Press, 2001); and an article on Our Lady of Refuge parish in Long Beach, California, from *The Tidings* (Archdiocese of Los Angeles), May 13, 2005. See also Kurt Baer, *Painting and Sculpture at Mission Santa Barbara*, Monograph series, vol. 3 (Washington, DC: Academy of American Franciscan History, 1954) and *Mexican Devotional Retablos from the Peters Collection*, ed. Joseph F. Chorpenning, OSFS, (Philadelphia: Saint Joseph's University Press, 1994).

Chapter 3: Lady of the Angels

California became a part of Mexico in 1821 following its independence from Spain. In 1848, at the end of the Mexican-American War, California was purchased in accordance with the Treaty of Guadalupe

Hidalgo, thereby becoming part of the United States; Mexico retained the territory of Baja California. Los Angeles was incorporated as a municipality on April 4, 1850, five months before California achieved statehood.

On the conflict about the city name, see the *Los Angeles Times* story by Bob Pool, "City of Angels' First Name Still Bedevils Historians," March 26, 2005. On this and for more background on the early religious history of the area, see Michael Engh, SJ, *Frontier Faiths: Church, Temple and Synagogue in Los Angeles 1846–1888* (Albuquerque: University of New Mexico Press, 1992).

Other useful sources include J. Thomas Owen, "The Church by the Plaza: A History of the Pueblo Church of Los Angeles," pt.1, *The Historical Society of Southern California Quarterly* 50 (March 1960): 5–28; Diana Serra Cary, "Our Lady Queen of the Angels," *St. Anthony Messenger* (August 1962): 8–11; Jack Miles, Peggy Fogelman, and Noriko Fujinami, *Robert Graham: The Great Bronze Doors for the Cathedral of Our Lady of the Angels* (Venice, CA: Wave Publishing, 2002); and Michael Downey, *The Cathedral at the Heart of Los Angeles* (Collegeville, MN: Liturgical Press, 2002).

The older Our Lady of the Angels statue in the present cathedral was originally commissioned in 1961 from Florentine artist Eugenio Pattarino for the Minor Seminary in Mission Hills by Archbishop James Francis McIntyre.

For a recounting of the life of Fr. Virgil, see Mario T. Garcia, *Padre: The Spiritual Journey of Father Virgil Cordano* (Santa Barbara, CA: Capra Press, 2005).

Chapter 4: Our Mother

On Our Mother of Good Counsel, see Marion Habig, OFM, "Pope, Counsel, Reunion and Mary," pp. 23–26, *The Marian Era: World Annual of the Queen of the Universe*, vol. 4 (Chicago: Franciscan Herald Press, 1963).

For changes in the doctrine about limbo, see the International Theological Commission's document titled *The Hope of Salvation for Infants Who Die Without Being Baptized* (April 20, 2007).

The 1939–1990 *History of the Chinese Center in Los Angeles* was self-published in 1990. The more highly produced sixtieth anniversary booklet, *St. Bridget Chinese Catholic Center*, was published in 2000, available at the parish.

For an enlightening discussion of the medieval Mary as esteemed for her bodily, maternal role, see Donna Spivey Ellington, *From Sacred Body to Angelic Soul: Understanding Mary in Late Medieval and Early Modern Europe* (Washington, DC: Catholic University of America Press, 2001).

The light-skinned European canons of beauty that dominate Marian images, no matter the culture in which they function, are certainly questionable. Among many others Timothy Matovina, Ada Maria Isasi-Diaz, and Robert Orsi have commented on the way that popular devotional practices often provide a sanction for patriarchal and colonial cultures. Representative of Asian feminist critiques is *Off the Menu: Asian and Asian North American Women's Religion and Theology* edited by Rita Nakashima Brock, Jung Ha Kim, Kwok Pui-lan, and Seung Ai Yang (Louisville: Westminster John Knox, 2007).

The story about Loyola Marymount appears in longer form in my *Seasons of a Family's Life: Cultivating the Contemplative Spirit at Home* (San Francisco: Jossey-Bass, 2003).

Chapter 5: Immaculate Heart

A different version of this chapter was given as a paper at the 2011 Annual Conference of the Mariological Society of America and will appear in an upcoming issue of the Society's journal, *Marian Studies*.

The work Ruth refers to is Elizabeth A. Johnson, *Truly Our Sister: A Theology of Mary in the Communion of Saints* (New York: Continuum, 2003).

On the ministries of the early IHMs in California until 1940, see Marian Sharples's 1963 unpublished manuscript in the Immaculate Heart Community archives, *All Things Remain in God*. Because many of the principals in the conflict are still alive, documents relating to the disbanding of the Immaculate Heart Sisters held in the archives of the Archdiocese of Los Angeles are not available for public use. For a summary of events from the point of view of the present leadership of the ecumenical community, see Anita Caspary, *Witness to Integrity: The Crisis of the Immaculate Heart Community in California* (Collegeville, MN: Liturgical Press, 2003). For another perspective, see also Francis J. Weber, *His Eminence of Los Angeles: James Francis Cardinal McIntyre*, 2 vols. (St. Francis Historical Society, 1997). For historical newsprint articles that disapproved of the IHM decisions, see the April 15, 1971, issue of *The Wanderer* and the October 24, 1971, issue of *Twin Circle* located in the Mrs. Sutton Marian Clipping File at the Marian Library, University of Dayton.

The Mary's Day celebrations were the brainchild of Sr. Corita and other sister-artists in the late 1950s and 1960s. On the founding of the Daughters of the Most Holy and Immaculate Heart of Mary, see the essay from the Immaculate Heart Community archives by Juan Manuel Lozano, *The Immaculate Heart Sisters: A Historical and Doctrinal Study on*

Their Mission and Spirit in the Church (Claretian Private Printing, 1974). Other sources include *Book of Customs for the Daughters of the Most Holy and Immaculate Heart of Mary* (Province of California, 1914) and *Manual of Prayers, The California Institute of the Sisters of the Most Holy and Immaculate Heart of the Blessed Virgin Mary* (Los Angeles, 1947).

The quoted unpublished speech by Dr. Alexis Navarro, IHM, was given July 23, 1998, at Mount St. Mary's College, Los Angeles, California. It was supplied with permission by Dr. Navarro.

On early modern changes in the Virgin's image, see Donna Spivey Ellington, *From Sacred Body to Angelic Soul: Understanding Mary in Late Medieval and Early Modern Europe* (Washington, DC: Catholic University of America Press, 2001).

For a look at Mary's heart through a mid-twentieth-century lens, see John F. Murphy, "The Popes and the Immaculate Heart" in *The Marian Era: World Annual of the Queen of the Universe*, vol. 3 (Chicago: Franciscan Herald Press, 1962), 65–67, 88–91.

A contemporary perspective on the Immaculate Heart is offered by Sarah Jane Boss, "The Immaculate Heart of Mary: Visions for the World" in *The Church and Mary: Papers Read at the 2001 Summer Meeting and the 2002 Winter Meeting of the Ecclesiastical History Society*, edited by R. N. Swanson (Woodbridge, Suffolk, UK: The Boydell Press, 2004), 319–48.

Chapter 6: Our Lady of Hollywood

The quoted poem at the beginning of the chapter is from Armando P. Ibañez, OP, *Wrestling with the Angel: A Collection of Poetry*, rev. ed. (Los Angeles: Pluma Productions, 2001), 35. The August 28, 2006, *New York Times* article by Charlie LeDuff on the Hollywood nuns is found at www.nytimes.com/2006/08/28/US/28album.html?_r=0.

On the Our Lady of Covadonga image, see Msgr. Francis J. Weber, "The Madonna of Hollywood," *The Tidings* (Archdiocese of Los Angeles), November 26, 1982.

Today Mount Hollywood Congregational continues its progressive ministry. It identifies itself as "the first integrated church in Los Angeles . . . [with a membership that] represents a wide diversity of races, cultures, religious backgrounds and sexual orientations . . . which believe[s] in the power of peace and work[s] for nonviolent solutions to local, national and international problems." Its website is located at www.mthollywood.org.

On Fr. Peyton's crusade, see Richard Gribble, CSC, *The Life of Patrick J. Peyton, CSC: American Apostle of the Family Rosary* (New York: Crossroad, 2005).

Chapter 7: Mystical Rose

Sources consulted for this chapter include Meinard Geiger, OFM, "Our Lady in Franciscan California," *Franciscan Studies* 23:2:2 (June 1942): 99–112; Lawrence Scrivani, SM, "The Legion of Mary," in *Marian Studies* 54 (2003); *The Marian Dimension of Christian Spirituality: The 19th and 20th Centuries (Book III)* (Mariological Society of America: 2003), 102–16; and William M. Thompson, Jr., *Art of Home Visitation: Frank Duff's Priorities: The Legion Apostolate in America* (pamphlet, Marian Library Pamphlet Collection). For a recent biography of Frank Duff, see Finola Kennedy, *Frank Duff: A Life Story* (London/New York: Burns and Oates/Continuum, 2011).

The quotation at the start of this chapter is from Dante's *Paradiso*, 23.73–74.

The Litany of Loreto, although officially approved for liturgical use by Pope Sixtus V in 1587, continues to develop. New advocations having been added since that time, generally in response to some development in Mariology, in celebration of her protection, or as promoting values with which she is associated. These include Queen of the Most Holy Rosary (1675, after the Battle of Lepanto against the Turks), Queen Conceived Without Original Sin (1883, in response to the promulgation of the dogma of the Immaculate Conception), Mother of Good Counsel (1903), Queen of Peace (1917, at the time of the First World War and the Fatima apparitions), Queen Assumed into Heaven (1950, the promulgation of the dogma of the Assumption), Mother of the Church (1980, under John Paul II whose Marian devotion was central to his theology), and Queen of Families (1995: John Paul II was also a keen promoter of devotion to the Holy Family).

Pope John Paul II with his apostolic letter of 2002 *Rosarium Virginis Mariae*: On the Most Holy Rosary added the five Mysteries of Light to the traditional fifteen decades of the rosary.

On the rosary especially as it developed in the early modern period, see Nathan D. Mitchell, *The Mystery of the Rosary: Marian Devotion and the Reinvention of Catholicism* (New York: New York University Press, 2009).

The online Mary Page published at the University of Dayton has a useful article on the development of the title of "Rosary" to represent the prayer beads and the prayers spoken as they are fingered. See http://campus.udayton.edu/mary/questions/yq2/yq346.htm.

Readers interested in Marian prayers and their interpretation over the centuries might also enjoy Nicholas Ayo, CSC, *The Hail Mary: A Verbal Icon of Mary* (Notre Dame, IN: University of Notre Dame Press, 1994).

The 2008 *L.A. Times* article about the Mojave Desert apparitions can be found at articles.latimes.com/2008/may/13/local/me-virgin13.

Chapter 8: Star

On the Doheny family, consult Margaret Leslie Davis, *Dark Side of Fortune: Triumph and Scandal in the Life of Oil Tycoon Edward L. Doheny* (Berkeley: University of California Press, 1998) and Mary Ann Bonino, *The Doheny Mansion: A Biography of a Home* (Los Angeles: Edizioni Casa Animata, 2008).

On the study at Mary Star of the Sea in San Pedro, see Mary Clark Moschella, *Living Devotions: Reflections on Immigration, Identity, and Religious Imagination*, Princeton Theological Monograph Series (Eugene, OR: Pickwick Publications, 2008). Also useful is Moschella's *Ethnography As a Pastoral Practice: An Introduction* (Cleveland, OH: Pilgrim Press, 2008).

On the 1963 naming of St. Louise de Marillac church in Covina, see the *The Tidings* (Archdiocese of Los Angeles), December 4, 2009, from the Mrs. Sutton clipping file, Marian Library, University of Dayton.

Chapter 9: God-Bearer

The Eastern Rite Catholic Church's liturgical feasts that have Western analogues include January 6, known as the Holy Manifestation of the Divinity of Our Lord (Epiphany), the Purification of the Virgin on February 2 (in the West, the Presentation), the Visitation of Mary to her cousin Elizabeth on June 23, the Dormition of the Virgin on August 15 (the Assumption on the Western calendar), the Nativity of the Blessed Virgin Mary on September 8, the Patronage of the Most Holy Queen, Mother of God and Ever-Virgin Mary on October 1, the Maternity of St. Anne on December 9 (in the West, the Immaculate Conception celebrated on December 8), and the Nativity of Our Lord on December 25 (observed in consort with the Western church rather than the Eastern Orthodox churches which celebrate this mystery at Epiphany).

The contemporary scholars mentioned here are Charlene Spretnak, *Missing Mary: The Queen of Heaven and Her Re-emergence in the Modern Church* (NY: Macmillan Palgrave, 2004), esp. pp. 101–5 and Sarah Jane Boss, *Empress and Handmaid: On Nature and Gender in the Cult of the Virgin Mary*, (London/New York: Cassell, 2000) and *Mary: The Complete Resource* (London/New York: Continuum, 2007).

On the Byzantine pastor's comments, see *The Tidings* (Archdiocese of Los Angeles), April 27, 1962. This article is located in the Mrs. Sutton Clipping File, The Marian Library, University of Dayton.

Chapter 10: Perpetual Help

On Lourdes, see Ruth Harris, *Lourdes: Body and Spirit in the Secular Age* (NY: Viking Press, 1999) and Suzanne K. Kaufman, *Consuming Visions: Mass Culture and the Lourdes Shrine* (Ithaca: Cornell University Press, 2005).

On Ryoko Fuso Kado and his Lourdes grottos, consult *Encyclopedia of California's Catholic Heritage, 1769–1999* (St. Francis Historical Society, 2000), 427.

The Website of the Philippines national shrine of Our Lady of Perpetual Help is found at baclaranovena.org.

Chapter 11: Miraculous Virgin

On the Bicol Virgin, see *Ina and the Bikol People: A Journey of Faith* by Jose Maria Carpio (Archdiocese of Caceres, Philippines: 2002).

On Our Lady of Mount Carmel, see *Our Lady of Mount Carmel Church in Montecito, 1856–1988* (Los Angeles Public Library rare book room) and Joseph Cevetello "The Brown Scapular of Our Lady of Mt. Carmel," vol. 6, *The Marian Era: World Annual of the Queen of the Universe* (Franciscan Herald Press, 1965), 55–62, 111.

Among sources helpful in understanding Latino/a faith, see Roberto S. Goizueta, "Making Christ Credible: U.S. Latino/a Popular Catholicism and the Liberating Nearness of God," in *Practicing Catholic: Ritual, Body and Contestation in Catholic Faith*, edited by Bruce T. Morrill, Joanna E. Ziegler, and Susan Rodgers (NY: Palgrave Macmillan, 2006), 169–78. See also his "The Symbolic World of Mexican American Religion" in *Horizons of the Sacred: Mexican Traditions in U.S. Catholicism*, edited by Timothy Matovina and Gary Riebe-Estrella (2002), 119–37. These quotes are from pp. 123–25.

Peter Brown, *The Cult of Saints: Its Rise and Function in Latin Christianity* (Chicago: University of Chicago Press, 1981), is helpful for grasping the cosmo vision of early Christianity, which continues to inform Latino/a devotions.

On the power of images, see David Morgan, *The Sacred Gaze: Religious Visual Culture in Theory and Practice* (Berkeley: University of California Press, 2005); *The Lure of Images: A History of Religion and Visual Media in America* (NY: Routledge, 2007), 260–62, and his *Visual Piety: A History and Theory of Popular Religious Images* (Berkeley: University of California Press, 1998). See as well Colleen McDannell, *Material Christianity: Religion and Popular Culture in America*, (New Haven: Yale University Press, 1995). See also my introduction to and the essays in "Religion and the Visual" in *Journal of Religion and Society*, Supplement 8, v. 14 (2012), edited by Ronald Simkins and Wendy M. Wright and found at http://moses.creighton.edu/JRS/toc/current.htmlA.

On black madonnas, see Stephen Benko, *The Virgin Goddess: Studies in the Pagan and Christian Roots of Mariology* (Leiden: E. J. Brill, 1993) and Sarah Jane Boss, "Black Madonnas" in *Mary: The Complete Resource*, ed. Sarah Jane Boss (London: Continuum, 2007), 458–75.

Chapter 12: Lady of Victory

The introductory quotation is from Louis de Montfort, *True Devotion to Mary*, trans. Frederick Faber (Rockford, IL: TAN Books, 1985), 132.

A portion of the text of this chapter appeared in *Weavings* as "To Be Alert: A Rumination," *Weavings* 22, no. 6 (2007): 6–14.

Sources for this segment include James Alison, *Raising Abel: The Recovery of the Eschatological Imagination* (NY: Crossroad, 1996); Linda B. Hall, *Mary, Mother and Warrior: The Virgin in Spain and the Americas* (Austin: University of Texas Press, 2004).

E. Ann Matter, "Apparitions of the Virgin Mary in the Late Twentieth Century: Apocalyptic, Representation, Politics," *Religion* 31, no. 2 (2001): 125–53; Sandra L. Zimdars-Swartz, *Encountering Mary: From La Salette to Medjugore* (Princeton: Princeton University Press, 1991); William Christian. Jr., *Apparitions in Late Medieval and Renaissance Spain* (Princeton: Princeton University Press, 1989) and his *Visionaries: The Spanish Republic and the Reign of Christ* (Berkeley: University of California Press, 1996); Chris Maunder, "Apparitions of Mary" in *Mary: The Complete Resource*, edited by Sarah Jane Boss (Oxford: Oxford University Press, 2007), 424–57; and Nicholas Perry and Loreto Echeverria, *Under the Heel of Mary* (London/NY: Routledge, 1988).

On the Kolbe group, see Rosella Bignami, "Fr. Luigi Faccenda, OFM Conv, and the Kolbean Marian and Missionary Charism" in *Marian Studies* 54, *The Marian Dimension of Christian Spirituality: The 19th and 20th Centuries (Book III)* (2003): 146–55. See as well Judith Marie Gentle, *Jesus Redeeming in Mary: The Role of the Blessed Virgin Mary in Redemption According to St. Louis Marie Grignon de Montfort* (Montfort Publications, 2003).

On the Catholic Church in Vietnam, see *A World History of Christianity* edited by Adrian Hastings (Grand Rapids, MI: William B. Eerdmans Publishing, 1999), 3369ff. When the apparitions occurred in Vietnam, the first depictions of Our Lady of La Vang were fashioned after the French image of Our Lady at the basilica of Notre Dame des Victoires. Gradually, as the faith was inculturated, her image became more Vietnamese. See also *Keeping Faith: European and Asian Catholic Immigrants,* eds. Jeffrey M. Burns, Ellen Skerrett, and Joseph M. White (Eugene, OR: Orbis Books, 2000).

On traditionalist devotion, see Paula M. Kane, "Marian Devotion Since 1940: Continuity or Casualty?" in *Habits of Devotion: Catholic Religious Practice in Twentieth-Century America*, ed. James M. O'Toole (Ithaca: Cornell University Press, 2004), 89–130.

La Conquistadora in Santa Fe, known as Our Lady of Peace, is now interpreted as an image of the encounter of cultures that has resulted in the unique Catholicism of this part of the world. See the Archdiocese of Santa Fe website at www.archdiocesesantafe.org.

The Merton poem "La Salette" is found in *The Collected Poems of Thomas Merton* (New Directions, 1980), 130. The sole image of Mary's visionary encounter with two poor French cowherds at La Salette that I have discovered in the Los Angeles archdiocese is found among that series of apparition windows created in Munich in the mid-1950s by Franz Mayer and Company for the Pontifical Institute of Christian Art and installed at Immaculate Conception parish on James Wood Boulevard just south of downtown.

Chapter 13: Our Lady of Peace

The Picpus fathers (SSCC) have a cathedral in Honolulu, Hawaii, the Cathedral of Our Lady of Peace, which is the oldest cathedral in continuous use in the Unites States, consecrated in 1843. On that congregation in L.A., see Harold A. Whelan, SSCC, *The Picpus Story: The Sacred Hearts Fathers' Missionary Activity in the Sandwich Islands and Early California 1826–1856* (Pomona, CA: Apostolate of Christian Renewal, 1980). Another interesting detail about O. L. of Peace in the region is found in the Society of Jesus' designation of its former novitiate, founded in 1961, as *Nuestra Señora de la Paz*.

The pamphlet on Our Lady of Malibu was published by M/P Enterprises, Pacific Grove CA, n.d. The quote by the artist was taken from these pages.

For a modern treatment of Our Lady of Peace as patroness of nonviolence, see Jesuit John Dear's *Mary of Nazareth, Prophet of Peace* (Notre Dame, IN: Ave Maria Press, 2003).

The image that the people at Sacred Heart in Altadena identified as The Lady of All Nations is in fact more likely a variant of the image of Our Lady of Victory in the chapel of Notre Dame des Victoires in Paris. The Lady of All Nations was revealed to Ida Peerdeman, a seer in Amsterdam, between 1945 and 1959. In this representation the Virgin is standing alone on a globe in front of a cross with a large flock of sheep representing the people of the world gathered around her. The Lady of All Nations image has been associated with the prophecy of papal proclamation of Mary as Co-Redemptrix.

Chapter 14: Queen

For the theological foundations of Mary's regality, there is abiding value in the encyclical of Pius XII, *Ad Caeli Reginam*, October 11, 1954.

English translations of the Marian antiphon titles are *Alma Redemptoris Mater* (Loving Mother of the Redeemer), *Ave Regina Caelorum* (Hail Queen of Heaven), *Regina Caeli*, (Queen of Heaven Rejoice), and *Salve Regina* (Hail Holy Queen). The little pamphlet, *Book of Mary: Prayers in Honor of the Blessed Virgin Mary* (United States Conference of Catholic Bishops, 2002) contains these prayers and others with a description of their liturgical use. See also William G. Storey, *A Book of Marian Prayers: A Compilation of Marian Devotions from the Second to the Twenty-First Century* (Chicago: Loyola Press, 2011).

A brief but thorough treatment of the Virgin's queenship is written by Sarah Jane Boss, "The Development of the Virgin's Cult in the High Middle Ages" in *Mary: The Complete Resource*, 149–72.

Chapter 15: Our Lady of Sorrows

Segments of this chapter have appeared in earlier versions in my articles "Pursuing Mary in Los Angeles," *Initiative Report: Catholic Common Ground Initiative* 11, no. 3 (September 2007): 3–6, and "Circles of Sorrow," *Weavings* 25, no. 1 (Fall 2009): 22–30.

On the significance of practices of piety in Catholicism, see Elaine A. Peña, *Performing Piety: Making Space Sacred with the Virgin of Guadalupe* (Berkeley: University of California Press, 2011).

Chapter 16: Jesus and Mary

The opening quotation is from Pope John Paul II, *L'Osservatore Romano* Weekly Edition in English (November 22, 1995): 11.

On the devotion to the two hearts, see *The Theology of the Alliance of the Two Hearts: Documents of the 1997 International Theological Pastoral Symposium on the Alliance of the Hearts of Jesus and Mary (Book 1)* (Rome: Two Hearts Media, 1997).

Ivone Gebara questions the idea that Western Catholic Christianity is the divinely intended form of the Gospel in "A Feminist Perspective on Enigmas and Ambiguities" in Tomás Bamat and Jean-Paul Wiest, eds., *Popular Catholicism in a World Church: Seven Case Studies in Incul-*

turation (Maryknoll, NY: Orbis Books, 1999), 256–64. More recently Pope Benedict XVI has championed the idea that the form and teachings of the Roman Catholic Church, even as derived from encounter with Greco-Roman philosophy and culture, is in fact divinely intended. See also Ivone Gebara and Maria C. Bingemer, *Mary, Mother of God, Mother of the Poor* (Maryknoll, NY: Orbis Books, 1989).

Resources for this chapter include Orlando O. Espín, *The Faith of the People: Theological Reflections on Popular Catholicism* (Maryknoll, NY: Orbis Books, 1997) and Anita de Luna, *Faith Formation and Popular Religion: Lessons from the Tejano Experience* (Lanham, MD: Rowman and Littlefield, 2002). See also Daniel G. Groody, *Border of Death, Valley of Life: An Immigrant Journey of Heart and Spirit* (Lanham, MD: Rowman and Littlefield, 2002).

Several modern magisterial statements about Mary have been collected together in *Mary in the Church: A Selection of Teaching Documents* (Washington, DC: United States Conference of Catholic Bishops, 2003). Included are Behold Your Mother: Woman of Faith, the 1973 pastoral letter of the American bishops; *Marialis Cultis*: For the Right Ordering and Development of Devotion to the Blessed Virgin Mary, Pope Paul VI's 1974 apostolic exhortation; and an encyclical and an apostolic letter from Pope John Paul II in 1987 and 2002: *Redemptoris Mater* (the Mother of the Redeemer): On the Blessed Virgin Mary in the Life of the Pilgrim Church and *Rosarium Virginis Mariae*: On the Most Holy Rosary. It is Paul VI's statements that most guide the pastoral approaches that I explore in this chapter.

See also the Vatican II document *Lumen Gentium*, Constitution on the Church, Chapter VIII entitled "The Role of the Blessed Virgin Mary, Mother of God in the Mystery of Christ and the Church." The 1963 *Sacrosanctum Concilium*, Constitution on the Sacred Liturgy, Chapter V, paragraph 103, states that "in celebrating this annual cycle of Christ's mysteries, holy church honors with especial love the Blessed Virgin Mary, Mother of God, who is joined by an inseparable bond to the saving work of her son. In her the church holds up and admires the most excellent fruit of the redemption, and joyfully contemplates, as in a faultless image, that which she herself desires and hopes wholly to be."

On the distinction between "devotions" and "popular piety," see the publication of the Congregation for Divine Worship and the Discipline of the Sacraments, *Directory on Popular Piety and the Liturgy: Principles and Guidelines* (Vatican City: 2001), nos. 7–10.

Also see the Catholic Bishops Conference of the Philippines statement issued on February 2, 1975, ANG MAHAL NA BIRHEN: Mary in Philippine Life Today: A Pastoral Letter on the Blessed Virgin Mary.

The fifth meeting of the Latin American and Caribbean Episcopal Conference took place at the Marian shrine of Aparecida, Brazil, in May 2007, and was attended by Pope Benedict XVI. It represents something of a change in attitude toward popular devotion.

The unscriptural imagined meeting between the risen Christ and his mother after the resurrection is engraved on the imaginations of Filipino Catholics by early modern Jesuit missionaries who took their cue from their founder Ignatius of Loyola whose Spiritual Exercises contain the reunion scene. On the Jesuits and Mary, see Thomas M. Lucas, SJ, "Virtual Vessels, Mystical Signs: Contemplating Mary's Image in the Jesuit Tradition," *Studies in the Spirituality of Jesuits* 35, no. 5 (November 2003).

On the present revival of traditional devotions, see James Martin, SJ, *Awake My Soul: Contemporary Catholics on Traditional Devotions* (Chicago: Loyola Press, 2004). For reflections on the liturgical celebration of Mary and the saints in a multicultural church, see Wendy M. Wright, "Discovering God's Presence in His Holy Ones: The Feasts of Mary and the Saints" in *Assembly: A Journal of Liturgical Theology* 37, no. 2 (March 2011): 18–24.

Chapter 17: New Creation
Sources for this segment include Virgil Elizondo, *Guadalupe: Mother of the New Creation* (Maryknoll, NY: Orbis Books, 1997); Timothy Matovina, "Theologies of Guadalupe from the Spanish Colonial Era to Pope John Paul II" in *Theological Studies* 70 (2009): 61–91; Simon Coleman, "Mary: Images and Objects" in *Mary: The Complete Resource*, ed. Sarah Jane Boss. (Oxford: Oxford University Press, 2007), 395–423; *Horizons of the Sacred: Mexican Traditions in U.S. Catholicism*, ed. Timothy Matovina and Gary Riebe-Estrella (Ithaca, NY: Cornell University Press, 2002); Jeanette Rodriguez, *Our Lady of Guadalupe: Faith and Empowerment among Mexican-American Women* (Austin: University of Texas Press, 1994) and her *Stories We Live— Cuentos Que Vivamos: Hispanic Women's Spirituality*, 1996 Madeleva Lecture (Mahwah, NJ: Paulist Press, 1996); Nancy Pineda-Madrid, " 'Holy Guadalupe . . . Shameful Malinche?': Excavating the Problem of 'Female Dualism,' Doing Theological Spade Work," *Listening* 44, no. 2 (Spring 2009): 71–87; and Thomas A. Tweed, *Our Lady of the Exile: Diasporic Religion at a Cuban Catholic Shrine in Miami* (New York/Oxford: Oxford University Press, 1997).

The literature on Guadalupe is extensive. Beyond the ones listed above, among the most helpful are D. A. Brading, *Mexican Phoenix: Our Lady of Guadalupe: Image and Tradition Across Five Centuries* (Cambridge University Press, 2001); Timothy Matovina, *Guadalupe and Her Faithful:*

Latino Catholics in San Antonio from Colonial Origins to the Present (Baltimore: Johns Hopkins Press, 2005); *Goddess of the Americas: Writings on the Virgin of Guadalupe,* ed. Ana Castillo (NY: Riverhead, 1996); Antonio Valeriano, *History of Apparitions of Our Lady of Guadalupe* (Mexico, 1969); Jacqueline Orsini Dunnington, *Guadalupe: Our Lady of New Mexico* (Santa Fe: Museum of New Mexico Press, 1999); Carl Anderson and Eduardo Chavez, *Our Lady of Guadalupe: Mother of the Civilization of Love* (NY: Doubleday, 2009), Kristy Nabhan-Warren, *The Virgin of El Barrio: Marian Apparitions, Catholic Evangelizing, and Mexican American Activism* (NY: New York University Press, 2005).

Also of interest, and representing the variety of approaches to the topic, are Eryk Hanut, *The Road to Guadalupe: A Modern Pilgrimage to the Goddess of the Americas* (NY: Jeremy Tarcher/Putnam, 2001); David Arthur Sanchez, "Guadalupan Iconography: A Post-Colonial 'Signifier of Resistance' of the Chicano/a Civil Rights Movement," *Listening* 44, no. 2 (Spring 2009): 88–99; Jeffrey S. Thies, *Mexican Catholicism in Southern California: The Importance of Popular Religiosity and Sacramental Practice in Faith Experience,* American University Studies Series 7, vol. 139 (NY: Peter Lang, 1993); Paul Badde, *Maria of Guadalupe: Shaper of History, Shaper of Hearts* (San Francisco: Ignatius Press, 2009); Franciscan Friars of the Immaculate, *A Handbook on Guadalupe* (1997); and Elaine A. Peña, *Performing Piety: Making Space with the Virgin of Guadalupe* (Berkeley: University of California Press, 2011).

On the Mexican chapel of Our Lady of Guadalupe in Hermosa Beach as an example of Mexican chapels, see P. A. Gazin, *Footprints on the Sand* (1991). For an ecumenical perspective, see Maxwell E. Johnson, *The Virgin of Guadalupe: Theological Reflections of an Anglo-Lutheran Liturgist* (Lanham, MD: Rowman Littlefield, 2002) and *American Magnificat: Protestants on Mary of Guadalupe* (Collegeville, MN: Liturgical Press, 2010) by the same author.

Chapter 18: First Fruits

Pius XII in his *Munificentissimus Deus* in 1950 defined the dogma of the assumption. Pius IX's *Ineffabilis Deus* of 1854 gave dogmatic definition to the immaculate conception. The Marianist order, through its Mary Page generated from the Marian Library at University of Dayton also has tried to make these dogmas accessible to a modern mentality. The website address is http://campus.udayton.edu/mary/mariandogmas.html. See specifically the short essay on the Immaculate Conception at http://campus.udayton.edu/mary//meditations/immac.html.

Sources for this chapter include Nancy Pineda-Madrid, " 'Holy Guadalupe . . . Shameful Malinche?': Excavating the Problem of 'Female Dualism,' Doing Theological Spade Work" in *Listening* 44, no. 2 (Spring 2009): 71–87; Lina Boff, *Mary and the Feminine Face of God: For a Marian Spirituality*, trans. Solymar Torres (Chicago, IL: Servite Coalition for Justice, 2007); Tina Beattie, *God's Mother, Eve's Advocate* (London: Continuum, 2002); Sarah Jane Boss, "The Doctrine of Mary's Immaculate Conception" in *Mary: The Complete Resource*, ed. Sarah Jane Boss (London: Continuum, 2007), 207–37, her *Empress and Handmaid: On Nature and Gender in the Cult of the Virgin Mary* (London/New York: Cassell, 2000), and her *Mary* in the New Theology Series (Continuum, 2003); Sally Cunneen, *In Search of Mary: The Woman and the Symbol* (Ballantine Books, 1996); Rosemary Radford Ruether, *Mary, the Feminine Face of the Church* (Westminster Press, 1977), Aurelie Hagstrom, "Advent, Mary, and Hospitality: Making Room for the Lord," *Ministry & Liturgy* 38, no. 7 (September 2011).

On visual images of Mary, see *Divine Mirrors: The Virgin Mary and the Visual Arts*, ed. Melissa Katz (Oxford: Oxford University Press, 2001); Alfred McBride, OPraem, *Images of Mary* (Cincinnati: St. Anthony Messenger Press, 1998); William Hart McNichols and Mirabai Starr, *Mother of God Similar to Fire* (Maryknoll, NY: Orbis Books, 2010); and Caroline Ebertshäuser, Herbert Haag, Joe H. Kirchberger, and Dorothee Sölle, *Mary: Art, Culture and Religion through the Ages*, translated by Peter Heinegg (New York: Crossroad Herder, 1997).

On recent developments in Marian thought set in historical context, see Lawrence Cunningham, "The Virgin Mary," in *From Trent to Vatican II: Historical and Theological Investigations*, eds. Raymond F. Bulman and Frederick J. Parrella (Oxford: Oxford University Press, 2006).